REAL WORLD GRADUATION

The Entrance Exam for Adulthood

(101 Questions and Answers)

Also by Edward D. Duvall

The Federalist Companion: A Guide to Understanding *The Federalist Papers*

This book contains a direct account of the historical events of the Revolutionary era from 1760 to 1788, emphasizing the causes of the war, its conduct, and the failures of the Articles of Confederation following the peace. It also shows the structure of the arguments presented by Jay, Hamilton, and Madison in their defense of the Constitution as contained in *The Federalist Papers*, and a cross-reference between the Federalist essays and provisions of the Constitution.

Can You Afford That Student Loan?

This book describes the basics of the student loan programs as well as the risks and benefits of student loan. It then provides a clear method by which the student can determine the affordability of a student loan. This is done using an extensive table of occupations and their starting salaries from the Bureau of Labor Statistics. Using some common rules for debt repayment, the book contains a unique nomographic method for determining what amount of loan is affordable when the payments come due, given starting salaries and repayment terms. It concludes with several examples that illustrate the most common issues regarding the affordability of student loans.

The Control and Manipulation of Money
Basic economics, and a financial and economic history of the U. S.

Part 1 discusses basic economics, including labor, capital, rent, money, and the banking system. Part 2 is a complete financial and economic history of the U. S. from 1775 to 2020. It is divided into 12 chapters; one describes the National Banking system (1862-1914), and one describes the Federal Reserve (1914-present). Each of the other chapters cover a certain period in U. S. monetary history, mostly aligned along the lines of the banking system in force. Each chapter includes data regarding: U. S. government revenues and expenditures, national debt, condition statements of the banking system, money supply, and consumer price / income indices.

A Solar Energy Estimator
A Simple Solar Panel Viability Model

The Solar Energy Estimator consists of a book showing the complete derivation of a model that calculates the energy savings and return-on-investment of a solar panel installation. An Excel® spreadsheet is provided that permits the user to make the actual calculations, using only a small number of inputs. It may be used for any non-commercial purpose.

https://fremontvalleybooks.com

Real World Graduation
The Entrance Exam for Adulthood
(101 Questions and Answers)

Edward D. Duvall

Fremont Valley Books, LLC
Queen Creek, AZ

10 May 2023

ISBN: 978-0-9845773-6-1

Published by Fremont Valley Books, LLC
https://fremontvalleybooks.com

Edward Duvall's blog: https://edduvall.com

To my wife, Mary
"The muscle car lady"

CONTENTS

1

Introduction

This book is an update to an original published in 2019 in which the questions and answers were in separate volumes. In this edition, some of the questions have been updated, and the questions and answers have been included in one volume.

As before, the book is intended for young people aged 18 to 23 who have completed or are close to completing their formal education. To you I say congratulations: you've done your time in school, and now you are ready to begin living as an independent person. Your teachers have spent all the time necessary to teach you the basic knowledge you will need from a purely academic standpoint. Unfortunately, the real world does not function in the neat, organized fashion as represented in the textbooks. The real world operates entirely differently.

Those of you who graduated after 2015 are probably the first generation to be exposed to the mainstream media constantly talking about "propaganda", "disinformation", "misinformation", "malinformation", "inauthentic information", "authentic information", and "conspiracy theories". All but the last have definitions [1] which may be summarized as follows:
a. Propaganda is usually produced by government, generally political, and similar to advertising
b. Disinformation is deliberately designed to cause harm
c. Misinformation is false, but without misleading intent
d. Malinformation is correct, but designed to harm a person's reputation
e. Inauthentic information is designed to hide its source
f. Authentic information is traceable to its source.

What about "conspiracy theory"? As recent history has shown, today's conspiracy theory is tomorrow's confirmed facts; in other words, something is called a conspiracy theory if it does not fit the desired narrative, ideological mandate, or propaganda. Before we go any further, check out the authors of reference 1. Notice that the first one and the last three gave only their first name and last initial. Page 1 of reference 1 proudly notes that the last one, "Katie M." works for the Northern California Regional Intelligence Center and the other three (Peter M., Laci F., and Michael G.) all work for the Federal Bureau of Investigation (FBI). Why would these four individuals be hiding their identities as the authors of a publicly available document? Maybe they don't actually exist. Maybe the entire document is itself propaganda and/or disinformation. Maybe asking that question will get you labeled as a conspiracy theorist.

I digressed on that subject to warn you that it will be necessary to filter out a great deal of useless garbage in the course of making appropriate decisions now that you are out of school. The next chapter contains 101 questions designed to show how the real world that you are entering differs from how you've been taught about it. It is an informal introduction to the important issues you will confront during your lives. To make it more interesting, I have eliminated the essay format, and have instead adopted a multiple-choice question format (or as my generation called it, "multiple guess"). The answer follows immediately after each question so that you may check to see how well you are prepared for the adult world.

It is not like those "closed-book" tests you had in school. You are encouraged to use every means available to answer the questions. After all, you will be doing the same thing for the rest of your life: checking with friends and family, researching things on the internet, and reading published papers by knowledgeable experts. There are several questions in which I have cited references; it will be helpful if you consult those to see if I've misrepresented anything.

References

[1] Peter M., Sam Alexander, Adam Cambridge, S. Renee Farner, Robert Kang, Stephanie Kiefer, Kawika Takayama, Christopher Vallandingham, Laci F., Michael G., and Katie M. "Combatting Targeted Disinformation Campaigns: A whole-of-society issue", Analytic Exchange Program (AEP) 2019, Oct 2019, p. 4

2

101 Real World Questions and Answers

Question 1: Investment Strategies

What investment strategy is best to promote long-term prosperity for persons aged 18 to 25?
a)   A mixture of stocks and bonds
b)   Gold, silver, other precious metals, jewels
c)   Real estate
d)   Fine art
e)   A mixture of the above.

Answer to Question 1

This is a trick question. None of the answers are correct because all of them require investments in order to acquire them. Investments can be made only out of savings, and savings is what is left after you have met your living expenses. For average persons aged 18 - 22, there is little in the way of excess after living expenses. Therefore, it is necessary first to invest in yourself.

You are the only thing that you are guaranteed to have for the rest of your life. As my father told me, "Education is the only thing they can't take away from you."

The real answer is that you should always invest in yourself, meaning you should get as good an education as you can afford. That does not necessarily mean to go to college, or get into the elite private schools. Contrary to what our so-called "education experts" tell us, college is not for everyone. A life of useful work that pays the bill is for everyone. It is true that we live in a technological society, and an education that is based on math and some sort of technology will usually command higher wages in the long run. But many people find they would rather work the "blue collar" jobs. If you are happier doing that kind of job, all well and good. The important point is to get the most training for the profession you have chosen, and find a job you enjoy.

This is true even if you have to go into debt to get that education or training. Make sure you don't go too deeply in debt because you will spend many years paying it off when you should be at that time investing for your retirement. Here is a good rule of thumb. Research the annual entry-level income of the profession you are trying to become qualified for. That annual salary amount is approximately the maximum debt you should enter into in order for that education to pay off financially. The only exceptions are the legal and medical professions, which can tolerate higher debt levels because the average income potential over time is much higher.

The socialists demand that you not invest in yourself; socialism is founded on the notion that your life should be pre-determined by "experts" who will guide and regulate you at every turn. Don't fall for it. Obtain the best education you can for the profession you prefer, and make sure that you are able to do for yourself without coercion by either government officials or corporations.

-- § --

Question 2: Important Influencers

Which of these societal forces have the most influence on the basic attitudes, behavior, and overall morality of a society?
a)   Government officials
b)   Teachers
c)   Religious leaders
d)   Friends
e)   It varies from person to person, but one the above has the most influence.

Answer to Question 2

This is a trick question.   None of the given choices is the correct answer.

Government officials do not have nearly as much power to influence basic attitudes, or behavior, or morality as they may think. They may instill an attitude of cynicism by their constant lying or by the consistent incompetence. They can pass tax laws with the intention of coercing certain behavior, and may sometimes coerce behavior directly. It has been proven over and over again that no government can legislate morality; it did not work with Prohibition between 1919 and 1933; it does not, and will not, work with regard to the "drug laws" or the "gun laws". The government is a fairly weak societal force.

It is true that teachers have a great deal of opportunity to instill basic attitudes into their students, especially when it is considered that teachers spend more time with children than do their parents. But in the end, the teacher can only instruct (or indoctrinate, as the case may be); they can require that the student memorize facts and pass a test, but they can't make the student believe any of it.

Religious leaders can only present the facts of their theology; ultimately the decision to embrace or reject religion is a matter of faith. They can have great influence on overall morality, but they are not the most powerful force behind it.

Friends can only exert "peer pressure", a temporary fad at best.

The correct answer is that parents have the greatest impact on the overall morality of a society. It is parents who teach, or fail to teach, their children how to live as actual humans, starting very early in the child's life. The fact that parental guidance starts so early (almost from birth) is what causes parental actions, good and bad, to have the greatest overall influence on attitudes, behavior, and morality. Children above all learn by observation, and parents are the people they watch the most in their early formative years. So, if you plan to be a parent, remember that what you instill in your children when they are young is how they will live when they are adults. As it says in Proverbs 22:6:

"Train a child in the way he should go, and when he is old he will not depart from it."

How they are trained as children is a good predictor of how they will live as adults, which in turn will determine what kind of nation we will have thirty years from now.

There are people who claim that families "cannot do it alone", and "the government needs to help raise children". There is even a prominent American village idiot who wrote a book claiming that "it takes a village to raise a child". No it doesn't, as demonstrated by several millennia of history. It takes parents, preferably two, but one will do, who have a vested interest in their children. It is the socialist faction that above all wants to replace the family with a government institution so that children can be indoctrinated into giving up freedom as soon as possible.

-- § --

Question 3: Collectibles

In 1979, a certain woman bought a large number of popular "collectible" dolls. It was commonly believed at that time that these dolls would increase in value over time, and as such, were considered by some to be a worthwhile investment. In fact, some were suggesting that a $5.00 doll purchased in 1979, if kept in its original packaging, would find buyers in 1999 (20 years later) at a price of $100.00 or more, far in excess of the effects of inflation. This means that these dolls were expected to increase in value about 16.1% per year (in so doing, their value would double every 4.47 years, and would be worth 20 times what they were purchased for at the end of 20 years). If the effects of inflation were also considered, the dolls would be expected to sell for a lot more in 1999. However, in 1999, the woman who bought the dolls found that there was virtually no demand for them, other than their usual value as children's toys. She has been offered $1.50 each by another collector, which will represent a considerable loss to her. What actions should be taken?

a) The woman should sell the dolls for $1.50 each, and then sue the person who sold her the dolls in 1979 to recover the other $98.50 each (plus whatever extra is due owing to inflation).

b) The woman should sell the dolls for $1.50 each, and then sue the person who sold her the dolls in 1979 for $3.50 each; that way, she at least recovers her investment.

c) This woman will have to take the loss, but the state or federal government should pass a law prohibiting the sale of "collectible" dolls.

d) Because collectibles always increase in value over the long run, she should hold onto them and make even more per doll than the original $100.00 estimate. Her inability to sell them at a profit now is only a temporary setback.

e) This was a case of questionable behavior by the original seller. This woman will have to take the loss. But, in order to prevent this from happening to other people, the state or federal government should pass a law requiring background checks and permits for anyone who manufactures or sells dolls.

Answer to Question 3

This is a trick question. All of the provided answers are wrong.

The most important thing to remember when this woman decided to sell the dolls: every item is worth what she can get for it, nothing more and nothing less. Let's review the history of the dolls. In 1979, the woman bought them for $5.00 each. Why were they priced at $5.00? Because the buyer and seller agreed on the price; the seller got the most he could, and the buyer paid the least she could. They valued them equally, and the seller agreed to part with each doll in return for $5.00. Had they not agreed on the price, the sale would not have been made.

But why did the woman pay $5.00 each for them? She apparently bought them because she had been told they would increase in value because they were "collectibles". What is a "collectible"? It is something that people like to collect; i.e., to spend their money on, even though they may not have a practical use. Old stamps, obsolete coins, old cars, and baseball cards are typical items that people have collected as a hobby or because they happen to like these things, although they do not have any particular use or any value to anyone else.

There is no guarantee that anything that is bought today can be sold at any later time. A person who bought a buggy whip factory in 1898 found selling buggy whips increasingly difficult, especially after the advent Henry Ford's Model T in 1908. Buggy whips simply became obsolete as the public switched from horse-drawn carts to cars, and the value of the buggy whip manufacturing business went close to zero. Likewise, there was no guarantee that anyone would place any value on the "collectible" dolls in the future. An item advertised as a "collectible" is likely to be something that will never have any value, except to the person who gets rid of them now to a person, like our woman, who falsely believed a mass-produced doll would become increasingly valuable just because a seller claimed it was "collectible".

Let's put this in more concrete economic terms. An "investment" is defined as part ownership of an enterprise that engages in acquisition and use of equipment and tools to: a) develop and produce items for sale; or b) construct buildings and infrastructure, both for sale at a profit. In other words, these are "capital goods", used to produce additional goods. Paying money to obtain stock (partial ownership) in a manufacturing company, or a video game company, or a mining company are investments because they use labor, talent, and equipment to produce items for sale. Note this definition excludes raw land, old cars, the home you live in, and dolls. None of these can be used to produce anything else, and are therefore either "speculation" or "expenses".

Secondly, if the stock market only increases in value at an average rate between 7% and 10% annually over the long term, why would anyone think a mass-produced doll would increase in value at a faster rate (in this example, a claim of 16% annual increase)? Our woman believed it because she did not do the arithmetic. She did not question the plausibility of the claim that dolls would have a greater investment potential than actual productive enterprises. A good rule of thumb is that when you buy something that is not obviously an investment (i.e., stock, business), it's yours. It is highly unlikely that you will ever be able to re-sell that item for more than you paid for it (excluding the effects of inflation). So, when you buy something, make sure you have a use for it, or make sure you like it enough to part with your money permanently to get it. Again, everything you buy is priced because that is what the seller can get for it. In the future, you will sell for what you can get for it, and most items bought for personal use decline in value over time.

Answer (a) is wrong because there was no guarantee that that the dolls would go up in value; it was merely wishful thinking. No one signed a contract promising to pay $100.00 for them in the future, so the courts have nothing to enforce. In fact, even the seediest lawyer will decline the case.

Answer (b) is wrong for the same reason; keep in mind that "collectibles" as such should not be regarded as "investments". The factory that produced the dolls was an investment for its owners, but the dolls themselves are not investments.

Answer (c) is wrong because the government should not interfere with basic economic agreements; the government cannot save a person from themselves. If it were to pass a law prohibiting sale of "collectible" dolls based on a complaint from a greedy buyer, it would soon find itself prohibiting sales of nearly everything, because someone somewhere will complain about every price. Then there would not be much of an economy.

Answer (d) is wrong because "collectible" is an advertising trick that is not enforceable; I can claim this book to be "collectible" if I want to, but that does not mean anyone will actually want to collect copies of it, or to pay for it in the future.

Answer (e) is wrong for the same reason (c) is wrong. There is nothing "questionable" about the seller's actions. The seller himself did not claim that they might be worth a lot more in the future; some other advertising or "popular fad" was at work to convince the buyer that they would. The fact that such a claim contradicts common sense does not make it "questionable". Secondly, buying and selling only by permits and regulation makes products more expensive due to the increased compliance overhead. Third, even if the seller has the permits, the buyer is not relieved of making good buying choices. The buyer can still be taken in by their own greed. It was the buyer's greed and willingness to believe in a fairy tale that led to the loss.

The important thing to remember in this example is that when you are buying something, it is worth (to you) what you are willing to pay for it. When selling, it is worth what you can get for it, which is to say, it is worth what someone else is willing to pay. If you believe that the government can or will protect you from every bad economic decision, you are asking for something that cannot be done.

But that does not stop the advocates of socialism from claiming they have the knowledge to protect everyone from their own bad decisions. All they desire is the absolute power to force their notions onto you, the unsuspecting chump. Don't fall for their claims: if they were that smart, they would not be socialists in the first place. Secondly, a little common sense on your part will serve to avoid most of these circumstances.

-- § --

Question 4: The "three-fifths rule"

Article I, Section 2 of the U. S. Constitution originally contained the following provision:

> "Representatives and direct Taxes shall be apportioned among the several States which may be included within this union, according to their respective Numbers, which shall be determined by adding to the whole number of free persons, including those bound to Service for a Term of Years, and excluding Indians not taxed, three-fifths of all other persons."

In this passage, "representatives" refers to the number of seats in House of Representatives in Congress, "Numbers" refers to population, "several States" refers to the State that ratify the Constitution and join the Union, "those bound to service" refers to indentured servants (those who had committed to a term of voluntary servitude in compensation for repayment of the voyage to America fronted by others), "Indians not taxed" refers to Indians on reservations, "other persons" refers to slaves, and "free persons" refers to anyone not in the "other person" group, i.e. not slaves.

This passage can therefore be clarified as follows: "Representatives and direct Taxes shall be apportioned among the States according to their respective population, which shall be determined as the sum of the number of a) all free persons, b) indentured servants, and c) three-fifths of slaves; specifically excluding Indians on reservations." In other words, representation in Congress was apportioned to the full population of all people in the state not on reservations, except for slaves, whose apportionment was at a fraction of only 60%. This is known as the "three-fifths" rule. This three-fifths provision was superseded by the 14th Amendment, which was ratified 9 Jul 1868.

Why did the Founding Fathers insert the three-fifths clause regarding slaves?
a) Most of the Founding Fathers were slave owners who had contempt for black people, and reduced the value of black people to 60% of a white person because it was a long-held tradition.
b) Most of the Founding Fathers were slave owners who had contempt for black people, and reduced the value of a black person to 60% of a white person in an attempt to deprive the slaves of their fair share of welfare payments.
c) Even the Founding Fathers who did not own slaves were racist, and reduced the apportionment of slaves to 60% of a white person to suppress the political influence of the black slaves in the Southern states.
d) The members of the Democratic Party insisted on this provision before they would allow a ratification vote in the Southern states.
e) Each of the Founding Fathers had different motives, but these motives were generally a combination of a), b), and c).

Answer to Question 4

This is a trick question. All of the answers provided are wrong.

Answer (a) is wrong for two reasons: 1) the provision originated in 1783 as explained below; and 2) the provision applied to slaves, not to all black people (there were many free black people in the states).

Answer (b) is wrong because the Constitution was developed and ratified in 1787 and 1788; "welfare" payments did not begin until the 1960's.

Answer (c) is wrong because slaves were considered property, and thus had no political voice. Slaves did not get to vote, did not get to send representatives, and were prohibited from engaging in any type of political activity.

Answer (d) is also wrong for two reasons: 1) the Democratic Party did not exist for another 12 years; and 2) although it is true that the members of the Democratic Party founded, sponsored, and protected the Ku Klux Klan, and adopted and enforced the Jim Crow laws, these activities did not start until after the Civil War, approximately 90 years after the Constitution was debated and ratified.

Here is the explanation of how the "three-fifths" provision came to be, and why answers based on race are wrong. In 1778, (during the Revolutionary War) the thirteen American states proposed a mutual defense confederacy against Great Britain called the Articles of Confederation. The Articles were adopted and put into force with the ratification by the last state (Maryland) on 1 Mar 1781. The eighth Article contained a provision whereby the Confederacy would raise money and pay its obligations based on the relative value of the lands and buildings held by the respective States [1]. In other words, the central government was financed under the notion of property taxes upon the States, but this notion only determined the amount each state should pay. Each State was allowed to raise the tax by any means determined by the state legislatures. This turned out to be difficult to implement in practice, so various amendments were introduced such that the tax became proportional to population instead of property. The northern states therefore wanted to count all the slaves in the south equally with free persons, as that would increase the amount of tax to be paid by the southern states, and reduce the amount that could be levied on the northern states. The southern states objected to that proposal, arguing that slaves were not nearly as productive as free persons, and so the state should not be forced to pay taxes as if they were. Several compromises were proposed on how to count people, and finally a three-fifths ratio for slaves was proposed by James Madison on 18 Apr 1783. The Articles of Confederation required unanimity of the states for amendments, and this proposal failed to get the required votes (New York and New Hampshire rejected it). The original provision continued under the Articles. Note that the "three-fifths rule" was originally proposed in 1783 as a compromise on a taxation issue, not apportionment. There was no "apportionment" under the Articles of Confederation, since each state had one vote in Congress.

During the debates on the Constitution in 1787, the same issue came up, except now it also centered on the number of seats each state would get in the House of Representatives as well as direct taxation. During debate on 16 Jul 1787, James Wilson proposed the old 18 Apr 1783 amendment (which was not adopted under the Confederacy) as a means of reaching a compromise between the competing factions, proportioning both direct taxation and representation in Congress [2, 3, 4]. So, the three-fifths rule was a political compromise designed to settle issues of how much taxes each state would pay to support the federal government; having nothing to do with moral judgment on the relative value of black people, racism, or the Democratic Party's long-standing contempt for black people.

Contrary to claims by some that the three-fifths rule increased incentives for slave-owners, it turned out to be a means to reduce the political power of those states having a large concentration of slaves by reducing the number of seats in the House of Representatives. The three-fifths rule did not lead directly to the demise of slavery, but it did prevent the situation from becoming worse. As the number of southern states increased, the number of congressional seats held by slave states also increased. However, the three-fifths rule reduced the number of seats they would have had if slaves had been counted as full persons; this prevented the southern states from obtaining enough votes to amend the Constitution in such a way that slavery would always be allowed.

This original provision's effectiveness as a tax measure was superseded in practice by the use of tariffs to fund the government and later by the 16th Amendment (which permitted a personal income tax). The apportionment aspect was superseded directly by the 14th Amendment, which reads as follows:

"Representatives shall be apportioned among the several States according to their respective numbers, counting the whole number of persons in each State, excluding Indians not taxed"

Were those who adopted the 14th Amendment racists because they continued to exclude Indians on reservations? No: those Indians did not become citizens until the early 20th century, and therefore at the adoption of the 14th Amendment, were not qualified as citizens to be counted in the apportionment.

The main point to remember in this example is: don't blindly trust socialist political hacks in their claims about racism and other people's alleged motivations. Don't believe that all white people who believe in the Constitution are racist because the Founders were racist, and the Founders were racist because they adopted the three-fifths rule. The rule was adopted as the best economic and political compromise that could be reached at that time, not for racial reasons. It may well be that some of the Founders did regard black people as inferior, but that sentiment was not the source of the "three-fifths" rule. If anything, the three-fifths rule retarded the growth of slavery. Examine the historical facts for yourself.

[1]   James Bryce, *The American Commonwealth*, New York: Macmillan Co., 1907, Vol. 1, pp. 692-698
[2]   James Madison, *Notes of Debates in the Federal Convention of 1787*, Athens, OH: Ohio University Press, 1966 (reprinted 1976), p. 103
[3]   Jonathan Elliot, *The Debates in the Several State Conventions on the Adoption of the Federal Constitution as Recommended by the General Convention at Philadelphia in 1787, Together with the Journal of the Federal Convention*, [commonly known as "*Elliot's Debates*"], Philadelphia, PA: J. B. Lippincott & Co., 1881, Vol. 1, pp. 205, 206
[4]   Edward D. Duvall, "Regarding the Three-Fifths Rule", contained in *Historical Essays*, Queen Creek AZ: Fremont Valley Books LLC, 2023; https://fremontvalleybooks.com

-- § --

Question 5: College Costs

A study by the U. S. Department of Education in 2006 [1] reported that college tuition, fees, and room and board are continuing to rise. The data in Figure 5-1 shows the costs of tuition, fees, books, and room and board for in-state students attending public four-year universities, living on-campus.

School Year	Tuition & Fees ($)	% Increase in Tuition & Fees	Room and Board ($)	% Increase in Room and Board
1998-1999	3640	-	4985	-
1999-2000	3768	3.52	5144	3.19
2000-2001	3979	5.60	5342	3.85
2001-2002	4273	7.39	5675	6.23
2002-2003	4686	9.67	5918	4.28
2003-2004	5363	14.45	6316	6.73
2004-2005	5939	10.74	6649	5.27
2005-2006	6399	7.75	7025	5.65

Figure 5-1

A separate study [2] concluded that a college graduate with a 4-year degree in 2005 will earn 63% more than a person with only a high school diploma (approximately $57,000 per year vs. $35,000 per year). This means, on average, that a college graduate earns approximately 75% more over their working lifetimes ($2.1 M vs. $1.2 M) as compared to a person with only a high-school diploma. Given the costs of a college education shown in Figure 5-1, and the earnings benefits of a college education, what is a good federal policy regarding college costs?

a)   The federal government should ensure all tuition, fees, and room-and-board is free.

b) Congress should enact price controls on tuition, fees, and room and board to keep the annual rate of increase at or below the rate of inflation.

c) Congress should pass a law requiring that tuition costs be frozen at the rates that prevailed during the freshman year.

d) Attendance at college should be mandatory so that everyone's income will rise.

e) Some combination of a), b), and c) should be adopted to improve the current system.

[1] Digest of Education Statistics, 2006, (NCES 2007-017), U. S. Department of Education, Washington DC: Institute of Education Statistics, Table 319 (Jul 2007)

[2] National Center for Education Statistics (NCES), 2004, Table 14-1; NCES 2006, Table 22-1 (based on U. S. Census Bureau, Current Population Survey, and U. S. Census Bureau, 2006, PINC-03.

Answer to Question 5

This is a trick question. All of the answers are wrong.

Answer (a) is illogical, because nothing is free and the federal government does not actually pay for anything. Everything the federal government pays out has either come from the taxpayers or is added onto the national debt to be paid by future taxpayers. So, if option (a) were enacted, everyone who pays taxes would indirectly pay for the tuition of all students. Taxpayers without children or those whose children do not go to college would be forced to pay for something from which they and their children do not benefit. Meanwhile, while those who attend college will receive the free benefit as well as the benefits of from higher wages over their working lifetime. In other words, this policy amounts to public costs but private gain. Shall the children of the wealthy be educated at public expense, paid for by the people of the lower and middle economic classes?

Answer (b) cannot work because the cost of something cannot be determined by arbitrary fiat. If the cost dictated by Congress is below the actual cost of providing the service, the private colleges will simply close. A college education will either become even more difficult to obtain (i.e., only those with influence or connections will be able to get in to the few remaining schools), or of lesser quality. Likewise, public colleges will either require a greater amount of funding to maintain its standards, requiring more taxes to be paid by many who will not benefit, or will lower the quality of the education provided. It is exactly the same phenomena that prevailed when the Soviet Union placed price controls on bread at 2 kopeks per pound. They discovered that bread cannot be produced for 2 kopeks per pound, even in a slave-labor command system. Price controls always lead to shortages if the commanded price is below the cost of production. Therefore, although the official price of bread was 2 kopeks per pound, there was never any available for purchase by the typical person (except on major holidays commemorating the Revolution). The Communist Party ruling elite, however, got all the bread they wanted.

Answer (c) will not work because the colleges will simply adjust their freshman-year rates to include the expected increases over the four years, plus a little more for insurance in case their estimate is low. The average tuition rates will actually increase slightly faster than they otherwise would.

Option (d) cannot work because it forces many people to do something they either do not want to do or are not capable of doing. Coercion is always bad policy. The trend will be that the standards will have to be watered down to prevent so many from flunking out; in the end the quality and thus the value of a college education will sink to the current value of a high-school diploma. Note also that room and board cost more than tuition, yet this proposal does nothing to address it.

This should be looked at in a whole different light. If it is true that a college education is worth $900,000 over one's working lifetime, the investment is well worth it. If one started college in 2002, the total cost of tuition would be approximately $23,000. If one took out a loan, and ended up paying $75,000 for the interest and principal, the return on investment over one's working lifetime is still a factor of 12 (900/75). This is a very good investment. It assumes, of course, that one majors in a field for which there is some demand (unlike anthropology, ancient Chinese art, gender studies, or the social benefits of rock 'n roll). Keep in mind that $6,399 per year for tuition is $17.53 per day, a figure that is not overwhelming for most people. We should be thankful that a college education is as cheap and as beneficial as it is.

One word of warning is in order, however, regarding the taking out of "student loans". Formerly, up until the early 1990's "student loans" were made through a cooperative government/private industry system in which the government partly subsidized the loan by in effect paying part of the interest. It did this by requiring lenders to charge a lower interest rate than they otherwise could, and providing the lenders with other offsetting incentives (through tax breaks or exemptions). The government also restricted the amount that a student could borrow. So, a student could borrow nominal amounts at fairly low interest rates, the net result being that the student would be able, after graduation, to pay the loan back to the lender. But, Congress decided to "improve" the program by allowing greater amounts to be borrowed; sometimes students borrowed so much that they had great difficulty paying it back. Also, many students abused the system by defaulting on the loans. In response, the government passed legislation such that student loans cannot be discharged (forgiven) by a bankruptcy determination; the student is now liable for the loan repayment no matter what other financial problems he has. The government (now the initiator of all student loans) has the advantage: it is certain to always get repayment unless the student dies. As a result, the student has to be wary of the risk: taking out a very large student loan means that he or she could conceivably end up with very large debts which they must pay regardless of other financial pressures. Therefore, one should restrict their borrowing on student loans unless: a) it is only for a nominal amount, or b) is to obtain an education in a field that will result in a high-paying job, such as engineering, mathematics, physics, chemistry, nursing, medicine, etc. Do not borrow heavily to get a degree in library science or sociology because the economic payback (the subsequent job) will not cover the cost of the loan necessary to obtain it.

Figure 5-2 [1] shows how this works in practice; that is, how the amount borrowed, the number of years of the term of the loan, and the required monthly payment are related. The left panel shows the monthly amortization of a $1,000 loan at various interest rates over various terms of the loan. The legend API means "annual percentage rate", (i.e. the interest rate on the loan). For example, a loan of $1,000 at 4% for 12 years has a monthly amortization of about $8.50 (actually, $8.76). The right panel shows the total monthly payment as a function of the monthly amortization. Combined, these two show how much the monthly payment would be over a given number of years at a given interest rate. The dashed lines show two examples.

Suppose you have calculated that you have to borrow $25 K (K = $1,000) in order to get the degree you desire from the school you want to attend. But suppose you are only willing to pay $360 per month in repayment, and you can borrow money at 10% interest. How many years will you have to repay? Starting on the right panel, start at $360 on the x-axis, and go up per the short dashed line to where it intersects the $25 K line; then read across to the left panel until it intersects the 10% interest line. Then read down to get the required number of years to meet these conditions. In order to meet this repayment schedule, you will have to take the loan out for about 8 years and 9 months. In reality, the lender will require an integer number of years; for 8 years, $25,000 at 10% comes to a monthly repayment of $379.36, and for 9 years comes to $351.97. Figure 5-2 gives you a sense of where the answer lies.

A second example is demonstrated by the longer dashed line. Suppose you are only willing to make payments for 10 years, and you can borrow at 6% interest. How much will your monthly payment be if you must borrow $40 K? Start on the left panel at 10 years, read up to the 10% interest line. Then read across until you find about where the $40 K line would be (you can interpolate between $25 K and $50 K by eye). Then read down until you get about $450 per month (actually $444.09). Conversely, you could easily answer the question of how much you can afford to borrow if you can borrow at a certain interest, and only want to pay a given amount monthly for a certain number of years. This chart can also be used to find the total payment for different loan amounts at different rates for different terms. Just solve each one separately and add the results.

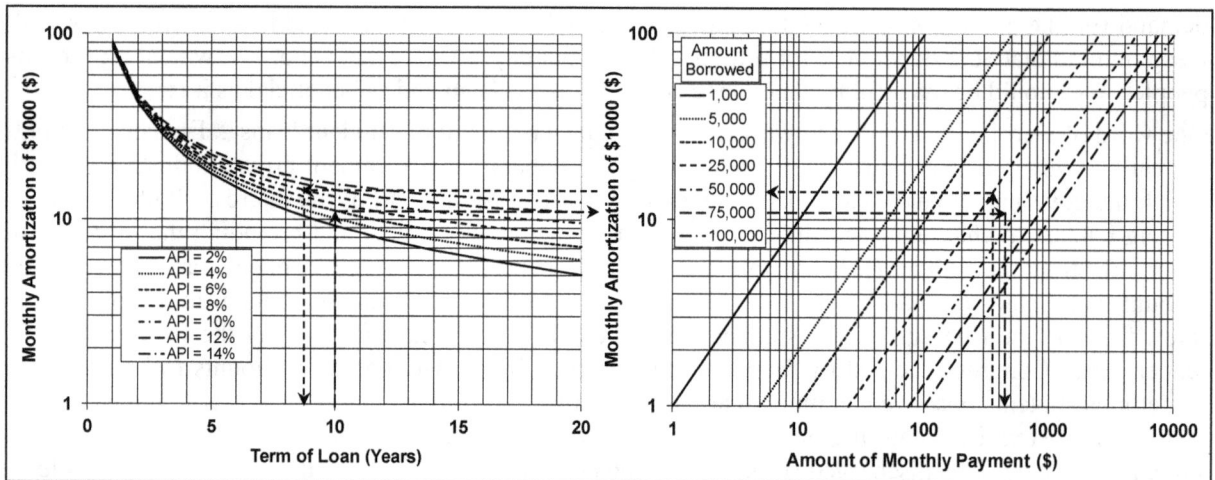

Figure 5-2: Nomograph for Student Loan Repayment

Don't be fooled by the education mafia that demands that you run up large student loan debts to obtain a diploma of questionable value. You would be surprised to learn how little actual employers care if you attended an "elite" school; a college education shows that you have mastered the basics of a subject, and have the capacity to learn what the employer needs. Don't be fooled by socialists who claim the higher education is a "civil right" or there is some "moral imperative" to provide free higher education. If the socialists get their way, the value of a degree will evaporate in the same way that socialism causes all things of value to evaporate.

[1] Edward D. Duvall, *Can You Afford that Student Loan?*, Queen Creek, AZ: Fremont Valley Books LLC, 2011, https://fremontvalleybooks.com

-- § --

Question 6: Donating to Charities

A person wishes to donate $100 to a charity. What percentage of the $100 will actually go to the cause for which the charity was established?
a)   All of it (100%) will go for the cause, because that's what charities are legally required to do.
b)   None of it (0%), because all charities are rip-offs.
c)   There are always some expenses associated with fundraising, but these are regulated, and charities are required to spend more than 90% of contributions on the cause.
d)   There are always some expenses associated with fundraising, but these are regulated, and charities are required to spend more than 80% of contributions on the cause.
e)   There are always some expenses associated with fundraising, but these are regulated, and charities are required to spend more than 70% of contributions on the cause.

Answer to Question 6

This is a trick question. None of the answers are correct.

Charities are not required to spend a certain amount on the cause; they are only required to report their revenue and expenses accurately on IRS Form 990. Some charities are very efficient; some are a complete waste of money. A survey [1] in 2004 found that the average fraction actually going to the cause after expenses for a wide range of charities was 84%. There were some very good ones with 100% going to the cause (Brother's Brother Foundation, Children's Hunger Fund, and a few others), while some were very inefficient (William J. Clinton Presidential Foundation at 31%, Philadelphia Museum of Art at 49%, and the Humane Society of the U. S. at 57%). A more recent survey [2] indicates that the Midwest Food Bank, MAP International, and the Billings Food Bank are all very efficient, while the Children's Charity Fund, Firefighters Charitable Foundation, and the Committee for Missing Children are all very poorly run.

So, if you want to evaluate which are the best charities, and whether they can be trusted with your donation, find out how efficient they are at fundraising and what fraction of received donations actually goes to the cause.

[1]   William P. Barrett, "America's Most (and Least) Efficient Charities", Forbes Magazine (Forbes.com) 23 Nov 2004
[2]   https://www.charitynavigator.org

-- § --

Question 7: Gauging Inflation

A reputable economic research organization conducted a survey of prices in 2004. They found that median prices of the following items increased as follows:
1.   Unleaded gasoline, from $1.59 per gallon to $1.88 per gallon; an increase of 18.23% [1]
2.   Single-family homes, from $170,483 to $191,738; an increase of 12.46% [2]
3.   Soybeans, from $6.00 per bushel to $9.67 per bushel; an increase of 61.16% [3]
4.   Flour, 5-lb bag, from $1.44 to $1.50; an increase of 4.10% [4]

From these statistics, what is the approximate inflation rate from 2003 to 2004?
a)   The inflation rate should include only the data for gasoline, soybeans, and flour, since those are common products that people use directly or indirectly every day; the inflation rate is approximately 27.83% = ((18.23 + 61.16 + 4.10)/3).
b)   Only the data for single-family homes should be used, since homes are purchased on long-term mortgages (usually 30 years), and are therefore a better predictor of long-term inflation. The long-term inflation rate is the most important metric. Therefore the inflation rate for 2003-2004 is approximately 12.5%.
c)   Only the data for unleaded gasoline should be used because it is the only one of these that most people have to buy directly. Most people do not buy homes every year, and the prices of soybeans and flour are not useful because they are only components in items purchased by most people (i.e., flour is used in making bread, but there are other costs besides flour that contribute to the increase price of bread, such as sugar, butter, and fuel). Therefore, the inflation rate for 2003 to 2004 is approximately 18.23%.
d)   All of the data should be used, but not equally weighted, since some of these are purchased frequently, some infrequently, and some are used more than others. For example, gasoline is purchased frequently, and homes infrequently. No data was provided on the pro-rated amount of usage, so the most that can be inferred about inflation during this period is that was somewhere between 4.10% and 61.16%.
e)   Only the data for soybeans and flour should be used, since they are basic commodities that are used in a large number of products, and represent structural trends in the economy. Therefore, the inflation rate was approximately 32.7% (the average of 61.16 and 4.10).

[1]   Energy Information Administration, https://www.eia.gov/dnav/pet/pet_pri_gnd_dcus_nus_w.htm, Series history (file = PET_PRI_GND_DCUS_NUS_W.xls).
        Within the file, see series EMM_EPM0R_PTE_N_US_DPG
[2]   Federal Housing Finance Agency, Quarterly Average and Median Prices for States and U. S.: 2000Q1-2010Q2, file = state_statistics_for_download.xls, available at:

https://www.fhfa.gov/DataTools/Downloads/Pages/House-Price-Index-Datasets.aspx#mpo

[3] Macrotrends, https://www.macrotrends.net/2531/soybean-prices-historical-chart-data; the data points are for 7 Apr 2003 and 19 Apr 2004

[4] St. Louis Federal Reserve, Economic research, Average Price of White Flour, series APU000070111, available at: https://fred.stlouisfed.org/series/APU0000701111. The data points are for Oct 2003 and Oct 2004

Answer to Question 7

This is a trick question. All of the answers are false.

The question asks about the rate of inflation, but only gives data on the rise in prices. A rise in prices can come about by many different causes: a) an increase in demand with a fixed supply; b) a reduction in supply with fixed demand, c) buying by optimistic speculators; d) reduction in supply caused by accidents, hurricanes, floods, tornadoes, and droughts; e) increased cost due to new regulations; and many others. But natural prices also can decrease if: a) supply is greater than demand; b) demand drops in the presence of the same supply, or c) less capital is wasted in unnecessary regulations.

Inflation is an entirely different thing and has a different cause. Inflation is due to an expansion of the money supply in excess of the needs for production and clearing the market of that which is produced. It is not an increase in prices per se; it is the reduction in the buying power of the unit of currency, which means that, because each dollar is worth less, it takes more of them to buy a certain thing, and prices increase. The rise in prices of products is one symptom of inflation. Note the difference: a normal price increase is due to economic factors; inflation is due to government or central bank manipulation of the currency by printing more currency than is required for the economic exchange requirements of the economy. Only governments and central banks in control of the money supply can create inflation; inflation cannot be caused by industries, farmers, unions, workers, Wall Street, or any other economic participants, although the government would like you to blame any or all of them. The general, underlying rise in prices, which robs the working person, is always due to government and government-chartered banks, like the Federal Reserve.

True inflation is always marked by a general rise in all prices with the other natural effects upon prices added on to it. It is very difficult to separate out which part of a price change is due to true inflation of the currency, and which are induced by naturally-occurring economic effects. It is therefore easily camouflaged, and a great deal of ink and videotape is used to mask the fact that governments and their central banks are responsible for a reduction in the value of a dollar and the resulting reduction in the standard of living for the average worker. The most reliable indicator of true inflation was the publication of the "M-3" statistics by the Federal Reserve, which showed how much new currency was being printed. It has now been discontinued (care to guess why)?

So, there was insufficient data provided in the question to determine what part of the increase in prices was due to inflation and which are due to other normal causes. Typically several years' worth of data is required to estimate the monetary inflation rate. The main point here is: don't be confused by the much-advertised "Consumer Price Index". It is a measure of the increase in prices of an averaged composite of a mix of commodities, and cannot separate out the debasement of the currency from other normal causes.

Don't be taken in by socialists who claim that inflation is an invention of capitalists devised to rob the working person. It is true that inflation does so in the long run; it is not true that inflation is only practiced in free-enterprise economies. The socialist wants you to believe that the free-enterprise system is evil, and that only the government can rescue you from its effects. But, as I have noted above, even in free-enterprise economies, inflation is always engineered by government or government-chartered institutions. If socialists take over the banking industry directly, how likely is it that inflation will disappear? Historically, inflations has been used more frequently, and to a greater extent, in socialist nations than in free-enterprise ones. We need look no further than Zimbabwe or Venezuela for the most recent examples.

-- § --

Question 8: Success by Polling

A reputable pollster takes an opinion poll of 1000 people. The poll consists of only one question, and it is about the probable success of a proposed government policy. None of the respondents were familiar with the policy, but were familiar with the issue that the policy addressed. The respondents of the poll are asked to give their opinion as one of the following choices. The percent of the respondents that gave each answer is indicated in parentheses. The choices were:

a) Virtually no chance of success (3%);
b) Small chance of success (31%);
c) Good chance of success (64%); and
d) Virtually guaranteed success (2%).

The reputable pollster calculates that his margin of error is about 4%. How accurate is the poll as an indicator of how successful the policy will be if it is enacted?

a) The probability of success is 96% (100% - 4%), because the answers have to be corrected for the pollster's estimated error.
b) The policy will be 64% successful because that choice got the highest percentage.
c) It has a good chance of succeeding because that choice got the highest percentage, but is not necessarily 64% probable.
d) The probability of success is always 50-50 no matter what the poll says.
e) The policy will never be enacted because the people who responded to the poll did not achieve the required two-thirds (66%) majority in their opinion.

Answer to Question 8

This is a trick question. None of the answers are correct.

The polling scenario in the question is typical: it asks the people to respond to a question they do not understand. Therefore, the answers are all irrelevant, and the margin of error is infinite. Polls are often used this way to play into people's desire to give their opinion. They delude themselves into believing that their answer matters. Of course, their answer does not matter, because the success of the policy will be whatever it is. But the results of such a meaningless poll can be used by clever politicians, bureaucrats, and corporations to con the public into believing that if majority of people in a poll have confidence in a particular policy, it is probably a good policy to pursue. It also works the other way: if the people who answer the poll do not have confidence in a certain policy (never mind they do not understand it), those who are opposed to the policy will use the poll results as ammunition against it. A pollster is considered reputable if he faithfully tabulates the answers he has received, and counts them accurately. No matter how reputable the pollster is, polls are usually fixed in one of many underhanded ways. This example is only one of them.

The thing to remember from this is that poll results are relevant only if the respondents understand the effects of a policy. The results of the poll indicate only its popularity, not its chances for success or its accuracy. There was a time when nearly everyone believed the earth was flat. Had a poll been taken then, and people asked if sailors would fall off the earth, a high percentage would have agreed with the pollster's choice that they would. There was a time when nearly everyone believed that supersonic flight was impossible. Had a poll been taken then, most people would have agreed with the pollster's suggestion that aircraft approaching the speed of sound would disintegrate or disappear. There are people now who believe the earth is going to be destroyed because people use gasoline in their cars. Current polls indicate that most people believe the earth is going to be destroyed because of too much carbon dioxide in the atmosphere resulting from the burning of fossil fuels such as gasoline. There is no such evidence.

Trick polls are a favorite of socialists because they can ask uneducated people (in effect): would you like to have something for free? Of course, uneducated people do, because they don't get around to thinking about who will actually pay for it. Nothing of value is actually free. Don't be fooled by socialists claiming that socialism is workable because the polls show that people believe the false claim that things of value can be produced for free. The fact that some poll respondents may be attracted to the idea of getting something for nothing does not mean that socialism will actually result in free things. Everything of value must be paid for in some way or another; which is the one topic socialists do not want to talk about.

Another trick practiced by the socialists is to commission polls when emotions are running high due to some famous crime or tragedy. Common examples include gun-control polls after a mass shooting (as if they are actually all that common); a defective medical device scare; medications that were tampered with; and corruption by bank officers.

-- § --

Question 9: Hospital Surcharges

Consider the following fictional scenario. Suppose a certain surgeon perfected a surgical procedure involving the treatment of a certain heart disease. This procedure increased the survival rate for this particular disease from nearly zero to nearly 100%. It is widely used throughout the medical industry to treat this particular disease and its complications.

A certain person had this type of heart disease. He had the procedure performed on an emergency basis after being brought in unconscious in an ambulance, and subsequently made a full recovery. Reviewing the hospital bill, the patient noticed a $50 surcharge annotated "Originator's surgical procedure usage fee". The insurance company informed the patient that his insurance policy does not cover this fee. It turns out, upon further investigation, that this $50 is going to the surgeon who developed the original procedure as a type of royalty; i.e., a payment for the use of the procedure. What is the best argument the patient can make to the insurance company and/or hospital for not paying the $50?
a) That he did not know about it before treatment, so he should not have to pay.
b) That it is likely another one of those arbitrary charges the hospitals always add, so it should be deducted off the bill as a routine matter.
c) That he cannot afford it.
d) That the procedure was not provably necessary in his case.
e) That the procedure is so common that people should not have to pay it.

Answer to Question 9

This is a trick question. All of the answers are false. This patient should not make an argument at all; he should be glad to pay the $50 and be thankful that some smart guy discovered a procedure that saved his life.

A patient who chose argument (a) is a tight-fisted excuse-making moron. How could he have been informed if he was brought in unconscious? If he was conscious and was informed, would he have declined the surgery? Sure he would, he says (now that he is alive because of it).

Answer (b) is wrong because the hospital bill states clearly that it is a fee to the creating surgeon.

The patient who uses argument (c) is a lying hypocrite, for surely at some time in his life he paid $50 for parking at a baseball game, or paid $50 to get into a State Fair, or spent $50 on lottery tickets, or perhaps routinely spends $50 over the bar on a Friday night after work. But he begrudges a doctor a lousy $50 for the procedure that saves his life?

The patient who uses argument (d) is the guy who thinks he knows more about medicine than the doctors, and the lawyers he hires are also dumb enough and arrogant enough to think they know more than doctors. If he's so smart, why didn't he do his own surgery before he ended up unconscious?

The patient who uses argument (e) is an ingrate who knows the value of money but not of important things; he denigrates the importance of a discovery, and for him, a very necessary procedure. Also, he seems to value his life at less than $50. It's worse than that. Suppose the patient was a rock musician. If he claims he should be excused from paying a doctor's royalty because the procedure is now popular, does that mean that he should not obtain royalties on his music if it becomes popular? Of course not; he would demand (rightfully so) every penny due to him in royalties.

Always consider the relative importance of what the bill is for. Sometimes smart people who do important things deserve a few extra bucks by way of commissions and royalties, even if they're not an athlete, movie star, or musician.

The socialist would make all the false claims above, and probably a few more. A socialist only values the lies that allow him to gain more power, which is why they hold Karl Marx and Vladimir Lenin in such high esteem. They denigrate any sort of individual initiative, such as the example here of a surgeon inventing a successful procedure. A socialist believes the government is entitled to claim ownership of everything despite having done nothing, simply because (they want you to believe) that governments always know best.

-- § --

Question 10: Predicting Bailouts

A Savings-and-Loan bank crisis in the 1980's and 1990's required a government bailout. Major automobile companies (Chrysler and General Motors) have sometimes required government bailouts. In the 2007-2009 bailout, many banks (Washington Mutual, IndyMac), mortgage companies (Fannie Mae, Freddie Mac), and financial institutions (Bear Stearns, American International Group) required government bailouts.

"Fannie Mae" and "Freddie Mac" are nicknames for two government-sponsored entities (GSE) that buy residential mortgages; the goal being to stimulate home-buying. In the 2008 bailout, the losses to the taxpayers for bailing out these two organizations will range between $221 billion and $363 billion [1].

Bear Stearns, a long-standing investment bank specializing in mortgage securitization, was sold to JP Morgan Chase in an emergency sale to avoid a formal bankruptcy that would negatively affect the rest of the economy. The New York Federal Reserve bought $29.97 billion of Bear Stearns' "assets" to get them off the balance sheet, and then lent $28.82 billion to JP Morgan to finance the purchase of Stearns [2].

American International Group, an insurer of mortgage contracts, borrowed $182 billion in bailouts from the Federal Reserve; with the taxpayers liable if they fail to pay it back [3].

Morgan Stanley and Goldman Sachs converted to bank holding companies in order to obtain access to emergency funding from the Federal Reserve to stay afloat and avoid collapse [4]. Goldman Sachs required loans totaling $67.5 billion, while Morgan Stanley required loans of $96 billion.

How can one predict in advance which segment of the economy will require a bailout?
a) The ones with the highest CEO pay will require the bailout, because the CEO takes all the money out of the company.
b) All companies who operate in accordance with for-profit capitalism.
c) Only foreign companies require bailouts, because they borrow too much American money and fail to pay it back on time.
d) They are not really bailouts because the government pays for it.
e) All of the above.

[1] Phil Angelides, Chairman, *The Financial Crisis Inquiry Report*, New York: Public Affairs, 2001, p. 322

[2] ibid., pp. 290, 291

[3] ibid., p. 350

[4] ibid., p. 362, 363

Answer to Question 10

This is trick question. All of the choices are wrong.

Answer a) is wrong because none of the bailouts were correlated to CEO pay (although many of the CEOs of companies requiring bailouts made hundreds of millions of dollars).

Answer b) is wrong because without a profit motive, there would be no industry or economic activity above bare subsistence. Do you expect to work for free, or do you expect to be paid so that you can enjoy the benefits of your expenditure of time and talent? Your wages are the "profit" from your work: and that same attitude throughout the economy had led to the establishment of the civilization that we enjoy.

Answer c) is wrong because it is the U. S. that is borrowing from foreigners, which we add onto our "national debt".

Answer d) is wrong because the government only has what it can get from taxpayers; if a government loan or bailout goes bad, the government will raise your taxes to pay for it (or add it to the national debt for your descendants to pay).

The correct answer is: there are three categories of businesses that are guaranteed to receive bailouts:

a) Those that are highly regulated by the government and can show that their failure is a result of bad government policies;

b) Those whose failure will lead to a large number of angry Democratic party voters who may be willing to change to voting Republican; and

c) Politically well-connected companies and industries that ignore risk, confident that their friends in Washington (in both political parties) will save them from their incompetence and/or corruption.

Those in the first category usually require bailouts because they engaged in business decisions that were not rational; they were not rational because the chief regulator (Congress) actively encouraged or mandated that they engage in non-rational business practices. But for a time, business was good, and great profits were being made, and the Securities and Exchange Commission (SEC) regulators and Congress looked the other way. An example of this category is the Savings-and-Loan (S&L) collapse of the 1980's and 1990's. The S&L's were small private banks that accepted deposits and mostly lent money on mortgages. Throughout the 1950's and 1960's, these S&L's financed many residential mortgages at fairly low interest rates. The capital to finance the mortgages came from deposits from members, for which the S&L's paid interest. Interest on savings accounts was not regulated until 1966, when Congress decided to limit the amount that could be paid on savings accounts. This affected the S&L's more than commercial banks, since the commercial banks always had access to the Federal Reserve for contingencies. The S&L's did not have this luxury. The 1970's were a bad period economically: high energy prices, slow growth, high inflation, and high interest rates. The high interest rates meant that S&L depositors withdrew their money to make more profitable investments. But the S&L's could not compete because the interest they were allowed to pay was fixed. The income from the long-term mortgages previously issued at low interest rates combined with an inability to attract depositors led to a financial problem. Rather than correct the error that Congress made in 1966, Congress initially ignored the problem. But because so many mortgages were financed by S&L's there was considerable pressure to keep the S&L's in business. The federal insurance company that was to pay off depositors in case an S&L failed (FSLIC) was underfinanced. But allowing the S&L's to go out of business was not attractive, since it would prove that Congress was derelict in its duty to fulfill guarantees it had made. So, in 1980, Congress de-regulated the S&L's, meaning the regulators could now allow the S&L's to engage in higher-risk investments with their depositor's money. The hope was that they could earn enough in these higher-risk, higher-reward ventures to cover the losses elsewhere (i.e., from the long-term mortgages made in the 1950's and 1960's). The S&L's made high-risk real estate investments that failed, and the raising of interest rates in the early 1980's to correct the Federal Reserve's previous error of undue expansion put the S&L's into serious financial problems. Many of them were facing failure from the mid-1980's to the mid-1990's. The government then had to bail them out at a cost of about $130 billion of taxpayer's money. Here we mostly see bad government polices and some high-risk behavior by the S&L's.

Examples of the second category include the large automobile manufacturers: the Chrysler bailout in 1979 and the "structured bankruptcies" of both Chrysler and General Motors in 2008 and 2009. Chrysler's problems in the 1970's were mostly due to Chrysler's unwillingness to respond to the public demand for more fuel-efficient vehicles, given the rise in gas prices throughout the 1970's. Chrysler also decided not to try and raise capital from the public, relying instead on its own resources; this led to a debt financing problem. Chrysler was saved because many of its workers and those of its suppliers were union members, and Chrysler's failure would be a political problem for the Democratic Party. Hence it was bailed out with a loan $1.5 billion of taxpayer's money. Fortunately, Chrysler did make some significant changes, revamped its lineup, cut costs, improved sales, and was able to repay the federal government early. Overall, the government made a profit of about $500 million on this transaction.

The causes of the 2008 bailouts of General Motors and Chrysler are similar: high debt, falling sales owing to production of vehicles the public did not want, and high cost union labor. This again was clearly a political problem, since most of the workers are union members. The first $17.4 billion bailout was authorized 19 Dec 2008. There was a series of additional bailouts between Feb 2009 and Jun 2010; the total "invested" using taxpayer money was about $80 billion. In the end, GM ended up being 60% owned by the U. S. Treasury and 40% by private investors; Chrysler became jointly owned by the Italian carmaker Fiat and the United Autoworkers Union. Chrysler paid off its portion of the bailout in 2011; GM repaid part of its bailout, but the U. S. government wrote off $14 billion in losses.

An example of the third category is the bailout of financial institutions in 2007 through 2009. The main causes were:
a)   Government-mandated mortgages granted to people who could not afford them (called "subprime")
b)   A considerable amount of undetected corruption in the writing of those mortgages
c)   Willing and knowing suspension of risk assessment by large financial institutions
d)   Creation and sale of poorly-understood bundled securities known as "collateral debt obligations" and "credit default swaps" and
e)   Assumption on the part of the financial institutions (who should know better) that the housing boom of 2002-2006 would continue indefinitely, which led to undue assumption about future potential.

These financial institutions had to be bailed out because their collapse would affect the rest of the economy (so we are told), but actually they were bailed out because of close political connections and the fact that part of the problem was itself a result of unwise government policies regarding home ownership rates. On 3 Oct 2008, bailouts totaling $700 billion was authorized, but this was later reduced to $475 billion. Of the $475 billion authorized, $426 billion was actually "invested" in loans and other guarantees. In the end, $441 billion was repaid by these institutions, resulting in a profit of $15 billion; however other ancillary programs related to the bailouts will result in a $38 billion loss.

To summarize, bailouts occur when bad government policies lead to bad financial outcomes, or when a political party risks losing votes, or when politically-connected insiders come to believe they are so big and important that their friends in high places will never allow them to fail. This is "crony capitalism": in good times, the corporations keep all their profits; in bad times, the losses are covered by the taxpayers. A good indicator of which industries and firms will eligible for bailouts when necessary is to examine political contributions to members of certain Committees in the Congress, and contributions to their favorite Political Action Committees. The most important committees for implementing and managing large-scale bailouts in the House of Representatives are the Budget and Financial Services; in the U. S. Senate, it is the Banking, Housing and Urban Affairs, Budget, and Finance Committees.

But the main thing to recall here is that no small business will ever get a bailout because they simply do not matter to the political elite. Only the companies that are so incompetent and so large that their failure would negatively impact the general economy can get a bailout. So long as they have the right political and personal connections, they will continue in business, even at taxpayer expense. Raises and promotions all around; the penthouses, champagne, limousines, and fancy parties continue as always.

Disregard any talk you hear from socialists and progressives that the U. S. economy is too "capitalist", and requires more regulation. If the economy were truly capitalist, there would be no bailouts, and these incompetent and/or corrupt companies would get the "reward" they deserve: to be out of business. Don't be fooled into thinking that the socialists would prohibit bailouts; socialism thrives on cronyism, crooked backroom deals, and massive institutionalized corruption. That is because socialism requires business decisions to be made based on political considerations instead of economic ones.

-- § --

Question 11: Income Tax Fairness

Some in Congress in 2006 proposed an income-tax modification bill that would have provided a 5% across-the board reduction in federal income tax rates. The bill mandated that the highest marginal income tax rate would have been reduced from 38% to 33%; the next rate from 25% to 20%, and the lowest from 10% to 5%. Capital gains rates would remain unchanged. Critics have claimed that only the very rich would benefit from this measure. They were joined by Mr. Ralph Thompson, estimated to be the nations fourth-richest person, who came out in opposition to the tax cut, saying, "Neither I nor any other wealthy people need an income tax cut." But people who favor the tax cut claim that the working people will benefit because they will have more money in their pocket. For example, the single person working a full-time job (40 hours per week) at $6.50 per hour (just over minimum wage of $5.75 per hour) would have their marginal rate reduced to 5%, so they would have received a tax cut of approximately $4.67 per week after the combined standard deduction of $8,750. Does this income tax proposal unfairly benefit the wealthy or unfairly penalize the working poor with regard to income tax rates?
a)   It unfairly benefits the rich because they will pay less in income taxes.
b)   It unfairly benefits the rich because they don't need the extra money, as Mr. Thompson said.
c)   It unfairly penalizes the poor because it left the minimum wage unchanged.
d)   It unfairly penalizes the poor because the proponents of the tax cut are lying: the extra $4.57 won't buy much and isn't necessary.
e)   All of the above are true to some extent.

Answer to Question 11

This is a trick question. None of the answers are correct.

The arithmetic works like this. This person works 40 hours per week at $6.50 per hour, which is $260 per week. Assuming a 52 week work year, his total income is 52 x $260 = $13,520. His standard deduction is $5,150, plus there is a personal exemption of $3,500, for a total deduction of $8,650. So his taxable income is $13,520 - $8,650 = $4,870. At the old rate, he would pay $4,870 x 0.10 = $487 in federal income taxes. Under the new rate, he would pay $4,870 x 0.05 = $244, a difference of $243 per year. Or, dividing the $243 by 52 weeks per year, he would get a tax cut of approximately $4.67 per week.

Answer (a) is wrong because this proposal only reduces the amount of unfairness already imposed on the rich. To be fair with regard to income tax rates, the rich should pay the same rate as the poor. If this proposal was to be enacted, the rich will still pay more than six times the rate of the poor, so if anything, it is still unfair to the rich.

Answer (b) is wrong because it has nothing to do with fairness one way or the other. Also, the proposal deals with taxes on income, not wealth. The wealth held by the rich will not be affected one way or the other by a change in the income tax because the income tax is imposed on what is earned in a given year. On the other hand, wealth is the accumulation of income from past years (upon which income taxes have already been paid). It is true that the rich will end up with more money from their current income, but how is that unfair? Why is it unfair for the rich to keep most of their income after paying taxes? If a person makes a higher income, does that not suggest that his time is more valuable than someone who makes less? To suggest that everyone's time should be valued equally is to say that an hour of your time on a basketball court is just as valuable as an hour of Nikola Jokic's time on the court. Would an hour of your time in a recording studio be as valuable as an hour of Paul McCartney's or Sean Combs' time? People are rich because they inherited it, they married into it, they have great talent, or they had a good idea, worked hard, and earned it. None of those are unfair.

Answer (c) is wrong because it is irrelevant to the question at hand. The bill before Congress did not address the minimum wage any more than it addressed the capital gains rate.

Answer (d) is wrong because the extra $4.67 per week is still $4.67 the person will keep instead of paying it to the government. The fact that $4.67 per week (or $243 per year) is not a particularly large sum does not make it unfair. Why is it unfair for the poor to pay less in taxes? If it is "unfair" for the poor to pay less in taxes, it must be "fair" for the poor to pay more in taxes, right? Hopefully there aren't any voters who are dumb enough to embrace this line of reasoning. The reason the tax cut appears so small for the working poor is that their taxes are very low to start with.

Under this proposal, both the rich and the poor will have more money to spend; the rich will simply have more than the poor (as always, that's why they're called "rich"). Of these, answer (d) is the worst one, because the logic requires one to believe that even a small income tax cut is bad, even for the poor. Note that the $8,650 is the income of a person working part-time at about 28.9 hours per week at the $5.75 minimum wage. Such a person would pay no income tax because his income equals the sum of the standard deduction and personal exemption. In other words, answer (d) embraces the false concept that anyone making more than the minimum wage must be rich, and therefore undeserving of a tax cut.

This is one of the many disadvantages of a personal income tax: it fosters class warfare under the guise of "fairness". There is nothing "fair" about any citizen being required to divulge, under penalty of perjury, their income status to irresponsible bureaucrats at the Internal Revenue Service. Secondly, "fairness" is the wrong way to look at taxes because it ignores how income and wealth are created and utilized. The poor spend nearly all their income on living expenses; the rich use nearly all their income on either luxuries or investments. Expenditures for luxuries represent an increase in economic activity (someone has to supply them) and thus indirectly cause an expansion of employment. Investment creates opportunity for people to start their own businesses (including the poor) and also expands economic opportunity within existing businesses, which also benefits the middle class and the poor alike.

This debate shows the general degree of economic ignorance in America. The truth of the matter is, aside from any particular notion of "fairness", as societies generally become more prosperous, nearly everyone enjoys a higher standard of living than the previous generations. It is also true that those who have the most wealth will tend to gain more as the society continues to prosper, hence the saying "the rich get richer". But it is not generally true that as the rich get richer, "the poor get poorer", as is commonly stated. As societies become wealthier, the standard of living slowly increases, even for the poor.

The progressives (socialists) would have you believe that those with high incomes should be taxed such that their net income after taxes would only be slightly larger than those making the smallest amount. That is the socialist system: everyone (except for the political ruling class) ends up either poor or just above poverty. The reason that socialism fails is that it attempts to use slogans and brute force instead of economic reality. Economic reality shows that economic progress can occur only by expansion of capital; capital has to come from savings; savings is the difference between income and expenses; and if everyone has only enough income to meet their immediate expenses, then there can be no savings, no capital, and no economic progress. That is why the Soviet Union collapsed, and why Cuba, North Korea, and Venezuela are economic basket-cases. It also explains why the vast majority of people in Communist China will spend their lives walking behind a water buffalo, scratching out a subsistence living.

-- § --

Question 12: Reporting Storms

There are about 85 named storms worldwide each year [1]. Prior to 1950, hurricanes were not officially named. Hurricanes were given official names after 1953, and the minimum sustained winds necessary to qualify as a hurricane was 74 MPH [2]. In 2002, tropical storms also began to be named (having sustained winds greater than 38 MPH) in an effort to legitimize claims of "man-made global warming" [3, 4, 5]. Thus, the number of named storms has grown over time, due to the lowering of wind speeds used as the criteria. Every such storm, whether a tropical storm, or hurricane, has the same characteristics: strong winds, large waves impacting the shore, and a lot of rainfall. Why does every TV news outlet feel it is necessary to send a reporter to the beach before and after every storm to show viewers that this one will cause high winds, large waves, and heavy rainfall, exactly like all the others that have occurred during the past 100,000 years?

a) TV was not around for the first 99,960 years of hurricanes and tropical storms, and the news networks are trying to catch up.
b) TV anchors deserve a chance to do a little surfing.
c) So there will be a photographic record of the damage, for insurance purposes.
d) To conduct interviews with the local people, who can describe what they expect or what they saw afterward from the storm.
e) Some combination of c) and d).

[1] "Number of category 4 and 5 hurricanes has doubled over 35 years", University Corporation for Atmospheric Research, 16 Sep 2005 press release
[2] The National Oceanic and Atmospheric Administration (NOAA); https://oceanservice.noaa.gov
[3] "NOAA inflating storm numbers and aiding political campaign for carbon restrictions", The National Center for Public Policy Research press release, 30 Nov 2007
[4] 2007 Hurricane Season: In Like a Lamb, Out Like A Lion?, The National Center for Public Policy Research press release, 30 Aug 2007
[5] 2007 Hurricane Update, Have Records Been Broken?, The National Center for Public Policy Research press release, 10 Sep 2007

Answer to Question 12

This is a trick question. All of the answers provided are wrong.

The first reason TV networks send reporters to the beach whenever a storm comes ashore is that they have an enormous amount of airtime to fill, and looking at rain is easier than reporting events of real news interest. Answers a) and b) might be true, but do not relate to the question (since neither is "necessary"). Answer c) is false because the news corporation is not interested in insurance claims, unless it is their facility. Answer d) is false because the locals are going to tell the news reporter what everyone already knows: there will be strong winds, large waves, and a lot of rainfall.

A second reason for coverage of hurricanes is that it gives the news networks an opportunity to advance the notion that the weather is worse now than in previous centuries because mankind has affected the climate. They have an advantage in convincing the dummies: there is no video of hurricanes in any century prior to the 1900's. Therefore, any claim can be made about the relative severity of the weather because there are no means of drawing direct comparisons (and little reliable data recorded prior to about 1880).

We are seeing more serious effects from this phenomenon. In the past (prior to cable TV), news segments were fairly limited, and the anchors were able to get out the facts of a story, with only a small amount of time for editorializing (which was clearly labeled as such). But with "so much air time to fill", and active 24 hours a day, the "news" often turns to gossip, speculation, rumors, anonymous accusations, ignorant opinions, and pure ideology. It is becoming increasingly difficult for a viewer to get a straight story in chronological order, with actual facts, anywhere in the mainstream media. This trend is not good for the nation, or even for the media itself.

It is however helpful to the advocates of socialism. Without a contrary opinion being allowed, it is easy for the socialists to claim that your life must be handed over to them for absolute regulation because only socialism (being "scientific") has a plan for saving the planet. If the planet did need saving, the socialists are the wrong people for the job. No socialist nation has ever accurately calculated the number of ladies' size 7 shoes to produce. If they can't make that determination, how can they save a planet?

Don't be fooled: the weather goes in cycles on a scale measured in centuries, and there is no evidence that the weather is worse now than in previous eras. Scientists have compiled data based on ice cores and tree rings that suggest there was a warming trend in the Middle Ages (about 900 to 1250 AD), and a sudden miniature Ice Age period between 1600 and 1750. There was a time, about 1000 AD when the southern part of Greenland was actually green; that is, warm enough to support agriculture and farming. The European colonists who lived there either died out or moved on in the late 1300's. There were probably two causes: the end of Norwegian shipping, upon which the Greenland settlers depended for supplies, and the cooling of the climate, which precluded a continuation of agriculture in Greenland [1].

The fact that storms were not named prior to 1950 is the perfect ruse for the socialists to claim that the increase in the number of named storms is "proof" that mankind is changing the weather very rapidly and therefore the socialists must take over your life under the guise of restraining "man-made global climate disasters". The same people were claiming in the 1970's that global cooling would lead to mass starvation due to crop failures by the year 2000, none of which happened.

[1]   Knut Gjerset, *History of Iceland*, NY: The Macmillan Company, 1925, pp. 93-114

-- § --

Question 13: Team Jerseys

A sports fan (father of three young children) is in a clothing store and finds a jersey from his favorite major league sports team in his size that is on sale at $75.00. It normally sells for $100.00 (i.e., the $75 represents 25% off regular price). The jersey is a genuine one, authorized by the major league franchise (not an imitation). Why is this jersey a good deal?
a)   The sports fan can show his support for the team whenever he wears it.
b)   If he wears it to a game, the players will appreciate that he is one of their fans.
c)   He can use it to teach his children the value of teamwork.
d)   The jersey may become a valuable collectible in the future.
e)   Some combination of all of the above.

Answer to Question 13

This is a trick question. All of the answers are wrong.

This is a bad deal, because he is actually buying a $10 jersey with a $65 logo, which is the licensing fee paid to either the league, the franchise, or the owner of the franchise.

Answer a) is wrong because a team performs as well as it does depending on the abilities of the players and coaches, regardless of how many people support it or wear their licensed jerseys.

Answer b) is wrong because the players, all of whom make much more than the average person, are too busy laughing at people paying $75 or $100 for a $10 jersey. If anything, their laughter would cause them to play worse.

Answer c) is wrong because a jersey does not teach team work per se; that has to be done by example.

Answer d) is wrong because it can happen only 100 years from now, assuming the jersey in question has never been worn, and is one of very few surviving at that time (not likely).

If this father wanted to spend the $75 on something important, a better choice would be to spend the day with the kids, buy them a few small toys and a round of ice cream. The best football in America is not played among the college ranks or the NFL: it is with the kids in the backyard.

-- § --

Question 14: Lobbying Congress

Consider the following fictional scenario.

Congressman A received a total of $161,000 from a consortium of oil and gas companies, consisting of $118,000 in direct campaign contributions and $43,000 to his Political Action Committee (PAC). Congressman B received a total of $68,000 from a legal lobbying group that supports expansion of civil lawsuits, consisting of $53,000 in campaign contributions and an additional $15,000 in contributions to his PAC. Congressman C received a total of $258,000 from an environmental lobbying group, consisting of $204,000 in campaign contributions and $54,000 to his PAC, which is another environmental lobbying group. Congressman D received a total of $380,000 from a group devoted to increased regulation of "conservative talk radio", consisting of $346,000 in campaign contributions and $34,000 to his PAC. All four of these Congressmen were lawyers before they ran for Congress.

A bill came before Congress which contained the following provisions:
1. A reduction in natural resources leasing fees, which will save oil and gas companies $24,000,000. This is the outcome desired by Congressman A's donors.
2. An increase in the deductibility of rent and expenses for legal offices, which will result in a $138,600,000 savings to lawyers because they will pay less in income taxes. This is the outcome desired by Congressman B's donors.
3. An extension of the amount of federal land to be controlled and administered by environmental groups along with a federal grant of $102,700,000 to cover administration, lobbying, education, and other costs. This is the outcome desired by Congressman C's donors.
4. A provision in which a portion of the advertising revenue from certain talk radio shows (totaling $47,200,000) is to be turned over to a federal agency to investigate the political ideology and financial condition of talk radio hosts. This is the outcome desired by Congressman D's donors.

All four of the Congressmen voted for the bill. Which Congressman's actions constitute the worst examples of bribery?
a) Congressman A, because he seeks to protect the predatory for-profit oil and gas industry, which seeks to pollute the entire earth.
b) Congressman B, because the contributions he received constitutes a conflict of interest (he was a lawyer himself before he ran for Congress).
c) Congressman C, because the amount that was given to the environmental PAC will be devoted to lobbying, part of which will be probably be donated to Congressman C next year.
d) Congressman D, because his donors seek to reduce the free speech rights of conservative talk radio hosts.

e) All of them are equal offenders, because the principle involved (trading favors or creating laws for money), is immoral and illegal. The problem is not the exact amounts of money that changed hands.

Answer to Question 14

This is a trick question. None of the provided answers are correct. None of this as described constitutes bribery.

Although the statements in this scenario are fictional, the process described is very real. Everything in this scenario is perfectly legal because Congress has passed many laws which make these arrangements legal. There is no corruption to be found here. Congressmen routinely take money in contributions from various rent-seeking groups, and then pass laws that directly or indirectly benefit those same groups. Far from being considered illegal, immoral, or unethical, it is how Congress operates because Congress has found it beneficial to operate this way. It is how Congress rewards their friends (those who demand some special benefit) and punishes their enemies (the taxpayers and those who cannot afford lobbyists).

There is one exception. Such activities can be considered illegal if and only if a particular donation was devoted to getting a particular provision passed, called a "quid pro quo" (a Latin term meaning "something for something"). In other words, if Congressman A received $10,000 for the sole purpose of voting for the bill in question, that would be considered possible bribery. But so long as the lobbyists never demand any particular vote on any particular bill, the lobbyist can actually write the language of the bill for their benefit, make contributions to the Congressman, have him vote for the bill and encourage other members to vote for it, and receive the benefits they wrote into the bill. All this is done legally because the contributions were not explicitly tied to that one vote.

There are two lessons here. The first is that everything given to these interest groups will come out of the taxpayer's pockets. In the natural resources example per Congressman A, the taxpayers will be deprived of leasing fees that belong to the people in general. In the civil suit example per Congressman B, lawyers will get a reduction in the amount of taxes they pay, which means the revenue has to be made up from increased taxes elsewhere. In the environmental example per Congressman C, regulatory power and taxpayer money is given directly to an interest group simply because they demand it. In the free speech example per Congressman D, the lobbying group gets a new federal agency to investigate, intimidate, and persecute their ideological opponents at taxpayer expense.

The other lesson is that Congressman B should raise his rates. To see why, it is necessary to consider the benefit-to-cost ratio from the point of view of the lobbyists. If the lobbying group spends $68,000 to obtain favorable terms under a new law that will save them $138,600,000, then the benefit-to-cost ratio is 138,600,000 divided by 68,000, which comes to 2038.23. The lobbyists desire to maximize the benefits from the money spent on lobbying, otherwise lobbying is a waste of money.

Consider the benefit-to-cost ratios of these four scenarios. Congressman A's donors received $24,000,000 in benefits at a cost of $161,000, and ratio of 149.06. By similar calculations, it is easy to see the benefit-to-cost ratios are 2038.23, 398.06, and 124.21 for Congressmen B, C, and D respectively. This shows that Congressman B gave away far greater benefits in relative terms than did the other three. Congressman B works cheap, and was a "good find" for the lawyer's guild. No doubt he will be rewarded with a full partnership in the law firm of his choice after he retires from Congress.

This is not to say that all lobbying is bad. If a lobbying group uses its influence to protect the rights of citizens (e.g., to defend the rights called out in the Constitution), then such lobbying is beneficial. Then the question becomes: if all Congressmen have sworn an oath to defend the Constitution, and so have all other government employees, why is such lobbying necessary? Because no government is ever satisfied with the power it has. This is especially true of "progressives" and socialists: their goal is to maximize their power and minimize your rights, and even reduce your rights down to privileges to be doled out as convenient for them.

-- § --

Question 15: Legal Short-Term Earnings

The most effective plan to adopt for earning a lot of money legally in a short period is:
a) Lottery tickets
b) Games of chance (legal gambling) at a casino
c) TV game shows
d) Church bingo
e) Timing of investments in the stock market

Answer to Question 15

This is a trick question. None of these choices are a reliable way to obtain money in a short period.

Answer a) is wrong because the probability of winning a lottery with a large prize is very small. For example, the probability of winning the big prize in a state-run lottery depends on the structure of the game, meaning how many numbers the player gets to choose from an array of numbers. Some games are structured as 6/49, in which the player chooses six numbers between 1 and 49. The probability is:

(6 x 5 x 4 x 3 x 2 x 1) divided by (49 x 48 x 47 x 46 x 45 x 44) = 720 / 1.006834752E10, which comes to one chance in 13,983,816 = 7.1511E-08, which is the same as 0.000000071511. Likewise, for a simpler game of 5/22, the probability would be (5 x 4 x 3 x 2 x 1) divided by (22 x 21 x 20 x 19 x 18) = 120 / 3,160,080 = one chance in 26,334 = 0.000037974. But keep in mind that players are induced only by large prizes, which can be issued only if a large number of people play, and so the game must be made more difficult. That is, in order for large prizes to exist, the probability of winning has to be kept very small such that more players buy tickets, and the prizes continue to increase week after week because it takes several weeks for the probabilities to come into play such that someone finally gets the winning numbers. That is why simple games (such as picking numbers from 1 to 100) have small prizes. At the other extreme, the Powerball lottery can work up to very large prizes because the probability of winning the big prize is somewhere around 1 in 175,000,000 = 5.7142E-09 = 0.0000000057142.

Answer b) is wrong because the "games of chance" at casinos are engineered to provide the casino, playing as the "house", a slight edge. In games of pure chance such as roulette or dice, the player must guess correctly many times in a row in order to win a significant amount over what they bet. In Blackjack, the probability of winning is higher for a skilled player than an unskilled one, but the edge enjoyed by the house will cause all players to lose in the long run. In the short run as considered here, a player can win but not by planning to go in and win; it is purely a case of short-run good fortune, guaranteed (by the house advantage) to disappear as quickly as it came as more hands are played.

Answer c) is wrong because the probability of winning a TV game show depends on the probability of being chosen to appear on the show. If it is a game of skill (general knowledge as in "Jeopardy", "Who Wants to Be a Millionaire", or experience at shopping as in "The Price is Right"), a player may do well. But the overall probability of winning, when contemplating how to earn a large amount of money in a short time, is very small because the probability of getting onto the show is very small.

Answer d) is wrong because the probability of winning at church bingo (which will not involve a large amount of money anyway) depends on the number of "cards" being played. Suppose that the church operates the game truly as a charitable event, that is, it does not play as the "house"; all the prizes are awarded to players in the audience. If so, the probability depends on the number of customers that play. If you are the only player, only you can win, and eventually (even if it takes nearly all the numbers being called), you will be the winner. If 100 bingo cards are being played, each card has an equal chance of being the first to meet the bingo requirements, and the probability that you will win is 1 in 100, that is, 0.01. Likewise, if you are one of 10,000 cards that are being played, your probability of winning is 1/10,000 = 0.0001.

Answer e) is wrong because...wait a minute; we pause here for a commercial interruption....

> Wouldn't you like to live like the rich and famous? Wouldn't you like to have a private jet, a summer home on the Riviera and a winter home in Aspen? Wouldn't you like to have the biggest yacht in the harbor? Wouldn't you like to be invited to the A-list parties with all the other successful people? Well now you can! All you have to do is become skilled at day-trading in the stock market, and you too can enjoy untold wealth. Build your wife that dream house she's always wanted! Buy a fleet of Ferrari's, one for each day of the month! Become known as the one guy from your hometown who made it big! Send your children to the finest universities! No more trudging to a boring job every morning: day trading can be done in the comfort of your own home! Day trading stocks, bonds, and commodities futures is simple once you learn the secret tricks shown in the upcoming "Don't Wait - Get Rich Today Working the Market" seminar. Tickets are only $699 per person. First come, first served! Hurry, seats are going fast and we can offer this low, low price only for a short time! Act now, and don't miss out on this fantastic opportunity! Live the life of your dreams! Make your reservation today!

We've all seen those ads. But I'll tell you their "secret trick" for free. The "secret trick" is: all you have to do is be able to guess or infer what the market will do tomorrow, or in the next hour, or in fifteen minutes from now. You can either rely on guesswork or you buy an avalanche of data from some company and hope to make enough sense of it to buy and sell stocks profitably. All you have to do is guess or infer correctly about 80% of the time. See how simple? Anyone can do that. Except --- no one can do that. The market depends on the choices of millions of people spending billions of dollars every day, and you, the individual, cannot hope to do better than the aggregate of investors, which is "the market". The same is true of any scheme that depends on "timing the market". The market cannot be timed; it is subject to the truth, the false rumors, the actual needs, the phony desires, the greed, the generosity, and above all, the arbitrary whim of millions of investors. Can you benefit from occasional lucky guesses? Can you "diversify and spread the risk" and make money? Sure, but you will not get rich quick either way.

As a wise person once said, "The way to end up making a small fortune in day trading is to start off with a large fortune."

The correct answer to this question is: there is no way to develop a "plan" to get rich legally in a short time. All of the possible answers posed in the original question have either: a) a very small chance of success; b) a very small monetary prize; or c) can occur, but only in an unplanned way. This last category does happen, but purely by accident and coincidence.

-- § --

Question 16: Jim Crow

Slavery in the Southern states was abolished in the U. S. after the Civil War with the ratification of the 13th Amendment to the Constitution on 6 Dec 1865. However, racism continued to be a problem, as exemplified by the so-called "Jim Crow" laws that began to be passed in the Southern states during the late 1880's. The Jim Crow laws consisted of provisions such as [1, 2]:

a. Whites and blacks were segregated in restaurants, theaters, hospitals, public transportation, schools, and libraries. The facilities provided for blacks were generally inferior to those provided for whites.
b. Literacy tests were applied to black voters, but exemptions made for illiterate whites.
c. Poll taxes were imposed on black people, but waived for whites.
d. Marriages between whites and blacks were prohibited.
e. Curfews were imposed only on black people.

f.   Railroading of black people into long jail sentences for minor infractions and then paroling them to large landowners, who worked them as slaves.

g.   Occasional lynching's by the KKK and other white supremacy groups to keep the black people in fear (approximately a total of 4,950 lynching's occurred between 1880 and 1968)

h.   Black people were prohibited from owning guns.

Based on the above facts, what were the primary underlying objectives of the Jim Crow laws?

a)   Allowed the Republican Party to suppress the black voters and keep them in fear because they could not defend themselves.

b)   Allowed the Republican Party to take advantage of black people by keeping them in poverty relative to whites.

c)   Allowed the Republican Party to perpetuate the falsehood that black people were inferior and could not be trusted.

d)   Allowed the Republican Party to keep the black people isolated and ignorant by preventing them from achieving the same educational level as the whites.

e)   All of the above.

[1]   Ronald L. F. Davis, Ph. D, "Creating Jim Crow: In Depth Essay", available at: https://agaul.weebly.com/uploads/3/7/8/0/3780214/jimcrow_lesson.pdf

[2]   Clayton E. Cramer, "The Racist Roots of Gun Control", *Kansas Journal of Law and Public Policy*, Winter 1995, available at: https://www.claytoncramer.com/scholarly/racistroots.htm

Answer to Question 16

This is a trick question. All of the answers provided are wrong.

But all of the answers are correct if the phrase "Republican Party" is changed to "Democratic Party". It was the Democrats who enacted and enforced the Jim Crow laws in order to suppress black people's progress from slavery to freedom [1]. They were in effect from about 1890 to 1968. In 1968, a greater fraction of Republicans than Democrats in Congress voted for the Civil Rights Acts (signed by Democratic President Lyndon Johnson because he was backed into a corner politically). Under the Civil Rights Acts, the federal government took responsibility for enforcing equal treatment of black people in some southern states, which gradually ended the legal aspect of the Jim Crow era.

It was the same Lyndon Johnson, as Majority Leader of the Senate, who had blocked a vote on an identical bill in 1957. It was only when change became inevitable that he signed it as President.

The Democratic Party has waged three large-scale attacks against black people in America. The first was slavery itself, including the justification for it based on "inferiority" of black people. The second attack was the institution and enforcement of the Jim Crow laws. Both of those attacks ended, one by a Civil War, and one by black people standing up for their rights. Through both of those attacks, the black people held together by maintaining strong family ties and by adhering to the Christian faith. The third attack was the "Great Society" programs of the 1960's. The Democratic Party made black people the test cases for their socialist political control experiments under the pretense of relieving poverty. It is a very subtle and so far very successful attack, because it has served to greatly weaken the black family, (and to a lesser extent, the influence of the Christian church in the black community). This attack continues, as those programs are all now ingrained into federal policy.

Don't be fooled by all the talk from progressives and socialists in the Democratic Party about how they are working day and night for "racial equality". The Democratic Party has always hated black people and they always will, except on Election Day when black people can be fooled or intimidated into voting for Democrats. The new plantations (large Northern cities run by Democrats) are not much different than the old ones (large Southern cotton farms run by Democrats).

[1]   The American Civil Rights Union, "The Truth about Jim Crow", 2014, available at:
      https://theacru.org/wp-content/uploads/2015/02/ACRU-the-truth-about-jim-crow_v2.pdf

-- § --

Question 17: Unusual Behavior

A famous Hollywood movie star/celebrity concluded that he was born as the wrong sex because he was attracted to other men. He had a sex change operation and changed his name from William to Jessica. After the sex change, she found that she was no longer attracted to men, but was now attracted to women. This has turned out to be very confusing for her and her fans. What is the best course of action to address this unusual behavior?
a)   Have a sex change back to a man and announce he is gay.
b)   Maintain her sex as a woman, but live like a man and date women.
c)   Undergo extensive therapy to find out why he/she thought she/he should have been a female in the first place.
d)   Become a lesbian, since that is her present orientation.
e)   Change his/her name to Dale, Kim, Robin, or Gene to get in touch with her masculine side (since these names are commonly given to both boys and girls).

Answer to Question 17

This is a trick question. There is no correct answer because the premise of the question was "how to address this unusual behavior".

For celebrities, especially those in the drama business, the behavior as described would not be considered particularly unusual.   The course of action taken by celebrities who find themselves in this kind of situation follows a well-known pattern. Usually the celebrity will attempt to portray themselves as some kind of victim, begin a foundation or activist group, demand that everyone else undergo "sensitivity training", and do whatever they can to draw attention to themselves. There might even be a movie script in it.

It should be kept in mind that celebrities as such are a dime a dozen, especially now that there are so many TV channels and opportunities for musical acts. The prime objective of a celebrity is to stay in the public eye, which is best done by staging publicity stunts like the ones described. Nearly everything a movie star or TV star does is a publicity stunt.

The latest publicity stunt used by many TV and movie celebrities is the promotion of socialism. They want you, the regular person, to believe that socialism is good for you, and that if implemented, we'll all be equal. Do you actually believe you will make as much money as TV and movie starts if socialism is implemented? Of course you won't --- movie stars aren't going to take a pay cut, and you don't have the talent that they have. The celebrities will retain their large salaries and fine homes and privileges since they are the "useful idiots" that every socialist needs to keep the people pacified. Nothing will change for them. However, under socialism, you will become a peasant.

-- § --

Question 18: Suppressing Rats

Consider the following fictional scenario. A certain city of 250,000 people was consistently overrun with rats. It was estimated that there were about 20 times as many rats in the city as there were people. The rats continued to be a health nuisance, and many children had to be treated in local hospitals due to rat bites and the diseases they carry. Over the past ten years, the citizens had voted for, and paid, special taxes to be allocated to fighting the rat problem, totaling $150,000,000. (This works out to about $60 per year for ten years for each city resident.) The city sanitation department was in charge of suppressing the rats, and sometimes made some progress. They routinely proclaimed great successes, but over the long run, the reality was that the rat population continued to grow.

A certain wealthy man decided to take some action. He convinced a local radio station to announce a "bounty" on rats, amounting to $2.00 per pound for any rats, dead or alive, payable in cash to any resident of the city who showed up at the city dump with the rats on a certain day. This was widely advertised over a two-week period; on the chosen day, many city residents arrived at the city dump with about five million dead rats. This was far greater than the total number of rats killed by the city forces in the past ten years.

The average weight of the rats was about 1.5 lbs each; this initiative cost the wealthy man about $15,000,000 all total. The wealthy man paid the bounty in cash as promised. The total expense was about one-tenth of the total cost of the special taxes paid by the residents over the past ten years.

Then, to embarrass the city, the wealthy man arranged for all the dead rats to be dumped on the sidewalks in front of City Hall late on a Sunday night. When the City Hall workers come to work the next morning, they could not get into the building because of all the dead rats blocking the entrances. Naturally, the Mayor and City Council members were furious, and called a press conference to denounce the private rat killing effort. The mayor demanded that the wealthy patron have the rats removed, which was refused. The city ended up removing the rats and burned them in a neighboring incinerator. What is likely to happen next?

a)   An investigation will be conducted into how the tax money appropriated for the unsuccessful city-run rat suppression initiative was spent to see if there was any waste, fraud, or abuse of the taxpayer's money.

b)   The head of the sanitation department will resign for his failure to get the rat population under control, even though the taxpayers had paid $150,000,000 in taxes for that purpose over the previous ten years.

c)   The Mayor will resign in disgrace for letting the rat situation get out of control.

d)   The Mayor will remain in office, but will announce that he will not run for re-election.

e)   Both a) and b) will occur plus either c) or d).

Answer to Question 18

This is a trick question. None of the answers are correct.

Here is what is likely to happen:

a)   The Mayor and City Council will call a joint press conference and denounce the rat kill-off as a dangerous action that put the health of the citizens at risk. Note: City Hall will be in the position of claiming that there was no health hazard when the rats were alive, biting small children. They will appear to claim that the rats became a health issue only after death, when they were put on the sidewalk used by City Hall employees. This attitude indicates a massive degree of arrogance and hypocrisy, neither which are problems for a typical City Hall. The Mayor and Council members will also decline to answer why they didn't stop the private rat-killing initiative beforehand if they thought it was so dangerous.

b)   The Mayor will ask the local police and the FBI to conduct a full investigation into the motives, finances, and personal relationships of the wealthy patron, the employees of the radio station, and the trucking company hired to deposit the dead rats in front of City Hall. All are subsequently demonized by the Mayor and Council members for being "cowardly, extremist anti-government types with possible ties to terrorism" and "infiltrators seeking to lower the public's opinion of the government".

c)   The wealthy patron will be sued for the cost of the rat removal, and will subsequently be prosecuted for conducting a sanitation operation without a license.

d) The wealthy patron will be sued by the government employees union for attempting to eliminate government jobs.
e) The wealthy patron will be sued by an animal rights group for genocide.
f) The head of the sanitation department will receive a raise and promotion to Special Advisor to the Mayor.
g) The Mayor will take credit for ridding the city of rats, and will run for Governor.

The important point to remember is that corrupt, incompetent, and inefficient governments will do what is necessary to protect themselves and their friends from embarrassment. If your local government is corrupt, incompetent, and inefficient, never participate in any attempt to do anything useful, unless you can keep it secret before and after. There's no future in it.

-- § --

Question 19: Speech Restrictions

Suppose a prominent black civil rights leader had made public speeches like these in 1993:

"Only after the white virus destroying the quality of life of black people has been eliminated can we hope to promote cooperation between the remaining races, which will then be founded on a common understanding."

"Honkie parasites on one hand ripped off the black people without a second thought, and on the other hand instigated people of color to violence. The misfortunes of black people have become a continuing objective for these white trash crackers, and it was unfortunately made possible because of the large number of desperate unemployed black people that mistakenly supported the international trade treaties, which further benefitted the rich honkies."

What is the proper amount of government regulation or actions that should be adopted to address speech of this sort?
a) Public speeches of this sort should first be subject to review by qualified people to determine if they are acceptable for public consumption. If a proposed speech is considered acceptable, then the speech could be made. However, neither of these two fragments is acceptable, and both should be prohibited.
b) These fragments are obviously racist, and should be prohibited by appropriate legislation.
c) These fragments indicate both racism and mental illness, and the person who made these statements should be examined to determine his mental health. If he is found to be of sound mind, he should be prosecuted for racism or hate speech.
d) The person making these statements should be prosecuted for hate speech unless he can prove he is mentally ill and therefore not responsible for what he says.
e) Because of the First Amendment, it is difficult to pre-empt speech solely because some find it objectionable. For radical opinions like these, a one-size-fits-all approach won't work, but the government should consider some appropriate remedy, tailored to specific cases. However, such remedies should be civil (i.e., fines and restrictions) instead of criminal (imprisonment).

Answer to Question 19

This is a trick question. All of the choices given are false.

As far as I know, no such speeches were given by a black person in 1993. In fact, the speech fragments in the question are actually modified paraphrases of speeches made by Adolf Hitler in 1939. In fragment (a), change "white" to "Jew", and "black" to "German", and you have a good sense of what Hitler actually said about the Jews. In fragment (b), change "honkie", "cracker", and "white trash" to "Jew"; "black" to

"German"; and "international trade treaties" to "Bolshevist Revolution", and you will have a good sense of what Hitler claimed about the impact of Jews on German society [1].

So, Hitler was obviously an idiot, any black person who would make a speech per the fragments is an idiot, and any white person who would make the opposite comments about black people is an idiot. Even so, all of the given choices regarding government actions are still wrong. It is clear that speech of this type is not beneficial and may be hurtful (but only to those who care what idiots think). The speech itself may be bad, but the fact that it exists is good. It is good because the speech you like, but which is opposed by others, also exists.

Suppose, in imitation of fragment (a), a Moslem said: "Only after the Christian virus infecting the quality of life of the people has been removed can we hope to establish cooperation between the remaining religions, which shall be built upon a common understanding." Would you really want the government to "protect" you from this speech? Such stupidity can be defeated only if the stupidity is known to the public.

In answer (a), if a system of censorship and review is in place, these sentiments by the Moslem (or white race-baiter or black race-baiter or Adolf Hitler) would not be widely known. Secondly, what criteria would be used to determine what is "acceptable"? Maybe the censors would disapprove everything they personally did not like (which would affect many things you do like); maybe the racists and religious fanatics would seek to obtain positions on the censorship boards. Note also, in answer (a) (if you chose it), you have appointed yourself the power to find that "neither of these is acceptable" and "should be prohibited". Who made you the Lord High Scrutinizer? What's that you say? You're British, and regulation of speech works well in your country? We would not wish to offend Moslems, now would we, ye residents of Merrie Olde Londonistan?

Answers (b), (c), (d), and (e) all have a similar fatal flaw, in that someone, somewhere, has to determine what is "hateful", or what "alleged thought" is sufficient proof of "mental illness". What is hateful, or what is mental illness will be in the mind of the government regulator, not in the mind of the subject. After all, the government regulator will have to either: a) use their experiences and moral judgment; or b) rely on a speech code, which in turn reflects the experiences and moral judgment of whoever writes the speech code. The regulator will regulate based on what he prefers, or on what a majority of other regulators prefer, or on what a majority of public opinion favors, or what a majority of government officials or academics consider "safe". Ultimately, any speech that some unknown unaccountable government regulator somewhere personally disagrees with will be considered "hate" or "criminal". None of these are a guarantee of correct determination: in the end, the regulation of speech leads to "freedom from speech".

There is an especial danger to answer (c). First of all, it has already been partially enacted under the "hate speech" laws. A person can be prosecuted for anything he said in the course of committing a felony, and anything he is suspected of thinking. It only applies as additional charges to an existing felony, but it will be a simple matter legislatively to extend it to all speech. When it is applied to all speech, it will have the effect of stifling all speech, since everyone will be facing bankruptcy for saying anything that offends someone with the right political connections.

The important point here is that the Founding Fathers were right when they decided that freedom of speech is the best remedy to sort out what is worthwhile and what isn't. If you have to tolerate things that you find offensive, pony up a little backbone and deal with it; meanwhile, no one gets to suppress your opinions either.

This is why socialists and "progressives" love speech codes: it allows them to determine and enforce what is acceptable, or more exactly, what conforms to their opinions. You, the regular person, are not allowed to have individual thoughts different than what the Most Exalted Socialist Masters dictate. Note that the speech codes are always changing, and of course exceptions are made when one of the Most Exalted Socialist Masters are caught violating it themselves. Speech regulation is all about the power to control thought, which influences actions, and to transfer power directly to the government, activist groups, and their cooperating corporations. It really is that simple.

[1]   For the actual text of Hitler's comments, see Norman H. Baynes, *Hitler's Speeches*, London: Oxford University Press, 1941, Volume 1, p. 743. Fragment (a) is a paraphrase of part of a speech Adolf Hitler gave at Wilhelmshaven on 1 Apr 1939; fragment (b) is similarly a paraphrase of one he gave in the Reichstag on 28 Apr 1939.

-- § --

Question 20: The IRS

Why is the agency that collects federal income taxes called the "Internal Revenue Service" (IRS)?
a)   It is responsible for answering taxpayer questions.
b)   It is responsible for printing all the forms and making them available online.
c)   It generates the revenue necessary to run the government.
d)   It advises Congress on the advantages and disadvantages of various tax policies.
e)   It is a combination of a), b), and d).

Answer to Question 20

This is a trick question. None of the answers are correct.

The IRS performs the functions cited in answers a), b), and d) along with several others, but they are not why it is called the Internal Revenue Service. It is called a "Service" to distract you, the taxpayer, from the fact that the IRS is actually an income tax enforcement bureau that has nearly arbitrary powers. It does not answer to Congress, or the President, or the courts, or the voters regardless of how much it abuses its powers. You are guilty before the IRS unless you can prove you are not; and you have to prove your innocence in the U. S. Tax Court if you disagree with the IRS's determination.

The IRS routinely gives incorrect answers to taxpayer questions. Too bad, you still have to pay taxes, penalties, and interest, even if you acted in good faith on IRS advice. Answer c) is wrong because the IRS does not "generate" revenue, it collects it from taxpayers.

There was a scandal in 2010 through 2012 in which IRS employees knowingly and willfully stalled approval of tax-exempt status for conservative political groups. No matter: no one was fired for this activity, no one was prosecuted, and no one was fined or went to jail. That was pretty good service, don't you think? Lois Lerner was fired, but only because she had become a public relations liability, not because anyone at the IRS thought she did anything wrong [1]. Her accomplices were unaffected, receiving the usual raises and promotions on schedule. IRS employees are at liberty to do anything they want to a taxpayer (with respect to the tax laws) all in the name of "service".

Don't be fooled by the names given to government agencies. The word "service" in the name of a government agency refers to the fact that you, the citizen, serve them. Likewise, the name of a government agency does not necessarily indicate their function. For example, the Department of Education does not actually educate anyone; the Department of Agriculture does not actually grow anything; and the Food and Drug administration neither raises food nor produces drugs. The Security and Exchange Commission neither provides securities nor performs exchanges. All of these, and the ones called "services", spend all their time regulating you, the citizen, and attempting to increase their power over you by "interpreting" the law to justify additional regulations.

Once again, it is easy to see why socialists and progressives desire to have as many overlapping government agencies as possible -- all the better to entrap you, my dear.

[1]   Staff Report, Committee on Oversight and Government Reform, U. S. House of Representatives, 113th Congress, "Lois Lerner's Involvement in the IRS Targeting of Tax-Exempt Organizations", 11 Mar 2014, pp. 3-5

-- § --

Question 21: Security of Property

The Mayor and City Council of a certain city desired to raise the amount of tax revenue received by the city. They made a secret arrangement with a mall developer as follows:

1. The city would designate a certain district of the city, consisting of 150 homes and a few small businesses as suitable for development. This district was selected because most of the homes are more than 30 years old, and it has excellent access to major freeways.
2. With the area so designated, the city would send notices to each homeowner and business owner that they had 90 days to move out of their homes, and the land turned over to the developer.
3. In order to save taxpayers money, the city would offer 85% of the current appraised values of the homes and businesses as compensation. On average, the homes in the affected district are appraised at $130,000.
4. The total amount paid to the homeowners by the city as compensation would be repaid by the developer. He would be allowed to collect an additional 2% surcharge sales tax on everything sold by stores in the mall. That way, the city would be repaid the amount given to the original homeowners, and also collect all the usual sales taxes.
5. The Mayor, City Council, and their respective staff members were to do all of the foregoing without any public hearings or notices until the formal designation letters were mailed to each affected resident.

The Constitution of the State in which this was to occur contains a "takings" clause, in which people are to be compensated for any seizure of property devoted to public use (i.e., the same as the Fifth Amendment to the U. S. Constitution). If this plan were enacted, which of the activities contained in the secret plan would violate both Constitutions?

a) A government entity entering into a secret financial agreement with a private entity.
b) Seizing property from a group of private owners and giving it to another private owner for the benefit of the new private owner (as well as the city).
c) Arbitrary designation of a certain district for unusual treatment simply because of the age of the homes and their location.
d) Forcing each homeowner to take a $19,500 loss on their property, since they will be paid only $110,500 for homes that were appraised on average for $130,000.
e) All of the above.

Answer to Question 21

This is a trick question. None of the elements of the secret plan violate either the law or the Constitution. There was a time when it would have violated the Constitution, and no such law would have passed, but the courts have solved that problem.

This process as described is now considered legitimate under "Eminent Domain" and "Tax Increment Financing". "Eminent Domain" originally meant that the government can take private property for public use, so long as the original owners were fairly compensated. Traditionally, the local government could take property from private individuals only if the objective was to build improvements for use by the general public: expansion of roads, canals, bridges, etc. However, in recent times, eminent domain has been expanded to allow the government to take from one private owner and give to another private owner simply because the new private owner promises to generate more revenue for the government [1]. Also, the government doing the taking gets to choose how much to pay the original owners for their property.

The process begins when the political entity designates the area to be seized as "blighted". This is actually a legal term, having nothing to do with the actual condition of the area. "Blighted" means that the entire area becomes subject to control by the local government. Once an area is declared "blighted", the current owners cannot sell their homes to another buyer: the homes are technically worthless because the entire area is now legally designated for "development". In other words, once the "blighted" designation is made, only one buyer is permitted (the government or a developer acting on behalf of the government), and only one entity sets the price (the government). "Tax Increment Financing" is the method in the latter case by which the city advances the money to the developer to buy the properties from the current owners. The mall developer is able to pay this loan back to the city because it is allowed to collect a special tax to be paid by the people who shop at the mall. In other words, the taxpayers pay twice (the original money given by the city, which came from the taxpayers), and through higher taxes such that the developer can repay the loan from the city.

Typically it is too expensive for the original owners to contest the amount they are to be paid, so they have no choice but to accept what the city offers as compensation for their homes and businesses. The alternative is to bankrupt themselves in legal fees by trying to sue the city.

Another twist on this scheme is for the government entity to set up a dummy corporation, usually with names containing the words "Progress", "Improvement", "Revitalization", "Empowerment", "Civic Action", "Opportunity" or similar innocuous titles, whose only purpose is to manage the paperwork required by the tax assessors' office to carry out the confiscations. The political entity (in this case, the city) then passes an ordinance permitting the dummy corporation to act in the political entity's behalf to perform the actual "eminent domain" procedure. This way the political entity can claim that it did not actually perform the deed; it was done by the dummy corporation. Then the same politicians who authorized the confiscation of private property at a net loss to the current owners can blame "greedy corporate interests" for destroying the lives of the affected people. Never mind that the corporation was created by the politicians for the express purpose of carrying out the politicians' conspiracy.

As for the $19,500 average loss on each home, those (former) homeowners should pony up some gratitude for the high quality local government that is doing what is necessary to increase government revenue in order to obtain more good government. The only remedy for this situation is not to own any property in an area with a convenient location that some developer with good political connections finds attractive for his use.

As bad as this situation is, it will be far worse under a socialist government. A socialist government pretends to respect private property only as long as it is politically convenient. A socialist government in this case will not have to go through the charade of a transaction, nor will it bother to pay any compensation at all. It will simply declare your property forfeit, put the developer's name on the deed, and send the county sheriff over to put you and your family out into the street. The developer will not be a private corporation. It will be another government agency tasked with "making a better community through promotion of equality".

[1] This was the situation in Kelo et al vs. City of New Haven, CT., in which residents sued the city for taking their property to give to another private entity. Although this should have been resolved within the state of Connecticut, an appeal was made to the U. S. Supreme Court, which ruled in favor of the city (545 U. S. 469 (23 Jun 2005)), on the grounds that "public purpose" is close enough to "public use", and that "economic development" is a suitable "public purpose".

-- § --

Question 22: Leading Stories

The editor of a local newscast has received four stories from his reporting staff on a certain day. The four stories concern a) an armed robbery in which two victims were stabbed, but not fatally; b) a local woman who claims to have proof that wearing white underwear causes skin cancer, although she has made many claims over the years and all of them have been proven incorrect; c) the Governor made a speech at a local hotel outlining his budget recommendations for next year; and d) the owner of a popular local restaurant was arrested for drug possession. Which of these stories will lead off that evening's newscast and why?

a)   The armed robbery story, because violent crime affects the most people in the community.
b)   The white underwear story, because it provides people with important information to help them protect their health.
c)   The Governor's speech, because it is required by law.
d)   The restaurant owners arrest, because people want to know if the restaurant will still be open.
e)   They will be broadcast according to the chronological order in which the four events occurred that day.

Answer to Question 22

This is a trick question.   All the answers are wrong.

Answer a) is wrong because violent crime does not affect most people in the community. It only affected these two victims.

Answer b) is wrong because the woman's claim is patently ludicrous on its face, and she has no credibility.

Answer c) is wrong because no states have passed such a law.

Answer d) is wrong because only a tiny minority of a city's population visits the restaurant in a given week, and so is not newsworthy.

Answer e) is wrong because it is the editor's job to decide what news is of greatest importance and broadcast in that order.

So how does the editor choose the lead story? The editor knows his audience, and has a sense of what types of stories are likely to attract the most viewers, which in turn allows the station to increase the advertising revenue. So, it is the editor's job to choose the lead story based on his estimate of which one will cause the most viewers to tune in, which increases ratings, which increases advertising rates. He does this based on his experience with the audience in that community. The armed robbery story will lead if it is likely that constitutes the latest in a series of crimes, which taps into the public's interest in general safety. The underwear story will lead if the editor believes he gets the largest audience with the outlandish and sensational. The Governor speech will lead if it contains dramatic changes from last year, or if the station (or editor) has a strong position of support or opposition to the Governor's agenda. The restaurant owner's arrest will lead if he is famous for something else besides owning the restaurant, especially if he can be represented as some sort of hypocrite. The selection of topics and stories on newscasts is based primarily on advertising revenue.

But of course there is an exception to this general rule: when the editor or management of the station has decided to infuse politics into "news" stories. Then the stories are chosen to advance a political agenda, not so much to report facts.

-- § --

Question 23: The Work Ethic

A certain person holds the following opinion on the work ethic: "Everyone should get off their butt, find a job, and do for themselves unless they can afford not to work, or they are too old, or too sick to hold a job." What is the fallacy in his reasoning?

a)   He is ignoring the fact that people should not have to work for less than they are worth.
b)   He is ignoring the fact that some people do not want to work and they shouldn't be forced; everyone has a right to basic necessities.

c) He is ignoring the fact that the world is interconnected now, and it is no longer necessary to "do for one's self".

d) He is ignoring the fact that "doing for one's self" is actually a form of selfish indulgence and smug self-satisfaction, which leads to the type of effete snobbery so harmful to community harmony.

e) This man is an extremist ideologue and his statement contains no evidence of logic or reason, so the question is irrelevant.

Answer to Question 23

This is a trick question. All of the answers are wrong.

Answer a) is wrong because an hour of a person's labor is worth what they can get for it; there is no objective determination of "worth". Wages and salaries are simply the price of labor. It is a factor in every product that is produced and every service that is performed. The total cost of producing something or providing a service is the combination of various labor prices with all the other costs: rent, materials, and machinery. If the end price of a product or service cannot be sold for more than the total cost of providing it, then the product or service will not exist. If wages are increased, then the costs of production will increase in proportion to the amount of labor that goes into production. Therefore, the prices you pay for those articles and services will also increase. Labor ultimately is worth what it can be re-sold for, not what some theorist claims it should be.

Answer b) is wrong because some people do not want to pay other people's bills, and they should not be forced to do so. The "right to basic necessities" for able-bodied people is a political concept calculated as a convenient excuse for "progressive" politicians to buy votes. There is no legitimate right to demand basic necessities from other people's pockets.

Answer c) is wrong because the interconnectedness of the world (whatever that means) does not pay your bills. Nor does it pay any other bills other than by generating revenue from some source (such as advertising). If it did, then "interconnectedness" is a self-perpetuating wealth-creating mechanism; if that were true, why isn't the internet free?

Answer d) is wrong because it consists of 100% psychobabble. Your friendly neighborhood progressive sociologists and socialists would like for you to embrace it, because if you adopt this mode of thinking, it will be easy for them and their corporate, government, and activist allies to bully you into believing anything.

Answer e) is wrong because this is not extremist rhetoric. History shows that this man's attitude, and its widespread belief and application in previous generations, has served to make America great. America became great because individuals were free to pursue their work choices with the satisfaction that comes from independence, and kept the fruits of their labor. America will decline in proportion to how far we drift away from this principle.

-- § --

Question 24: Islamic Terrorists

Why do famous Islamic leaders such as Osama bin Laden and Yassir Arafat never volunteer to personally undertake suicide bomber missions?

a) They are well educated in the will of Allah, and therefore are more valuable to Allah directing the work of others.

b) They serve as an inspiration to all Moslems, and therefore it is important that they continue to sacrifice in this life for the spreading of Islam, rather than taking the easy way out by transferring immediately to paradise in a suicide bombing.

c)   The leaders of Islam receive special revelation from Prophet Mohammed himself, and he told them that it is not their time yet.
d)   They cannot remember which button to push.
e)   The answer is some combination of a), b), and c).

Answer to Question 24

This is a trick question. All the given answers are wrong.

The goal of the modern jihad leaders is to remain on earth as long as they can because there are no baby billy goats waiting for them in heaven (if you know what I mean). Some jihad leaders instruct their followers that they will receive 72 virgins in paradise for all eternity if they die killing Christians and Jews. Just think, 72 virgins, who will presumably remain virgins for all eternity. Maybe they are highly skilled at serving lemonade. Maybe the mighty jihad warriors will be rewarded with eternity in the company of 72 elderly Catholic nuns with big wooden rulers. But the leaders like Arafat and bin Laden were in no hurry to get the 72 eternal virgins: they wanted to stay on earth as long as possible.

The modern Islamic "jihad" movement operates the same as all the other radical movements in history: the leadership convinces young, dumb, easily manipulated morons to do the dirty work while the leadership enjoys the fruit of other people's labor, besides what they can steal from the victims. In this case, bin Laden and Arafat enjoyed many pleasant years of molesting billy goats on earth. They also received a lot of publicity and wealth from those who supported the radical movement, but whose hypocrisy exceeded their courage. The same is true of those who led and supported the French Revolution in 1789, the Bolshevik Revolution of 1917 in Russia, Mao's revolution in China in the late 1940's, Castro's revolution in Cuba in 1959, and many other examples.

The modern socialist movement in America is no different. It depends on the energy of young, ignorant people to go out into the streets (such as ANTIFA) and gain attention for the movement, that is to say, help the socialist leaders acquire power. Once in power, the socialist leaders will continue to use the young and impressionable as a street army to intimidate anyone who opposes socialist policies, so long as it is necessary to do so.

-- § --

Question 25: Famous Phrases

Which of these are phrases found in the Constitution of the United States of America?
a)   "… separation of church and state…"
b)   "… government shall have the right …"
c)   "… people shall be entitled to general welfare …"
d)   "… right to rest and leisure …"
e)   Both a) and c).

Answer to Question 25

This is a trick question. None of the suggested choices appear in the U. S. Constitution.

Answer a), often cited by atheists, actually comes from a letter sent by President Thomas Jefferson to Nehemiah Dodge and others of "a Committee of the Danbury Baptist Association in the State of Connecticut" on 1 Jan 1802. The second paragraph reads as follows [1]:

> "Believing with you that religion is a matter which lies solely between man and his God, that he owes account to none other for his faith or his worship, that the legislative powers of government reach actions only, and not opinions, I contemplate with sovereign reverence that act of the whole

American people which declared that their legislature should "make no law respecting an establishment of religion, or prohibiting the free exercise thereof," thus building a wall of separation between church and state. Adhering to this expression of the supreme will of the nation in behalf of the rights of conscience, I shall see with sincere satisfaction the progress of those sentiments which tend to restore to man all his natural rights, convinced he has no natural right in opposition to his social duties."

It thus informs the Baptist group that the intent of the First Amendment is to prohibit the government from creating a state religion, compelling participation in any religion, compelling belief in any doctrine, or prohibiting belief in any doctrine, or otherwise interfering with private religious activities. Jefferson does not claim that the First Amendment mandates public atheism, as some would have you believe. If it did, why would Jefferson, having taken an oath to uphold the Constitution, write to members of a church?

Answer b) is incorrect because in the U. S. Constitution, the government was granted powers, whereas rights are simply regarded as intrinsic freedoms belonging to each person. In the American system, only persons have rights; governments can only have powers. The American system is a divided sovereignty, meaning that the federal government has certain powers, and the states have certain powers, but none of the powers granted to any government can interfere with the rights of a citizen. But in these modern times, many governments have knowingly and willfully violated the public trust by infringing upon individual rights to varying degrees.

Answer c) is incorrect; it is a common misuse of the statement in the Preamble to the Constitution, which reads:

> "We the People of the United States, in order to form a more perfect union, establish justice, insure domestic tranquility, provide for the common defense, and promote the general welfare..."

In this context, general welfare meant that the government was granted powers to do things that would benefit the people in general but could not practically be done by individuals (such as building roads, canals, and creating a Post Office). It has nothing to do with providing "welfare" to individuals (which is accomplished only by taking money out of the pockets of other individuals). The concept of public "welfare", or "safety net", is an entirely different idea, and is not contained the Constitution.

Answer d) is actually a quote from Article 119 of the 1936 Constitution of the Union of Soviet Socialist Republics [2]. This was nothing more than propaganda. History shows that there was not a moment of rest or leisure under communism, unless you were a member of the Communist Party. Incidentally, Article 122 of the same Constitution guaranteed that "women in the USSR are accorded equal rights with men". In other words, women were equal slaves to the all-seeing, all-knowing, all-directing socialist state.

[1] Merrill D. Peterson, ed., *Jefferson: Writings*, New York: Literary Classics of the United States, 1984, p. 510
[2] https://www.departments.bucknell.edu/russian/const/1936toc.html

-- § --

Question 26: Federal Budgets

Some political operatives stated during 2008 that there was a $5 trillion surplus at the end of the Clinton administration (20 Jan 2001). The total national debt as of 30 Sep 2008 was $10.024 trillion, per the official U. S. Treasury records [1], and Figure 26-1 shows the budget deficits for each year of the G. W. Bush administration (20 Jan 2001 to 20 Jan 2009) from the same dataset. Keep in mind that a trillion is 1,000 billion. The total of all the deficits during the G. W. Bush administration is $4.35 trillion as shown at the bottom of the table.

FY	Ending Date	Deficit ($)	Deficit ($ T)
2001	30 Sep 2001	133,285,202,313	0.1333
2002	30 Sep 2002	420,772,553,397	0.4208
2003	30 Sep 2003	554,995,097,146	0.5550
2004	30 Sep 2004	595,821,633,587	0.5958
2005	30 Sep 2005	553,656,965,393	0.5537
2006	30 Sep 2006	574,264,237,492	0.5743
2007	30 Sep 2007	500,679,473,047	0.5007
2008	30 Sep 2008	1,017,071,524,650	1.0171
Totals		4,350,546,687,026	4.3505

Figure 26-1: U. S. Federal Deficits, 2001-2008

A surplus of about $5 trillion when Bush came into office (20 Jan 2001) and a total debt of $10.024 as of 30 Sep 08 represents a $15.024 trillion increase in the national debt. Where did all the money go?

a)   George W. Bush, Richard V. Cheney, and all their crooked friends on Wall Street stole it.

b)   It was spent on the war in Iraq.

c)   It was spent on the war in Afghanistan.

d)   The rich people got tax cuts.

e)   Some combination of b), c), and d); and the jury is out on the possibility of answer a).

[1]   U. S. Treasury Department, Fiscal Data/Historical Debt Outstanding, available at: https://fiscaldata.treasury.gov/datasets/historical-debt-outstanding/historical-debt-outstanding

Answer to Question 26

This is a trick question. All the answers are false.

Regarding answer a), there is no evidence to date that the President, Vice President, or anyone on Wall Street actually stole any taxpayer money. (Congress may have given them money in the bank bailouts, but they did not steal it, and those transactions do not explain the issue here.) There are some dimwitted political activists who would have you believe that a President actually stole $5 trillion, proving that they have no rational arguments to make.

Answers b) and c) are also false because the money spent for the two wars is already included in the totals in the U. S. Treasury accounting system, and are thus reflected in the deficit figures.

Answer d) is also false because any shortfall of revenue (or gain in revenue) from tax increases or tax cuts are already reflected in the budget figures. (Generally, a tax cut results in more revenue to the federal government, as it frees up capital for investment, which in turn causes the economy to expand, with the resulting larger tax base).

The figures in the table are accurate. So where did the $5 trillion surplus that existed at the end of the Clinton administration go? Surprise, surprise, surprise: there never was a $5 trillion surplus; there has never been a surplus approaching that magnitude in any administration. The operatives who make this statement are either fools who cannot read numbers, or do not understand the difference between an asset and a liability, or do not understand the distinction between a plus sign and a minus sign. On the other hand, they may be lying because they think you are dumb enough to believe them. In reality, the national debt on 20 Jan 2001, the day Clinton left office, was $5.727 trillion. Notice: a debt, not a surplus.

It is not just the Democratic Party apologists for Bill "Perjurer in Chief" Clinton who adhere to this lie. It is repeated occasionally by those who were Republican members of Congress at the time [1]. This shows that both parties are content to lie about the true financial status of the nation.

Figure 26-1 shows a deficit for the year ending 30 Sep 2001; which is the last year of the Congressional budget passed while Clinton was president. Consider for example, what would happen if such a $5 tril-lion surplus did exist. It could only exist if the government had overtaxed the people by $5 trillion, because that is where all the money ultimately comes from. If the government had $5 trillion extra, don't you think there would have been a massive demand to have that money returned to the taxpayers? In the early 2000's, the total budget was about $2 trillion; so a $5 trillion surplus would represent a two and a half year period when no taxation would have been necessary, or conversely, a period of the same length in which the government would have sent large rebate checks equaling the amount that would normally be paid in income taxes. Do you recall anyone talking about a complete cessation of federal taxation in the early 2000's? Do you recall checks being mailed to taxpayers in the amount of their last two years of income taxes? Of course not: because there was never any surplus to be doled out.

The operatives who maintain this fraud do so because at the end of 2000, it was "projected" that a $5 trillion surplus *could* exist by 2020 *if* the Congress continued the policies of the late 1990's, *and if* the economy did not suffer any downturns (such as terrorist attacks, wars, or the bursting of economic bubbles such as the dotcom and mortgage fiascos). In other words, it required economic assumptions that have never occurred and never will occur, as well as the continuing good faith of politicians toward taxpayers. Try not to laugh too hard at that last phrase: *"the continuing good faith of politicians toward taxpayers"*. Enough said.

No government can hold on to a surplus of this magnitude, or of any real surplus. If they did, those funds would have to sit idle in some vault somewhere, of no benefit to the economy. In order for this $5 trillion surplus to exist, the nation would have to run upwards of twenty years of annual surpluses to accumulate it. What group of politicians could resist spending those surpluses on some useless crap, so long as they reaped some sort of benefit?

Don't be fooled by professional liars who rattle off phony projections as if they were established facts. Investigate the true numbers for yourself, as they are all published online by the U. S. Treasury Department.

[1]   Governor John Kasich of Ohio (R), a former member of Congress, stated this patent falsehood on *Fox News Sunday with Chris Wallace*, 15 Jan 2015.

-- § --

Question 27: Artistic Purpose

A group of artists has assembled samples of their work and have displayed them at public venues. Among the works is one that portrays child molestation as desirable, one that blatantly mocks Christians, one that ridicules the notion of hard work and sensible spending, and one that celebrates violence against women. All of them have high-scale production values. They are not cheap efforts designed only to get attention; they are serious artwork.

All of these works of art have themes that are contrary to traditional values, and in fact, turn out to be commercial failures. Why would artists knowingly and willingly spend their talents in this manner?
a)   They are trying to exceed the limits of what is protected by the First Amendment.
b)   They are trying to illustrate the obsolescence of the traditional moral values by example.
c)   It is usually the truly visionary people who tend to become artists; it is their job to instruct society.
d)   They are using reverse psychology to educate people that what they depict in their art really should be rejected.
e)   It is some combination of a), b), and c).

Answer to Question 27

This is a trick question. All of the answers are wrong.

Answer a) is wrong because none of these are limited by the First Amendment; all have been done before without censorship.

Answer b) is wrong because everyone already knows that people have sometimes failed to maintain the virtues of the traditional morality. But these failures do not prove that the traditional values are wrong or obsolete, it only means that the people who did not observe them may be hypocrites.

Answer c) is wrong because the truly visionary people are usually doctors, physicists, agricultural researchers, chemists, and engineers; they have changed society for the better far more than all the artists combined.

Answer d) is wrong because the actual goal among modern artists is to promote their alternate morality of "anything goes with no guilt or hypocrisy". In other words, the new moral code many artists subscribe to is not based on any high standards of behavior; it is based on the concept that the lowest form of behavior is as good as any other. The purpose of the artwork is to convince you (the normal person), that you are a primitive moron. The goal of many modern artists is to convince you to wake up and free yourselves from the guilt and hypocrisy of the good manners that your parents taught you.

Modern artists typically despise religious people and morality in general. If it were possible, they would line up all the religious people and kill them, without guilt or hypocrisy. But of course, the artists claim that you (the normal person) are a hypocrite if you were to criticize them for desiring to do so. If you (the normal person) do criticize them for any reason, you will be ridiculed and accused of "hating".

So it is with all forms of so-called "art" promoted by progressives and socialists. Their goal is to destroy traditional morality and the family unit, to be replaced by guidelines for dutiful little slaves and dependence on handouts from the government (which will actually be taken from your pockets).

-- § --

Question 28: For Your Convenience

A woman is shopping at a mall, and has a small bag of with one purchase from one of the various stores she has visited. She enters into another store, and sees a sign saying "Please leave all bags at the desk for your convenience", and a store employee informs her that all her bags must be left at the front desk while shopping. All the other shoppers are doing likewise. In what ways is this convenient?
a)   She won't have to carry that other little bag around with her in the store.
b)   She won't be running the risk of having someone steal from her bag while she is shopping.
c)   She will have more room in her cart.
d)   She will not run the risk of losing the small bag while shopping.
e)   Some combination of the above.

Answer to Question 28

This is a trick question; none of the answers are correct.

Since the shopper only had one small bag, neither (a) nor (c) is true.

Clearly (b) is not true, because leaving it at the front desk is an easy way for the store's employees to steal from her.

Answer (d) is not true because the bag can be lost at the front desk as easily as any other place.

This has nothing to do with her convenience, and everything to do with the possibility that the store manager believes that she may be a shoplifter. Having her leave her bags at the front desk is for *their* convenience, not hers. She was required to leave them there so that she would have a more difficult time shoplifting, as she would not be able to readily conceal things as easily.

When something is said to be "for your convenience", you can be reasonably certain that it is actually for someone else's convenience. The most notorious future possibility is the advent of "Central Bank Digital Currency" (CBDC). It is a method by which all transactions and record-keeping will be done electronically. The government will advertise it as a great convenience to the people: a) eliminating all that costly coinage; b) eliminating all that dirty Federal Reserve Note paper money, with the bacteria, viruses, and cocaine embedded in it; c) universal integration of your electronic device with the banking system; and d) everyone will have access to banking services. But it will be for the convenience of corporations and the government, not yours. You will no longer have any transaction privacy; everything you buy will be tracked. You will be prevented from buying more than a certain amount of things the government doesn't want you to have (such as meat or gasoline). The CBDC can be set up to have expiration dates such that you will be forced to spend everything you make and never accumulate any savings, and investments will be regulated as the government sees fit. See how "convenient"? Don't be fooled by claims of "convenience". Don't fall for the CBDC scam, as it will greatly reduce your freedom by eliminating your economic freedom.

-- § --

Question 29: Preservation of Rights

Article 2, Section 1 of the U. S. Constitution requires the President to take the following oath of office:

"I do solemnly swear (or affirm) that I will faithfully execute the Office of the President of the United States, and will to the best of my ability, preserve, protect, and defend the Constitution of the United States".

An integral part of preserving, protecting, and defending the Constitution is preserving the rights of the people. The rights of individuals specifically called out in the Constitution and its first ten amendments are:

1) Habeas corpus (right to challenge detainment)
2) Freedom of speech
3) Freedom of the press
4) Freedom of religion
5) Freedom to keep and bear arms
6) Freedom from bearing the expense of quartering soldiers
7) Freedom from arbitrary search and seizure (searches require warrants signed by a judge, with testimony under oath by the officials seeking the warrant)
8) Federal indictment only by grand jury
9) No double jeopardy (a person can only be tried once for the same crime)
10) Immunity from self-incrimination
11) Due process of law
12) Compensation for property allocated for public use
13) Speedy and public trial
14) Cross-examination of witnesses in criminal trials
15) Counsel for defense in criminal trials
16) Trial by jury
17) Facts found by a jury not reviewable by a court
18) Prohibition of excessive bail
19) Prohibition of excessive fines
20) Prohibition of cruel and unusual punishments

Also, rights not specifically mentioned are reserved to the people (individuals) or to the states. Based on your understanding of American history, which three would you rate as the worst Presidents with regard to preserving the rights of the people? The letter after their name indicates their party affiliation (F refers to Federalist, R indicates Republican, N indicates None, D indicates Democrat, D-R indicates Democrat-Republican, which later became the Democratic Party in the 1820's).

a)   Alexander Hamilton (F), Aaron Burr (F), and Benjamin Franklin (F)

b)   Richard M. Nixon (R), Gerald R. Ford (R), and George Washington (N)
c)   George H. W. Bush (41) (R), James E. Carter (D), and Thomas Jefferson (D-R)
d)   Walter Mondale (D), Barry Goldwater (R), and Alf Landon (R)
e)   Three among those listed in groups b) and c)

Answer to Question 29

This is a trick question. All of the given answers are wrong.

If you chose groups a) or d), please be advised that none of those six men ever served as President. Alexander Hamilton was ineligible to be President since he was not native-born (he was born in the West Indies). Aaron Burr was Vice President under Thomas Jefferson. Benjamin Franklin never held an office under the Federal Constitution. Walter Mondale served as Vice President under James E. Carter; Barry Goldwater was Senator from Arizona who lost the Presidential election to Lyndon B. Johnson in 1964; and Alf Landon, Governor of Kansas, lost the Presidential election to Franklin D. Roosevelt in 1936. It is true that Richard M. "I am not a crook" Nixon and Barack H. "Leading with my behind" Obama (and some others) committed crimes, authorized violations of the U. S. Constitution, or covered up for others' crimes, but they are small change compared to the truly criminal Presidents. The worst three Presidents in our history with regard to protecting the rights of the people are Abraham Lincoln, Franklin D. Roosevelt, and T. Woodrow Wilson.

Here is a list of Abraham Lincoln's violations of the rights of the people [1]:
a)   Suspension of habeas corpus (a power he usurped from Congress);
b)   Imprisonment without charge for disagreeing with Lincoln's war policy;
c)   Suppression of the press;
d)   Imposition of martial law, even in the Northern states
e)   Seizure of private property without compensation

Here is a list of Franklin Roosevelt's violations of the rights of the people:
a)   Forced confiscation of gold held by individuals in return for paper notes per Executive Order 6102, and the paper notes were immediately devalued;
b)   Imprisoned without charges about 110,000 innocent citizens of Japanese descent in internment camps based solely on their race;
c)   Attempted to undermine the Supreme Court by adding additional members sympathetic to his ideology (proposing the Judicial Procedures Reform Act of 1937)
d)   Implemented the National Industrial Recovery Act, which took control of the economy, and even prevented people from raising their own food.

Here is a list of Woodrow Wilson's violations of the rights of the people:
a)   Arrest and imprisonment for opposing U. S. involvement in WW I (Espionage Act of 1917, Sedition Act of 1918); 175,000 people were arrested during World War I
b)   Helped establish the Federal Reserve System (a central bank), which controls the economy indirectly
c)   Promoted and implemented the Federal Trade Commission, Clayton Antitrust Act, and the Adamson Act, all devoted to increasing the government's power over the economy
d)   Favored a Parliamentary system and administrative state, in which bureaucrats have arbitrary power
e)   Permitted his Cabinet secretaries to racially segregate government departments (which was an escalation of Theodore Roosevelt's policies)
f)   Implemented the Committees on Public Information; it's job was to propagandize and intimidate the people to implicitly trust the government
g)   Implemented the War Industries Board, which took control of the economy during World War I
h)   Rejected the principle of limited powers and the concept of personal inalienable rights, writing:

   "Every means, therefore, by which society may be perfected through the instrumentality of government, every means by which individual rights can be fitly adjusted and harmonized with public duties, by which individual self-development may be made at once to serve and to supplement social development, ought certainly to be diligently sought, and, when found, sedulously fostered by every friend of society. Such is the socialism to which every true lover of his kind ought to adhere with the full grip of every noble affection that is in him." [2]

When you strip away the high-class doubletalk, Woodrow Wilson is saying that every citizen should willingly submit to the soft socialism of coercion and intimidation, and be willing, in the interest of perfecting society, to accept whatever diminution of his rights that the government may seem fit to impose. But Wilson (a typical product of the Ivy League) was so stupid that he actually believed that society, consisting of flawed people, can actually be "perfected".

It appears that Thomas Woodrow Wilson was our worst President overall, yet many historians (many of whom themselves reject the U. S. Constitution) regard him as one of our best Presidents. When rating the conduct of Presidents of any other public official, the primary consideration is how well they protect the rights of individuals. It does not matter how popular they were, what political party they represent, who endorsed them, or who benefitted from their policies. In the long run, your rights are what matters most.

[1] Andrew P. Napolitano, *The Constitution in Exile*, Nashville, TN: Nelson Current, 2006, pp. 61-76
[2] Woodrow Wilson, *The State: Elements of Historical and Practical Politics*, Boston, MA: D. C. Heath & Co., (1907), Section 1519, pp. 631, 632

-- § --

Question 30: Anonymous Sources

Why do journalists publish articles using information from "anonymous sources"?
a)   To protect the identity of people who secretly provided vital information to the public, although it may not have been legal or ethical to do so.
b)   To protect the First Amendment rights of people who may be afraid of publishing or speaking out on their own.
c)   Because the media serves as the watchdog of a free society, and the people have a right to know about all the available information.
d)   Information from anonymous sources is generally more accurate than from open sources.
e)   It is primarily due to a combination of a), c), and d), although situations like b) do occur occasionally.

Answer to Question 30

This is a trick question. All of the answers are wrong.

Answers a) and b) are wrong because they pertain to "confidential" sources whose identities are known to the journalist; in that sense, they are not anonymous.

Answer c) is wrong because if the media were truly performing a watchdog function, they would publish only information that was corroborated by at least one or two reliable sources known to them. In other words, a respectable journalist would use the information provided "anonymously" only if it were verified by credible sources. In that case, the article is actually based on the credible sources, not the anonymous one.

Answer d) is wrong because there is no way to know if any information provided anonymously is correct or not until events demonstrate it one way or the other, or it is verified by credible sources known to the journalist. It cannot be assumed that information is more reliable simply because the person or organization that provided it does not want their name to be made public.

But truly "anonymous" information is frequently used by journalists because it has many benefits to the journalist. First, it gives rumor and innuendo a veneer of legitimacy; for example, a journalist may write, "anonymous sources have informed us that Famous Person X is under investigation, although we have been unable to verify it". The reader gets the message that Person X is to be suspected because they are being investigated. The reader is not likely to remember that the source is unknown, or that the journalist admitted that he has not confirmed it. But the reader has heard something negative about Person X, which was the goal of the "anonymous source".

Second, it allows the journalist to fill up a large amount of space by presenting claims, counter-claims, and denials without having to do the serious work of figuring out how much of it is true or relevant. In other words, the journalist fills the pages and airwaves with background noise that may contain very little that is factual or newsworthy.

Third, it provides the journalist with a means to interject his biases into his articles and broadcasts by mentioning information from anonymous sources that serve to advance the journalists' preferred view of how things are or ought to be. The advantage is that he cannot be accused of editorializing, since he actually is reporting on information that came to him.

Fourth, it provides journalists and editors with a veneer of legitimacy when publishing the most sensational and controversial claims and opinions; controversy generates interest; interest sells newspapers and airtime; all of which serves to increase advertising revenue and the journalists' fame.

There are many national so-called "news" outlets that function on this very basis. Test it for yourself: when you are watching the "news", focus on how much of what is reported is based on anonymous sources. You will find that many of the "progressive" outlets are willing to fill the airwaves with anonymous claims because the historical facts do not (and never will) conform to the "progressive" fairy-tale religion.

-- § --

Question 31: Super Bowl Victories

If the NFL team in a given city wins the Super Bowl, in what ways do the people living in that city and its surrounding suburbs benefit?
a)   Sense of accomplishment
b)   Increased economic opportunities
c)   Increased revenue from tourism
d)   Prestige
e)   All of the above

Answer to Question 31

This is a trick question. All of the answers are false.

As for sense of accomplishment per answer a), the players and coaches on the team certainly accomplished a difficult task, but the other people living in the city did not. They are simply spectators at most.

As for answers b) and c) there is no evidence that a city with a winning NFL team, or any winning team, gains any material economic or social benefits. A city does not become a long-term tourist destination because a sports team based there won a championship. If a city is a tourist destination, it is for other reasons: unique history (Boston, Washington), party life (Las Vegas, New Orleans, Miami), good vacation attractions (San Diego, Los Angeles, Miami, Buffalo), or access to wilderness areas (Seattle, Portland, Denver), among many others.

As for prestige per answer d), quick, which team won the Super Bowl after the 1996 season? Who cares? Assuming you remember which team did, does that city hold any actual prestige in your mind because a football team headquartered there won a championship that year?

-- § --

Question 32: Politician's Fears

What charge will cause the greatest amount of fear, anger, and resentment among politicians (as opposed to actual "statesmen")?
a)   Flip-flopper
b)   Liar
c)   Crook
d)   Ideologue
e)   They are equally afraid of all of the above.

Answer to Question 32

This is a trick question. All of the answers are false.

Answer a) is false because it implies that what he stood for before mattered, and what he stands for now matters, the question being why did he change his mind? "Flip-flopping" is the euphemism that one politician uses against a second one when the second one appears to have changed his policy or views on a certain issue. Politicians usually do not change their mind on policy. They simply appear to be "flip-flopping" because they were actually pandering to different groups. All it means is that he got caught telling opposite stories to different groups of interested citizens on the same subject. No politician cares if you can't keep his opinions straight: you are not a member of the ruling elite. Therefore, it doesn't matter to him if you think he's changing his mind as necessary to please the audience in front of him.

Answer b) is wrong because being caught in a lie implies that people are paying attention to what was said, even if it is false. Every politician demands to be heard, even if not believed. Politicians now believe that politics is war, and the methods used in war (mainly deception) are all a normal part of the process. Deceiving you, the voter, is probably one of the great satisfactions of being in politics. No politician cares if you believe him or not: you are not a member of the ruling elite; therefore, it doesn't matter if you think he's a liar.

Answer c) is wrong because it implies that what a politician does, and whether it is legal or not, is important to the politician. It is rare for a politician to be prosecuted for anything, except for making the political class look bad by engaging in the kind of overt corruption that everyone understands. A politician that stuffs cash in his suit coat pockets in the course of taking bribes is certainly in legal trouble because he is acting like a member of the Mafia. But there will be no legal trouble at all if the same cash is deposited in his campaign fund, or in his "Foundation", or "Initiative", or a trust fund, or one of his political action committee funds, where it may be drawn out as desired, all legal. Generally, prosecutors are not interested in prosecuting their friends and allies in government service. No experienced politician is afraid of being prosecuted. You are not a member of the ruling elite; therefore, it doesn't matter if you think he's a crook.

Answer d) is wrong because it implies that politicians take governing philosophy seriously one way or the other. Each politician accuses others of differing viewpoints as "ideologues", implying that the other guy is some sort of extremist. But each politician also regards each citizen as an extremist if they don't agree with the politician's views. No politician cares if you like his view of the legitimate role of government: you are not a member of the ruling elite; therefore, it doesn't matter if you think he's a power-mad crusader.

The correct answer to this question is "being regarded as irrelevant". Politics is the business of acquiring, using, and abusing power. A politician who is regarded as irrelevant can neither gain power, nor use power to change society, nor abuse power for his own benefit. That is their real fear; that is the one thing they are resentful about, and is the one thing that will cause them to explode in anger.

But it is not just the politicians who fear irrelevance; the bureaucrats fear it even more. That is why the bureaucrats are always hard at work creating more regulations and eliminating your rights, especially those who desire to advance the "progressive" agenda. The objective is to gain the necessary power to control conditions so as to make you dependent upon the government, while ensuring that they never have to be concerned about losing their jobs.

So, how do you reject a politician and a bureaucrat? Do for yourself and your family, taking care to never become dependent on them for anything.

-- § --

Question 33: Legislative Lobbying

"Lobbying" is the term used when a person or organization spends money and energy to influence legislators, administrations, and courts to adopt policies favorable to the person or organization. It has been estimated that a total of about $3 billion was spent by lobbyists in Washington in 2007, mostly in the course of influencing Congress. Among the groups that have lobbying activities in Washington are finance, insurance, real estate, medical, unions, trade associations (such as construction, firemen, police, miners, plumbers, electricians), industrial associations (such as automotive, tobacco), and the various ethnic, civil rights, and conservation activist groups. The influence of lobbyists has become so pervasive that often it is lobbying groups that actually write the legislation that Congress votes on. Generally, these legislative initiatives involve a change in tax conditions or status, or changes in the amount and type of regulation. Congress is supposed to be working in the interests of the people, but most legislation is pushed through due to the activity and influence of lobbyists. In what ways do lobbyists present a problem for the legislative function?

a) Congress opens itself up for legitimate criticism by accepting money, gifts, favors, and travel from lobbyists.
b) There is considerable risk that corporate interests will gain unfair tax advantages because they wrote the legislation for that purpose.
c) There is some risk that insufficient regulations will be enacted due to lobbying influence, because the legislation was written by those who will benefit from the change in regulation.
d) There is some risk that unions will engage in unethical activities because they get favorable treatment under the law, which occurs because they wrote the legislation for that purpose.
e) It is a combination of a), b), and c).

Answer to Question 33

This is a trick question. All of the given answers are false.

Answer a) is false because Congress is criticized frequently for being susceptible to lobbying influence, yet lobbying continues to increase every year. Therefore, Congress obviously considers the criticism unwarranted and unfair; if the criticism were considered legitimate, Congress would change the system.

Answers b), c), and d) are all wrong because having lobbyists write the legislation relieves members of Congress and their staffs from doing it; in fact it relieves members from reading the legislation before they vote on it. The member only needs to know which lobbyists favor or oppose it, and can cast their vote solely on that basis. Far from being a "problem", this is a great aid to members of Congress and their staff members.

It is great fun to criticize lobbyists and they do deserve some blame. But, lobbyists are not the core problem; they are only a symptom of it. The real problem is that Congress has arrogated to itself the power to legislate, tax, and regulate anything and everything, ignoring the limits of federal power contained in the Constitution. (The disease has now spread to some States and some large cities). Therefore, every organization that has an economic, political, or cultural stake in anything must be able to present their case to Congress through lobbying, in order to ensure that their interests receive a fair hearing. If Congress were to respect the original Constitution, it would not think itself qualified or empowered to legislate on so many issues, and lobbying would be far less necessary. The much-maligned lobbying industry does not just represent faceless corporate interests; the real-estate association, for example, represents the interests of realtors, who are actual people making a living in the real-estate industry.

The main point here is: don't buy into the notion that all lobbying is bad. Some lobbying benefits the public because sometimes it may prevent politicians from taking away your remaining rights. Lobbying is necessary only because officers of governments at all levels, especially the "progressive" ones, have assumed they are so smart that they are qualified and entitled to regulate every aspect of your life. The natural tendency of most politicians, especially the "progressive" ones, is to pass an ambiguous law (which they don't bother to read), and then hand off power to irresponsible, unaccountable, unelected, power-mad bureaucrats for enforcement. That is bad enough, but then your taxes are increased to pay for it. Lobbyists can sometimes curtail the worst impulses of the progressive political elite.

-- § --

Question 34: Wise Investments

Suppose you are 21 years of age and have $1,000 to invest. Which of the following investment strategies offer the greatest long-term financial benefits? Assume that the Prime Rate (the interest rate the Federal Reserve charges to the largest banks) is 5.2%. The banks in turn will lend money at 3% to 10% above the Prime Rate, depending on the credit-worthiness of the applicant. All of these investment strategies are legal in all 50 states.

a) You lend your $1,000 to an individual who promises to pay you 25% per year ($250 per year) interest on the principal. At the end of 10 years, you will receive $3,500, $1,000 of which is your original loan, and $2,500 is interest on the loan. The average annual return to you on this loan is 25%.

b) You lend your $1,000 to a corporation. The corporation agrees to repay you $600 the first year, $400 the second year, and $200 in the third year. In all, you will receive $2,200 over the three years, $1,000 of which is the original loan amount, and $1,200 is interest. The average annual return on this loan is 40%.

c) You give your $1,000 to a corporation, and they agree to pay you $100 per month (indexed for inflation) for life beginning when you turn age 50. Suppose your current median life expectancy is 57 years (meaning that people your age have a median life span of 57 more years). This means that half the people now aged 21 will die before they reach 78, and half will live to 78 or longer. If you fall in the median range for life expectancy, you will collect for 28 years starting on your 50th birthday. Indexing for inflation means that if inflation of the currency causes the dollar to be only half as valuable as it is now, the corporation will compensate you by paying $200 per month, i.e., you will receive $100 in today's buying power, not just $100. Assume that you are now 21 and you expect to live to be 78 (the median life expectancy). Then, you will receive the equivalent of $33,600 in present-year dollars, all of it in interest. The average return over the 57 years between now until time of death is 58.9% (although you will collect it only for the last 28 years of your life).

d) Go to the Off-Track Betting Parlor next Tuesday and bet the entire $1,000 on horse #3 in the fourth race.

e) Each of the first three options have varying benefits and risk, so it would be wise to split the $1,000 among the first three options (not necessarily equally).

Answer to Question 34

This is a trick question. None of the options presented are viable choices, because the first three are too good to be true, and the fourth one is not an investment.

If the Prime Rate is 5.2%, and the banks lend money at 3 to 10% above Prime, the banks therefore lend money at rates between 8.2% and 15.2%. Why then, would any person or corporation be willing to pay you between 25% and 58.9% if they borrowed from you, whereas they could borrow money from banks at much lower rates? The answer should be obvious: they wouldn't ask to borrow from you if they had sufficiently good credit to borrow from a bank. None of these choices make sense financially for a borrower with good credit, which means they are too good to be true for you, the prospective lender. If you are ever asked to lend money on these terms, reject the idea. The proposed borrower is either a crook who will steal your money, or they are desperate because they have very bad credit and there is virtually zero chance you will be repaid. Anything that sounds too good to be true (or practical) probably is. In fact, the first three offerings are so bad, that of the four options presented, rolling the $1,000 on a horse race actually has the best chance of returning something, even though the odds are unknown and probably low.

Don't be swindled by sales pitches offering something that is too good to be true. One common scam, still profitable after all these years, is one in which someone will offer to give you the winning numbers for a future lottery drawing in return for a $10 fee. Now put this in perspective: if someone knew the winning numbers, why would they share them with you? They would then have to share the prize with you, which would mean lower winnings for them. But dummies fall for this all the time. Anyone who offers you a deal that promises returns far above what can be reasonably expected is likely a con artist. Do a comparison against typical scenarios (like the interest rate in the example) and apply some common sense. You are not special enough to get breaks and deals as if you were Bill Gates, George Soros, a Rockefeller, a Clinton, or a Kennedy. You are nothing more than a mark.

-- § --

Question 35: The Source of Wealth

What is the source of wealth in the U. S.?
a)   The Federal Reserve, because it prints the money.
b)   The U. S. Treasury
c)   Banks
d)   The Stock and Commodities Markets
e)   There is no one source of wealth in the U. S.; all of the above together are the source of wealth.

Answer to Question 35

This is a trick question. All of the answers are wrong.

Answer a) is wrong because the Federal Reserve prints currency (not money); and said currency and even money are nothing more than representations of wealth that has already been created.

Answer b) is wrong because the U. S. Treasury, like any treasury, was intended to be storehouse for government revenues, which is actually wealth already created by taxpayers and given to the government. (However, the U. S. Treasury has become a place where officials add up how much of the wealth that will be generated in the future by Americans actually belongs to other countries.)

Answer c) is wrong because banks lend money, derived from existing wealth, or their credit, which is a way of expressing confidence in the utility of existing wealth. The money and credit are used to procure capital, from which further wealth is created. But the bank per se is not the source of wealth.

Answer d) is wrong because the stock and commodities markets are the means by which individuals and corporations can invest money, which comes from already-existing wealth, for the purpose of expanding it. But the market per se is not the source of wealth.

The correct answer is that all wealth comes from the work of nature as harnessed by man's labor and ingenuity. For example, the computer industry has provided many people with employment: the hardware builders, the software writers, the people who use the computers in their work, all the people who provide data to put into the computers, and the people who maintain the hardware and software to keep it all running. That employment has allowed those people to earn money, which they traded for either the comforts of the modern world, such as houses, cars, groceries, TV, etc., or for protection against potential future contingencies in the form of money and insurance policies. All of these things are the manifestation of the creation of wealth, which elevates the standard of living above bare subsistence.

The computer is one example of created wealth. But where did the computer come from? A computer consists of software (instructions) that directs the hardware (arithmetic processors and memory) what to do. Without hardware, there would be no need for software.

Where did the hardware come from? It is based on the microprocessor chip. The microprocessor chip is based on "transistors", which are electronic switches that are able to keep track of voltage levels in memory locations, upon which capability all software is based. Where did the transistors come from? A transistor is a small piece of silicon (the metallic component of beach sand) into which is embedded trace amounts of poisons like arsenic, gallium, and antimony. All of these are elements found in nature. How did they come to be combined into a transistor configuration? Because some engineers at Bell Laboratories in the 1940's were searching for a way to "transfer resistance" in electronic circuits, and in the course of their experimentation, discovered the switching and amplification properties of germanium and silicon "semiconductors". Why were they trying to "transfer resistance"? Because doing so would allow them to reduce the size and cooling requirements of the large relay and vacuum-tube computers of the 1940's. By the way, those computers filled several rooms, required several tons of air conditioning, were affordable only by large organizations and governments, and had less computing power than the pocket "scientific calculator" that can be purchased now for less than $25.

The researchers discovered that the transistors used as switches could perform all the required mathematical operations if they could be arranged into various "gates" (called AND, OR, NOR, NAND, EXCLUSIVE OR, and NOT). Mathematicians discovered that all the gates could be constructed from various configurations of NAND gates. The electronics designers established that these NAND gates could all be integrated on a large scale by a common transistor design and circuit configuration. So the race was on to pack as many NAND gates into as small a package as possible, while consuming the minimum power. This drive toward commonality led to a great reduction in overall cost, weight, and cooling requirements. Ultimately the process of miniaturization led to the microprocessor chip. The microprocessor chip led to the widespread availability of computers.

On the software side, engineers created common "instruction sets" called computer languages (such as Assembler, FORTRAN, c, c++, PL/1, COBOL, Pascal, Ada, Java, and many others) so that other people could write programs (applications) to allow people to communicate with the computer and tell it what to do. Thanks to the efforts of scientists and engineers who created all the refinements and improvements in silicon processing technologies, logic, and software, you can play a large number of video games on the internet, not to mention all the productive work that can be done now that could not be done with the old computers. More work that can be done means more work will be done, which means more people will be able to earn a living and save a little. So, in this computer example, wealth was created from the work of nature (refined beach sand and some naturally-occurring poisons), the ingenuity of scientists and engineers, and the labor of all those who use and maintain the many computers now in existence.

There are a very large number of like examples: moveable type and the printing press; eyeglasses; gunpowder; the steam engine; the cotton mill; heating oil; railroads, gasoline and the internal combustion engine; the airplane; and plastics are a few that come to mind. These inventions led to more than just a way to improve man's standard of living: they also altered history. Eyeglasses allowed people to work many years longer and support themselves. Moveable type allowed ordinary people to afford books and become educated, ending the monopoly on learning previously reserved to the clergy and nobility. Gunpowder ended the feudal system, since ordinary people had the means to defeat the tyrannical system of lords and knights. The steam engine and the cotton mill increased productivity and reduced the cost of transportation, releasing the people who formerly did those jobs to do more important and valuable ones. Heating oil made us all comfortable during the winter, and reduced the intensity and duration of flu outbreaks. Gasoline and the internal combustion engine spawned a vast industry that led to many people becoming firm members of the middle class. The same is true of railroads, airplanes, and plastics.

Wealth consists of all objects of value, that is, property, which may be converted to money if desired. But money is not wealth; it is only the medium used to either obtain or store wealth (i.e., anything that has value [1]). The important point is that wealth is accumulated only by saving and investing, because investment is possible only through the use of savings. Saving is spending less than one earns, and is therefore the means by which wealth is expanded.

But the progressive wants you to believe that any accumulation of wealth that comes from hard work and ingenuity is actually the result of government policy, and that all the benefits should accrue to every person equally (after the progressives take their cut). If the progressives and socialists ever get their way, hard work and progress will disappear because there will be no benefit to doing more than the bare minimum. As the Russian people said when they were slaves to the Bolshevik socialists under the Soviet Union, "They pretend to pay us and we pretend to work."

[1]   Amasa Walker, *The Science of Wealth*, Boston: Little, Brown, and Co., 1867, p. 7

-- § --

Question 36: 401(k) Withdrawals

The 401(k) system was set up such that people could save and invest their money prior to paying taxes, let the assets grow over time, then pay the taxes later when they started withdrawing it as early as age 59.5. However, early withdrawals are permitted for certain hardships with no penalty. Hardships are defined as large medical bills (as long as they do not exceed what can be deducted on your income tax), disability, and the splitting of a 401(k) account due to a divorce. Otherwise, early withdrawals are penalized at 10% of the withdrawal amount, and all income taxes on the amount withdrawn are due immediately. Aside from hardship cases, under what circumstances should the average person consider an early withdrawal from their 401(k), even though they have to pay taxes and penalties?
a)   To buy a house, or make a down payment on one.
b)   To buy a car.
c)   To invest in the stock market, buying individual securities, instead of staying with the generic mutual fund offerings in 401(k) programs.
d)   To pay for a honeymoon or other vacation.
e)   Both a) and c) are valid reasons.

Answer to Question 36

This is a trick question. None of the reasons given are good ideas for early withdrawal from a 401(k).

Answer a) and b) are wrong because it is better to rent a home if you can't afford to buy one out of current wages. Secondly, it is not wise to buy a car, which depreciates continuously, with money that is better used in your long-term interest.

Answer c) is wrong because the vast majority of regular people are not competent to invest in the stock market buying and selling individual stocks. Even the experts who do it full time do not produce consistent returns. The best strategy for a regular person is to invest in market-averaging "index funds" [1]. The experts who run the index funds buy and sell individual stocks on your behalf. For example, an S&P 500 index fund invests in those companies based on their market share or profitability. Let the experts work for you.

Answer d) is wrong because a short-term pleasure is less important than long term stability and security.

The 401(k) was devised to give working stiffs a chance to accumulate some actual wealth by contributing small amounts regularly and investing the money in stocks or bonds over a long period of time (30 to 40 years). Although the stock and bond markets fluctuate from year-to-year, over the long run, even modest amounts of regular contributions can add up to a large amount of money for retirement. The average return on a 401(k), so long as you don't mess with it, will far exceed the payout (if there is any) on your "Social Security retirement benefits". So the correct answer is: never take anything out of your 401(k); it is intended, and is best used, as a means of deferring gratification now (when you are able to work) so that you will have enough to live on in your later years (when you won't be able to work).

A good rule of thumb when you are working is: never take points off the board. That means that you never take money out of your 401(k), 403(b), Traditional IRA, or Roth IRA until you are about to retire, except for medical emergencies. Otherwise, those withdrawals will have a large negative effect on the accumulation of wealth in those accounts.

[1] There are many smart investment advisers who provide mostly the same solid long-term advice. One of the best is Paul Merriman, *Live It Up Without Outliving Your Money!*, Hoboken, NJ: John Wiley & Sons, 2008

-- § --

Question 37: The Point Spread

The San Diego Chargers are scheduled to play the Washington Commanders in a regular-season NFL game. If Washington is favored to win by 9 points (this is known as the "point-spread"), it is because:
a)   A team of reputable football experts have analyzed the respective player's abilities, and the majority of them have concluded that Washington is a better team, and will probably win by about 9 points.
b)   A team of reputable football experts analyzed the respective coaching strategies, and a majority of them have concluded that Washington will probably win by about 9 points.
c)   A team of football experts analyzed the health status of the most important players on both teams, and a majority of them have concluded that Washington will probably win by about 9 points.
d)   The politicians and bureaucrats in Washington are using their influence to intimidate the Chargers players, which usually helps the Commanders by about 9 points.
e)   Some combination of a), b), and c)

Answer to Question 37

This is a trick question. The "point spread" has nothing at all to do with the game or the teams or the players, or opinions expressed by football experts, or the influence of government officials.

The point spread is a gimmick created by gambling operations, legal and illegal alike. The objective of creating a "point spread" is to play upon the biases of the bettors in order to get them to place a large number of bets such that the total amount of money wagered on each team is about equal. Equalizing the amount bet on each team maximizes the net return to the gambling operator, whether it is a Las Vegas casino, a "betting parlor", or a local bookie. The gambling operation has no interest in the game or its outcome; it is interested only in taking a service charge for each bet or a fraction of the total amounts wagered. That is why the gambling operation always tries to increase the number of bets placed or total amounts bet, because that is where the money is (for them). The idea is to tempt the betting chumps to risk more of their money based on an entirely phony notion that the scores of competitive contests can be approximately predicted.

Here's how the "point spread" scam works. A gambling operation (called the "house") wins only if you lose. If you place a bet and win, then you win the amount wagered. If you lose, you lose not only the amount you bet, but also some additional percentage that goes to the gambling operation to cover their costs and make a profit. (Bookies normally take 20%, legal ones take less). Ties are counted as wins for the house. So, for gambling purposes, there are no ties, only winners and losers. The long run viability of the house depends on an equal amount of money (not bettors) being won and lost: the losers in effect pay off the winners, while the house gets a percentage of the amount lost. Here is where the point spread comes in: if a strong team is to play a weak team, clearly there will be more money bet on the strong team. Those bets are likely to win, but the house will not be able to cover those bets without an equal or greater amount being lost. Therefore, the house induces a larger number of people to bet on the weak team by giving points, that is, a score advantage for gambling win/loss score-keeping. The number if points assigned to the weaker team has nothing to do with an assessment of how much the weak team will lose by; it has only to do with inducing gamblers to perceive an advantage. The purpose of giving points is to get the gamblers (overall) to bet an equal amount of money on each team. The house obtains the money lost by the losers, uses it to pay the winners, and keeps the additional percentage taken from the losers as its profit. It has nothing to do with the prospective outcome of the game itself.

-- § --

Question 38: Policy and Regulation

What is the main benefit of being a government employee involved in policy or regulatory activities?
a)   The satisfaction that comes from performing useful services for the public.
b)   The satisfaction that comes from being part of the solution to the community/state/nation's economic problems.
c)   The opportunity to promote fairness and equality in the community/state/nation.
d)   The opportunity to manage the resources of the community/state/nation to improve the standard of living and quality of life.
e)   All of the above.

Answer to Question 38

This is a trick question. All the suggested answers are wrong.

The correct answer is that government employee whose job relates to policy or regulation is part of an organization for which there is no penalty for failure. Since there is no penalty for failure, government employees are largely immune from economic downturns and social forces, while retaining the advantages of competitive wages, good benefits, and generous retirement package. The downside is that the employee has to put up with a lot of internal bureaucratic infighting through his career, but it appears than many people are able to adjust to it.

Answer a) is wrong because most government "services" in modern times do not directly benefit the public. There was a time before the 1930's when governments restricted their activities to necessary functions: the local governments maintained a police force, a firefighting force, a public school system, and oversaw sanitation, water distribution, and kept the traffic lights working. The states had responsibility for education, roads, bridges, and other public facilities. The federal government concerned itself with defense, diplomatic relations, and other duties cited in the Constitution. But since the 1930's, the governments have made many promises and taken on more responsibilities, which they are increasingly finding they cannot fulfill. Most of the additional activities have become burdens to the people over the long run.

Answer b) is wrong because governments attempt to apply "one-size-fits-all" solutions to problems, and impose taxes and regulations to administrate it. History shows that governments are generally incapable of solving problems because the unintended consequences of their actions sometimes make problems worse, and sometimes cause new problems to be created. Most government officials propose to solve the problem they created by demanding an expansion of government to obtain more power over the people.

Answer c) is wrong because "fairness" cannot be adequately defined; every law and regulation will ultimately be unfair to someone, or at least will appear to be unfair. Anyone can find a lawyer who can make a claim of unfairness in some respect. Also, "equality" can exist only in a system of slavery or socialism, where every person ends up in the same place, regardless of their work ethic or talent.

Answer d) is wrong because only the creation of wealth can improve the standard of living; the creation of wealth depends on production, which is funded by savings.

Here is an example of government policies causing problems, but the government and its employees never having to answer for their failure. Social Security started off as a modest plan to prevent poverty in old age. When it was enacted in 1935, Congress set the "retirement age" at 65, which was 3 years above the median life expectancy. In other words, by the time one retired at 65, about 66% of the people born in the same year were already dead, and therefore were not going to collect anything. Benefits were paid by taxes levied on those who were still working via a "payroll" tax, which means that every worker pays the same percentage on their earnings up to some maximum. There were in 1935, about 15 people still working to pay into the system to pay the benefits of each person in retirement. Gradually the government decided to gamble that the economy could grow faster if retirees had more to spend. So, the government expanded the benefits for retirees, which required that the payroll tax rate and amount subject to tax be gradually increased from 1% on the first $3,000 of income in 1935 to 12.4% on the first $128,400 of income in 2018. Half is paid by workers, and half is paid by employers (the self-employed pay all of it).

At the same time, owing to the expansion of Social Security benefits, working people were induced into believing that they would not require savings of their own during retirement, so Americans began to spend most of their money instead of saving a portion of it. These trends did partly lead to an economic expansion (a consumer-driven economy), but caused far worse problems in the long run. As people live longer, they collect Social Security longer because the retirement age has been increased only slightly. The retirement age of Social Security was initially three years later than median life expectancy; it is now ten years before it (median life expectancy for people born in 1990 is about 76). The ratio of retirees to workers is down to 1:3 instead of 1:15. At the current Social Security tax rate, many of today's workers cannot afford to save for their own retirement. At the same time, the ratio of retirees collecting benefits to workers paying in will continue to increase, which means that the general trend is for benefits to decrease over time or for taxes to increase. Young people starting off have less money after taxes to save for themselves, and are faced with declining Social Security benefits when they retire. It is conceivable for people who retire in 2057 (i.e., born in 1990) that the benefits will be far less than what the person paid in over his working lifetime. But there is no penalty for failure by the government: Social Security will never be abolished, and no government employee will ever have to take responsibility for this fiasco.

No prescription medicine can be sold without obtaining approval from the Food and Drug Administration (FDA). Its charter is to perform testing to make sure that medicines are safe and effective. Obtaining that approval through the testing program may cost hundreds of millions of dollars and take several years. In the meantime, those who have diseases that a new drug may help are not permitted to obtain the new drug. Their lives may be at risk because the FDA's testing and review of manufacturer's tests takes a long time. On the other hand, the FDA may approve a drug that turns out to be harmful in some way. But who gets sued, the manufacturer or the FDA? Only the manufacturer: the FDA is exempted even though it failed in its main duty, which is to ensure the safety of medicines. See how convenient? The government never takes responsibility for its failures.

The 18th Amendment to the U. S. Constitution prohibiting production and sale of alcohol ("Prohibition") created the Italian Mafia, which smuggled in booze from overseas or manufactured its own. The Mafia corrupted governments and unions, and increased the cost of living in many cities, even after Prohibition was repealed in 1933. But no one in the government took responsibility for the fiasco.

The same is nearly true for government employees engaged in outright criminal activities. It is exceedingly rare for a government employee to be prosecuted for any crimes. It appears that one part of the government (the judicial system) is willing to cover up, excuse, and ignore the crimes of the other side (policy and regulatory). Hillary Clinton and the Biden family are the most famous examples. People who commit the same crimes, but are not government employees, are prosecuted regularly.

-- § --

Question 39: Media Standards

Media outlets such as newspapers, magazines, radio, and television are important sources of news and information to the voters. Because the success of a democratic republic requires voters to be well-informed, it is important for the media to report on issues in a truthful manner. The First Amendment to the U. S. Constitution states that "Congress shall make no law … abridging the freedom of speech, or of the press…". This means that the government is bound in principle, and the officers of the government are bound by oath, to recognize the pre-existing right of the media to be immune to governmental interference; that is, the media themselves are free to develop their own standards for accuracy in their reporting. Because there is no formal system or standardization imposed by the government, what standard have the media imposed on themselves? This question does not apply to the internet.

a) Media outlets impose a general prohibition on reporting facts unless they are provable.
b) Media outlets impose a general prohibition on expression of any opinions or biases by reporters, management, or editors. The only opinions that are allowed are those of readers in "Letters to the Editor" or by viewer emails in the case of radio and television.
c) When reporting "news", the media reports only the facts. The media outlet may be biased in their opinions, but those opinions are reserved solely to portions of articles or broadcast segments clearly labeled as "Opinion" or "Editorial".
d) Opinions of reporters and editors reflecting their personal biases are allowed within news stories, but are segregated in their own section, and clearly labeled as "opinion".
e) Although the exact practice varies from state to state, and from market to market, nearly every media outlet has adopted either c) or d) as an informal standard.

Answer to Question 39

This is a trick question. All of the answers provided are incorrect. Answer (a) is obviously incorrect: if the local TV station reports that a celebrity wore a green dress to an awards ceremony, or that a hurricane swept through the Bahamas, you can be reasonably certain that those events actually occurred because there are so many ways to independently verify that it occurred. Answers (b), (c), and (d) are all incorrect. It is true that Editorials and "Opinion columns" appear in broadcasts and newspapers, but those are not the only places that opinions occur.

Every media outlet is "biased" to some extent. Contrary to popular myths, media bias does not generally consist of reporting falsehoods as if they were true. The nature of media bias consists instead of cleverly mixing opinion with facts in such a way that you, the reader or listener, get an impression that is contrary to the facts. The media then is able to exert its biased influence, without being open to accusation of lying directly. The biased media outlets do not claim that an opinion is necessarily factual. The bias of the media is most efficiently propagated and concealed by using the following formula:

a. Find an opinion held by respected experts that support the media's bias, and reports the FACT that a respected person holds that OPINION. It is easy to find any desired opinion among the wide variety of "expert" commentators.

b. Supplement the opinion by a definition that is true, but not relevant, so long as this fact can be used to infer the validity of the opinion held by the quoted expert.

c. Cite some of the facts as they really are, but add an additional commentary that reinforces the bias.

Here are two examples of bias. Suppose one media outlet favors the tax policies of the current administration and desires to show that the tax policy is keeping the economy out of recession. The other opposes the tax policy, and desires to demonstrate that those policies are driving the economy into recession. The facts are as follows, as of November of the current year:

a. A recession is defined by two consecutive quarters (3-month periods) in which the Gross Domestic Product (GDP) declines.

b. The economic data for the last three quarters shows:
   1) Jun - Sep: GDP decreased 0.3%
   2) Mar - Jun: GDP increased by 0.6%
   3) Jan - Mar: GDP increased by 1.2%

c. Therefore, the economy is not currently in recession, but will be if the next two quarters (Oct - Dec and Jan - Mar) show negative GDP growth.

The media that favors the current policies will report the news as follows (both of these are fictional):

Economy Holding Stable
(Cleveland Pony Express, Nov 13, 2019)

The recent talk of recession appears to be premature, according to economic figures released today by the U. S. Bureau of Economic Analysis. Some economists had predicted a very steep decline in gross domestic product (GDP), but were surprised by figures showing only a modest 0.3% decline in growth rate. Economics professor James P. Silverlining commented, "In my opinion, this small 0.3% decline demonstrates the resilience of the economy in these otherwise competitive times. I was expecting much worse." The growth in GDP in the previous two quarters were positive (at 0.6% and 1.2% respectively). This one quarter of slower growth may well be a temporary lull in an otherwise healthy economic outlook. An economy is technically in recession when there are two consecutive quarters of negative growth in the nation's Gross Domestic Product (GDP). It is reasonably clear that the economic policies of the current administration have helped the economy avoid what could otherwise be a much bigger problem. We expect those same policies to contribute in the coming months to overcoming this minor glitch in the GDP.

Let us parse this passage. The first sentence is patently false, since the figures themselves say nothing about whether "talk of recession is premature" or not. They are simply economic figures. The second and third sentences are true but irrelevant, since they pertain to opinions held by those who happen to agree with the reporter at the Cleveland Pony Express. The fourth sentence is true, but note that the growth figures are given out of order, to imply that the rate of growth was increasing in the two quarters prior to the most recent quarter. The fifth sentence is speculation; it may be true, it may not, and the current figures neither support nor contradict it. The sixth sentence is a true definition of a recession. The seventh and eighth sentences are opinion and optimism.

The media that opposes the current policies will report it as follows.

Economy Nearing Recession
(Phoenix Courier, Nov 13, 2019)

With unemployment up and hard-working families struggling, economic figures released today confirm what most people already believe: that the economy is heading into recession. "It has been my opinion for some months now that an overall economic slowdown is in progress, and we should expect to be in recession sooner or later", says noted economics professor Dr. Hiram Firam. He also noted that there were widespread expectations that figures to be released later this month will show an increase in the unemployment rate. The outlook continues to decline, as numbers released today by the U. S. Bureau of Economic Analysis indicate that the nation's GDP declined by % from the growth reported in the previous quarter. An economy is technically in recession when there are two consecutive quarters of negative growth in the nation's Gross Domestic Product (GDP). It appears that the most recent quarter may be a transition between a normal economy and one in recession. These most recent figures show that the already gloomy economic trend is accelerating due to the policies enacted by this present administration. Look for more of the same in the months ahead.

Let us parse this example. The first sentence is patently false, since the figures simply are what they are. The figures do not "confirm" that the economy is heading into a recession, regardless of what people may believe about it. The second and third sentences are a factual report of an opinion held by someone who agrees with the reporter at the Phoenix Courier; the fact that this opinion was held is true but not relevant. Note also that the professor is speculating about another future report, not the one that is the topic of this article. The fourth sentence is true, but note that the author calls out "a decline of 0.9% from the previous quarter", conveniently omitting the fact that the most recent quarter was +0.6%. The fifth sentence is a true definition of a recession. The sixth sentence is speculation; it may be true, it may not; and the figures released today neither support it nor contradict it. The seventh and eighth sentences are opinion and pessimism.

Note that neither of the reports simply gives all the facts. Both provide opinions that are actually held by people who agree with the media outlet. Both give some of the relevant facts at hand, but are phrased in such a way as to bolster their preconceived notion. You might call this "practical creative writing".

In reality, bias exists in nearly every media outlet regardless of party preference. It is not so much a case of directly false statements; although these were easier to peddle in the past, the advent of the internet means that most blatantly false statements can be uncovered rapidly. Most of what we call bias is actually a result of false conclusions based either on unstated assumptions or a pre-conceived notion of what facts are relevant and which are not. In other words, very few media outlets are willing to spend the resources required to uncover all the facts or to present all of them. The picking and choosing of what is relevant constitutes the bias. It is difficult for a regular person get a suitably full picture to make up an informed opinion.

For example, in debates about the merits of tax cuts, some will claim that tax cuts always benefit only the wealthy, and tend to increase federal budget deficits. They typically cite the 1980's era tax policy under President Reagan as the benchmark. Others will claim that a tax cut always causes the economy to expand and the federal government gains revenue as a result. These people point to the 1980's tax policy under Reagan as a benchmark. Here is a case where neither side is willing to present at least a summary of all the relevant the facts:

a) The high marginal tax rates of the 1970's (up to 70%) caused a great deal of capital to be held by its owners or placed in bonds rather than invested in businesses, since the net proceeds from investing in capital production after taxes was less than could be obtained from guaranteed bond returns. In other words, there was idle capital available, but not the incentive to risk it.

b) President Reagan convinced the Congress to lower marginal rates, the most excessive of which were (logically) placed on the highest incomes; Congress also reduced the number of tax brackets and somewhat simplified the tax code. The benefit of a reduction in marginal rates is of most value to those who were formerly paying the highest marginal rates. Therefore, the wealthiest taxpayers received the greatest reduction of tax burden, although everyone obtained some tax cuts.

c) The tax cuts had three major results:

1) Wealthy people with capital to invest did so, since investing was now economically viable;

2) This additional investment created opportunity for people to start businesses, and hiring rose, increasing employment;

3) Poor and middle class people, with some relief, either spent or saved the additional money, which either caused consumer demand to increase or capital for investment to increase; both of which tend to expand the economy;

4) Overall tax revenue to the federal government increased dramatically.

d) With the expansion of the economy, employment increased, sometimes with higher wages, and the Federal Reserve saw fit to reduce interest rates. The result was general economic prosperity at all levels of the economy.

e) Congress, having made a political deal with a President of the opposite party, also radically increased the rate of federal spending; in fact the federal spending increased twice as fast as the revenue increase.

f) Although the federal government received more revenue, it spent even more than it had before.

g) Consequently, the federal budget deficits and the national debt increased dramatically.

h) Half of the spending increase was devoted to improving military readiness for national defense, and half was for social programs.

It is rare to find all these facts stated in one place at one time in any mainstream media report. Those with a preconceived notion that tax cuts are inherently bad in general emphasize fact g) while excluding the others. Those with a preconceived notion that tax cuts are inherently good emphasize b), c), and d) while excluding the others. Those who believe that expansion of government is inherently good but must be made affordable, emphasize f) and part of h) while trying to prove that a) is always irrelevant. Those who argue for more tax cuts emphasize c) and d) while pretending that a) is always relevant. In reality, the formula used by President Reagan (and earlier by President Kennedy) worked as applied to the conditions that prevailed from the early 1960's to the early 1980's; repeating this tax formula under different conditions will not necessarily lead to the same revenue results. At the same time, reversing the tax formula will not reverse the negative aspects of the spending formula. Instead of a careful analysis of what tax and spending policy should be for the conditions that prevail now, we usually get arguments over which facts from two or three generations ago are relevant because they appear to support a chosen political philosophy. This is what passes for journalism today, and we should not be surprised that the public is frustrated.

-- § --

Question 40: Burglary Rates

In 2007, there were a total of 2,179,140 burglaries in the United States, of which 67.9% were burglaries of residences [1]. There are 3,143 counties/parishes (Louisiana)/independent cities (including Baltimore and St. Louis) in the U.S., counting those for which the county governments have been eliminated (Delaware) or are planned for elimination (Massachusetts) [2]. There are 14,166 school districts in the United States (2007 data) [3]. From this data, which statistic indicates the greatest risk that your residence will be burglarized next year?

a) On average, a residence is burglarized in the U. S. every 21.3 seconds, because no matter where one lives in the country, it is possible that one's home will be burglarized in one of those 21.3 second average intervals.

b) On average, a residence is burglarized in each state every 17.75 minutes, because no matter where one lives in their state, it is possible that one's home will be burglarized in one of those 17.75 minute average intervals.

c) On average, a residence is burglarized in each county every 18.59 hours, because no matter where one lives in their county/parish/independent city, it is possible that one's home will be burglarized in one of those 18.59 hour average intervals.

d) On average, a residence is burglarized in each school district every 3.49 days, because no matter where one lives in their school district, it is possible that one's home will be burglarized in one of those 3.49 day average intervals.

e) All of the above indicate an equal risk.

[1] FBI Uniform Crime Statistics, 2007:
https://www.fbi.gov/ucr/cius2007/offenses/property_crimes/burglary.html
[2] n9jig.com/counties/county.html
[3] https://nces.ed.gov/surveys/annualreports/topical-studies/locale

Answer to Question 40

This is a trick question. All of the answers are false because they do not indicate risk per se. In fact, answers a) through d) are simply arithmetic conversions of the burglary rate for different political subdivisions. The total number of residential burglaries is 0.679 times 2,179,140 total burglaries, which comes to 1,479,636 residential burglaries. Given 365 days in a year times 24 hours in a day times 60 minutes in an hour times 60 seconds in a minute, there are 31,536,000 seconds per year. Dividing 31,536,000 seconds by 1,479,636 burglaries leads to the result of one burglary somewhere in the U. S. every 21.3 seconds, as indicated in answer a). Answer b) was derived exactly the same way; except with 50 states, the burglary rate would be (on average) one-fiftieth of the national rate, hence the interval between burglaries at the state level would be 21.3 times 50, which comes to 1065 seconds, which is 17.75 minutes. Answers c) and d) were done the same way (multiplying the 21.3 seconds for the whole U. S. by 3,143 counties to get 66,945 seconds = 1,115 minutes = 18.59 hours; and 14,166 school districts to get 301,735 seconds = 5,029 minutes = 83.81 hours = 3.492 days to obtain average burglary rates for county and school district subdivisions). So, answers a) through d) are identical; they are simply keyed to different geographic areas or political subdivisions. Note, however, they are illogical because they do not take population density into account.

But none of the answers indicate risk per se. The average rates assume that burglaries are entirely random, when in fact burglars are very careful to choose where to break in. Certain areas have higher crime rates than others; especially if there are many people in the area who are desperate for small quantities of money or things to sell in order to feed a drug habit. In those areas, the risk of burglary is higher than average. Likewise, some areas have low burglary rates (as in Texas and Arizona, where burglars often get a free one-way ride to the mortuary if the resident is home during the break-in). So in general, the "average rate" data shown in this question is useless for evaluating the risk to your residence. It is however, very useful for selling home alarm systems ("A burglary is committed every 21 seconds in America, get an alarm and feel safe"). It is also most convenient for those who desire to scare the public into giving up their rights for a promise of security (the favorite tactic of socialists and "progressives").

The important thing to remember is not to be deceived by overly broad statistics that probably do not apply to your situation.

-- § --

Question 41: The U. S. Dollar

The basic currency unit of the United States is called the dollar. The word "dollar" is a modification of the word "taler", which is a nickname for "thaler", which was the name of a coin minted by the Dutch which contained one ounce of 0.999 pure silver. Therefore, a dollar was originally devised in 1786 to designate a coin containing 375.64 grains of pure silver. There are 480 grains in a troy ounce, so the dollar consisted of 0.7825 troy ounces of silver. There are 31.103 grams per troy ounce, and therefore the dollar was 24.3406 grams of pure silver. Silver was traditionally regarded as 1/15th the value of gold, hence the dollar, although defined in silver, was equivalent to 1.622 grams of gold (which is equivalent to 25.31 grains of gold).

In 1834, the U. S. government decided to reduce the weight of gold in the gold coinage, so it altered the value of silver to be 1/16th of the value of gold, thus one dollar was devalued to 1.521 grams of gold. This put the dollar implicitly on a gold standard, although coins of both types circulated (and the dollar remained at 0.7825 ounces of silver).

In 1900, the dollar was formally converted to a gold standard, in which one dollar was worth 23.195 grains (which is 0.0483 troy ounces or 1.503 grams) of pure gold. The dollar was thus valued at 20.694 dollars per troy ounce.

In 1934, the dollar was devalued to $35 dollars per troy ounce of gold (13.71 grains or 0.02857 troy ounces or 0.8886 grams); In 1972, the dollar was devalued to $38 dollars per troy ounce of gold (12.63 grains or 0.026315 troy ounces or 0.8185 grams); in 1973 it was devalued to $42.222 per troy ounce of gold (11.36 grains or 0.02368 troy ounces or 0.73665 grams).

In modern times, dollars are issued as paper Federal Reserve Notes by the Federal Reserve Bank. The dollar is backed by the "full faith and credit of the United States Government". Therefore, the paper dollar, while itself is nothing more than paper and ink, is simply a representation of real value. How is the "full faith and credit of the United States Government" manifested when redeeming the paper dollars (in other words, for what things of value may paper dollars be exchanged at any Federal Reserve Bank)?

a) Gold, at the rate of 1/16th troy ounce per dollar.
b) Silver, at the rate of 0.7825 troy ounces per dollar.
c) Stock in the Federal Reserve banks.
d) Land held in trust by the Government, mostly in the western states.
e) The citizen may choose either gold at 0.02368 ounces per dollar per the 1973 gold standard, or silver at 0.7825 ounces per dollar per the revised 1834 silver standard.

Answer to Question 41

This is a trick question; none of the answers are true. Since 1933, the U. S. dollar has been what is known as a "fiat currency", which is paper currency that has no value in and of itself, and cannot be traded in for anything else of value. Former Chairman of the Federal Reserve Alan Greenspan confirmed in testimony before Congress that the U.S. dollar is in fact such a fiat currency [1]. If you attempt to trade your "Federal Reserve Note" so-called "dollars" into something of value at any bank, you will receive a vacant stare from the teller before she bursts out laughing, because Federal Reserve Notes are not redeemable for anything of actual value. Examples of "actual value" would be a commodity such as gold, silver, oil, land, or other items of value which would normally provide security for a paper currency.

The federal government routinely sells U. S. Treasury bonds that are denominated in Federal Reserve "dollars". The Treasury Bonds and the Federal Reserve Notes are backed by the "full faith and credit" of the U. S. Government. How can this be? If the dollars are not secured by commodities held by the government in trust, how would the federal government pay off a large holder of U. S. Treasury bonds if the holder will not be satisfied by more slips of worthless (Federal Reserve) paper? The holder of the bonds will be compensated through Congress' unlimited ability to levy a tax. In other words, the federal government does not have enough gold or other wealth to pay the bond holder, but you and all the other taxpayers do, because you have sufficient wealth (future earnings and savings) that can be taxed. The federal government does not hold stocks in profitable corporations that have actual value to pay the bond holder, but you and all the other taxpayers do. So, if the time should come when creditors lose faith in the Federal Reserve Notes and Treasury Bonds, and begin to demand actual payment in commodities for money lent, Congress will pay them by taxing all U. S. citizens as much as is required to pay the bond. The federal government will never give up title to the land in the western states, because that would constitute a loss of stature and sovereignty. The politicians will never allow the bonds to go into default, because that would constitute for them a loss of prestige. As usual, the taxpayers will pay the charges, plus interest, for the excesses of the Federal Reserve and the enabling politicians. Incidentally, the Federal Reserve is not an agency of the federal government; it is a consortium of private banks. It is called the Federal Reserve to give the illusion that you, the citizen, have a say through your representatives in Congress as to how the nation's finances are handled. In fact, there is no control of the Federal Reserve by Congress except for the occasional confirmation of an appointment made by the President. The most recent example is the confirmation on 5 Feb 2018 of Jerome H. Powell as the Chairman of the Board of Directors of the Federal Reserve System

The important point here is that the Federal Reserve is a leading member of the international banking cartel, and it does what is best for the cartel, not for the American people. It's claimed duty is to manage the money supply to prevent recessions, supervise the banking system, stabilize the value of the dollar, increase the general standard of living, and at the same time, to maximize employment [2]. These are mutually contradictory objectives. The Federal Reserve has in reality become a means to institutionalize inflation, which is a hidden tax on all working people, to finance the excesses of the federal government.

[1]   Alan Greenspan, Chairman of the Federal Reserve, in testimony before Congress, 11 Feb 2004: "We have statutorily gone into a fiat money standard, and as a consequence of that it is inevitable that the authority, which is the producer of the money supply, will have inordinate power." The "producer of the money supply" that Greenspan was referring to is the Federal Reserve, of which he was the head at the time.

[2]   *The Federal Reserve System: Purposes and Functions*, Washington DC: Board of Governors of the Federal Reserve, 1963, pp. 1 - 15

-- § --

Question 42: "No New Taxes"

During the Presidential election campaign of 1988, George H. W. Bush stated, "Read my lips, no new taxes". He was subsequently elected as the 41st President of the U. S. What did this statement mean regarding his intended tax policy as President?
a)   He would never raise income taxes if elected President.
b)   Since he said "read my lips", the statement was directed only at deaf people; so he meant that he would not raise income taxes on deaf people.
c)   "No new taxes" means he would not create any new category of taxes.
d)   If there are any tax increases, they will only apply to other people, not to you.
e)   A combination of a) and c).

Answer to Question 42

This is a trick question. None of the answers are correct, because Presidents do not raise taxes. Under the Constitution, only Congress has the power to raise a tax.

If we consider the answers as under our Constitutional system, in which all tax bills are passed first in Congress, all of the answers are still wrong. Answers a) and c) are still wrong because there is no way to prevent Congress from raising income taxes if it decides to do so by overriding a presidential veto.

Soon after George H. W. Bush was elected president, Congress passed a bill raising the income tax rates, and he promptly signed it into law in 1990. The bill also included new taxes imposed on boats, cars, alcohol, and tobacco. The fact that the government does not create new taxes does not mean it won't raise the rates on existing categories of taxation.

Answer b) is wrong because neither the increased tax rates nor new taxes contained an exception for deaf people. Therefore, even if we assign the least-constraining meaning to this statement ("I will veto any attempt by Congress to create any new categories of taxation on deaf people, or raise tax rates on deaf people"), we find that one of two things is true: a) either he was lying when he said it; or b) when push came to shove, he gave in to the demands of his politician friends, and threw the taxpayers overboard.

George H. W. Bush has not, to public knowledge, admitted to lying in this particular instance. But in general, even when you parse a politician's statement down to the etymology from the Middle French, you will find they are usually still lying. Why do politicians lie? For the same reason a cat licks his butt: no one expects any different behavior, and there is no penalty for it.

Answer d) is wrong because it is a rhetorical trick commonly used by politicians and bureaucrats of all types. If you chose d), you are exactly the kind of dummy the politicians and bureaucrats appreciate most.

You should keep in mind that most of those who have power, whether it is political within governments or economic through monopolistic corporations, are fully aware of the benefit (to them) of the occasional big lie. You should not rely on any of them for assurances of security or policy. It is especially true of progressives and socialists. The progressive/socialist has been trained to tell the lie that has the most immediate political benefit, even if he has to reverse it tomorrow. It simply doesn't matter to a socialist if he gets caught lying: he will insist that "ambiguity" is necessary, and he is doing it for the good of society.

-- § --

Question 43: Gold Coins

Gold has historically been recognized as the ultimate "safe" money because it never loses all of its value. On the other hand, many paper currencies throughout history have eventually become worthless. Some noteworthy examples are Continental dollar issued by Congress during the American Revolution (1777-1781), the German mark in 1923, the Yugoslav dinar in 1994, and the Zimbabwean dollar in 2008. Many people choose to hedge against paper currencies by purchasing gold coins as a form of insurance, which could be sold or bartered in the event the paper currency ever fails. Many types are offered for sale and advertised as follows:

a) "Authentic St. Gaudens $20 Double Eagles (originally issued between 1908 and 1929). A total of approximately 65,000,000 were originally minted. It is 34 mm in diameter, and contains 42.0 milligrams (mg) of pure gold. Each can be purchased for $29.95 US."

b) "Tribute proof $10 Liberty Head Eagles (originally issued between 1866 and 1907). Approximately 64,000,000 total were minted. It is 27 mm in diameter, and contains 21 mg of pure gold. Each can be purchased for $21.95 US."

c) "24 carat gold clad $10 Indian Head Eagles (originally issued between 1908 and 1933). Approximately 15,000,000 total were minted. It is 27 mm in diameter, and contains 19 mg of pure gold. Each can be purchased for $18.95 US."

d) "Private mint authorized $5 Indian Head Half Eagles (originally issued intermittently between 1908 and 1929). Approximately 14,000,000 total were minted. It is 21.6 mm in diameter, and contains 8.5 mg of pure gold. Each can be purchased for $19.99 US."

A famous company advertises these coins for sale on TV, radio, and newspaper ads, reminding the audience that these coins are rare and out of circulation, and that gold is always highly sought after both for its intrinsic value and in the form of beautiful old coins. The ad goes on to remind the audience that gold coins should be part of every investment portfolio. Which of these coins offers the best investment value?

a) The Double Eagle, because it is the largest physical coin and has by far the largest amount of pure gold.

b) The Liberty Head, because they were minted in the most distant past, which makes them more desirable.

c) The Indian Head Eagle, because it has the lowest price and is still contains pure gold.

d) The Half Eagle, because it is the rarest one (fewest were minted), which makes it more valuable.

e) It is best to have a variety of these coins as an investment. The prudent investor, or person who wants some insurance against a currency collapse, would be wise to buy some of each, but not necessarily in equal amounts. This is important to diversify one's gold investments, even more so than stocks and bonds.

The additional information required to determine the best investment value is as follows:

a. Suppose the current price of gold is about $1,450 per troy ounce.

b. There are 31.103 grams per troy ounce and 1,000 mg per gram (thus there are 31,103 mg of gold per troy ounce).

Answer to Question 43

This is a trick question. All the provided answers are wrong: none of these so-called gold coins are an investment. In fact, they are nearly worthless. To see why, it is an easy matter to calculate the actual amount of gold in each one. The formula for the number of troy ounces, W, of gold in each coin is:

$$W(oz) = \frac{X(mg)}{1} \frac{1(g)}{1000(mg)} \frac{1(oz)}{31.103(g)}$$

On the right side, the units of grams (g) and milligrams (mg) cancel since they appear in both numerator and denominator, and we are left with the formula for troy ounces on both sides:

$$W = \frac{X}{31103}$$

where W is the weight of gold in troy ounces, and X is the weight of gold in mg.

Using this formula, we determine that:

a) $20 St. Gaudens has 42/31103 = 0.00135 troy ounces of gold

b) $10 Liberty Head has 21/31103 = 0.000675 troy ounces of gold

c) $10 Indian Head Eagle has 19/31103 = 0.00061 troy ounces of gold

d) $5 Indian Head Half Eagle has 8.5/31103 = 0.000273 troy ounces of gold.

If the price of gold is $1,450 per troy ounce, the approximate value of the gold in each one is:

a) $20 St. Gaudens: $1.95

b) $10 Liberty Head: $0.98

c) $10 Indian Head Eagle: $0.88

d) $5 Indian Half Eagle: $0.40

No matter how much you pay for the coins, or even if you get two for the price of one, these are nearly worthless. The advertisers are using two tricks here. First, they call out the amount of gold in milligrams, which is a very small unit of weight, and which is unfamiliar to most Americans. A milligram is one-thousandth of a gram, and there are 31.3 grams in a troy ounce. Using a very small unit of weight, they can accurately use a fairly large number of those units, giving the (false) impression of a significant amount of gold in the coins. Secondly, they refer to the coins using euphemisms such as "authentic", "tribute", "authorized", and "gold clad", which have no actual legal meaning. If they were "genuine" coins, then they would be the real thing (and would be priced in the thousands of dollars each); these other euphemisms mean whatever the advertiser wants you to believe it means. Note also that the real coins were "originally issued in the 19th and 20th century", not these fakes that are being offered for sale. In this case, although not explained clearly, the advertiser's meaning of "authentic" is "a crude disk of bronze or lead painted over with tiny amount of gold".

It may be a good idea to own some gold. If you decide to do so, only buy true gold bullion coins from a reputable dealer. Before buying them, look up the current commodity price (bullion spot price) of gold and compare it to the asking price quoted by the gold dealer. The quoted price should be slightly higher than the spot price (which is the dealer's commission for storage and handling, same as any other merchant). In this case, if the spot-price of gold is $1,450 per ounce, a one ounce bullion coin should be priced a few percent above $1,450. You will pay more for true "rare" or "collectable" coins.

-- § --

Question 44: One-Year Investment

Suppose Christine has $1,000 to invest for one year only (she will cash out after 12 months), and is only interested in conservative investments such as mutual funds based on high-quality bonds that have a guaranteed annual return. She is presented with three options: a) Bond Fund A with a guaranteed return of 3% and no sales commission; b) Bond Fund B with a guaranteed return of 6% and a sales commission of 3%; and c) Bond Fund C with a guaranteed return of 10% and a sales commission of 7%. Nothing is zero risk, but assume for this example that the risk of all three options is zero. Sales commissions are always paid up-front. Choose the correct statement for this one-year investment:
a)   Bond Fund B is twice as good an investment as Bond Fund A (6/3 = 200%)
b)   Bond Fund C is 166% better as an investment than Bond Fund B (10/6 = 166%).
c)   Bond Fund C is 333% better as an investment than Bond Fund A (10/3 = 333%)
d)   Bond Fund C is a better investment than splitting the $1,000 between Fund A and Fund B in any ratio.
e)   All of the above are true.

Answer to Question 44

This is a trick question. All of the choices are wrong.

The benefit of an investment has to be evaluated on an absolute scale, not the relative scale of the guaranteed return. By an absolute scale, we are referring to the amount actually invested. In these examples, the amount invested depends on the sales commissions, paid up-front, meaning they are paid before investment is actually purchased. Bond Fund A has no sales commission, so the entire $1,000 is invested for Christine. The 3% sales commission in Bond Fund B brings her actual investment down to $970. The 7% commission for Bond Fund C brings her initial investment down to $930.

After the one year period, Bond Fund C will make 3% on the $1,000, and will be worth $1,030. Likewise Bond Fund B will earn 6% on the $970, and will be worth $1,028.20, and Bond Fund C will earn 10% on the $930, and will be worth $1,023.00.

Therefore all the answers are wrong for a one-year investment: Bond Fund B is worse than A, C is worse than A and B, and there is no way to make C better than either of the other two by splitting in any ratio.

These answers turned out this way because the term was only one year. If Christine could invest her money for a longer period, Figure 44-1 shows what would happen. The left panel shows the value of the respective Fund options over a ten-year period. The right panel shows the overall gain at the end of each year on the original $1,000 Christine had for investment. If we regard "better than" as equivalent to "gain made in dollars", it is seen from the right panel that Bond Fund B is twice as good as Bond Fund A after about seven years; Bond Fund C is 166% as good as Bond Fund B after about five years, Bond Fund C is 333% better than Bond Fund A after about six years. Fund C is guaranteed to be a better than any combination of A and B after about 15 months or so.

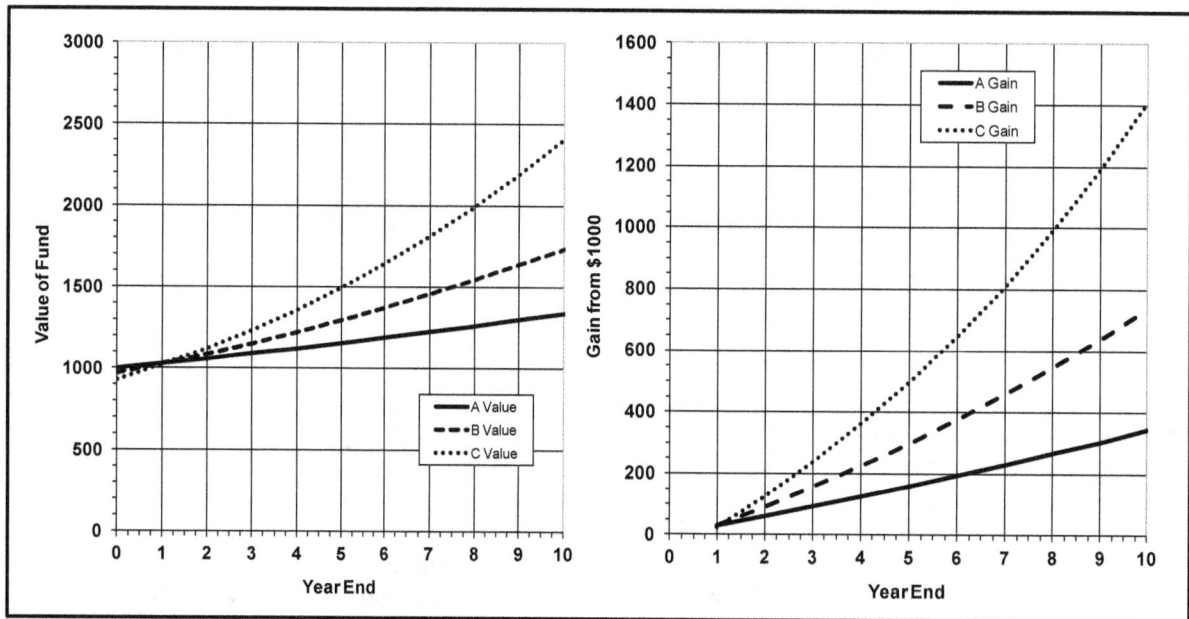

Figure 44-1: Returns on Investments

The important point here is to remember that numeric values such as rates of return have to be calibrated to an absolute, in this case, the amount actually invested   If someone makes a claim that something is "twice as good" as something else, make sure that the two measurements are to an absolute scale. For example, if an insurance salesman sells you a $100,000 life insurance policy, and tells you "it's twice as good a deal as a $50,000 policy", that is true only if the premiums and terms on the two policies are the same.   If they are sold over different terms or at different premiums, then you should compare the premiums and terms to a standard reference in order to make an accurate comparison.

Progressives and socialists would have you believe that all investments are nothing more than oppressing the poor. Never mind that Christine may have earned the money and saved it after expenses. The socialist believes that it is her duty to hand any excess income above her bare minimum living expenses to the government, who will distribute it to people unwilling to work. Thus the socialist claims to be acting in the interest of "social justice", which actually means the injustice of socialist robbery.

-- § --

Question 45: Assigning Blame

A wife had to go to a Garden Club meeting. She told her husband to stay home while she was out, and asked him to watch Channel 6 and get the winning lottery numbers. Also, she did not like the friends he was likely to hang out with (especially Bob). The husband was resentful of the way his wife had ordered him around. While his wife was gone, the husband noticed that they were out of beer, so he decided to violate his wife's wishes. He left the house to go and buy some beer. On the way, his truck ran out of gas. So he called his friend Bob, who met him where the truck was, and brought him a few gallons of gas. Bob went back home, and the husband continued onto the store. As he was going into the store, a mugger tried to hold him up. The husband refused to give the mugger his beer money, so the mugger shot and killed the husband. Who is to blame for the death of the husband?

a) The wife, for not treating the husband with respect, which provoked him into leaving the house. If he had stayed home, he would be alive now.
b) The husband, for leaving the house when his wife specifically told him to stay home.
c) Bob is at fault because he provided the gas that enabled the husband to get to the store where he was killed.
d) The husband, because he refused to obey the mugger.
e) Everyone in the story shares some of the blame except for the wife.

Answer to Question 45

This is a trick question. All of the answers are wrong.

Answer a) is wrong because although it is true that he would still be alive if he stayed home, that has nothing to do with how his wife treats him.

Answer b) is wrong because the husband is a big boy now and can decide for himself whether to leave the house or not. He did not sign up for slavery during the wedding ceremony.

Answer c) is wrong because Bob's assistance is irrelevant to whether the wife likes him or not, and is irrelevant to whether the husband went to the store or not; the husband was going there anyway.

Answer d) is wrong because no one is legally required to obey the orders of a criminal, although there are many politicians, bureaucrats, and police chiefs who would have you believe otherwise. In fact, there are some officeholders who are so stupid that they would try to put the blame on the storekeeper, the beer makers, the gas refiners, and the gun makers, pretending that somehow they influenced the outcome of this event. These idiots somehow manage to get their names on every ballot.

Answer e) is wrong because in a free society, everyone is responsible as individuals for their actions. In this case, all the blame falls on the mugger, as he is the only one who did anything wrong. All the other people in the story did nothing to contribute to the crime.

All the proposed answers are simple attempts to shift responsibility for the criminal's actions away from the criminal. They are consistent with the notion that crime occurs because "it's all society's fault" that some people are induced to commit crimes. But the true fact is that everyone is responsible for their own actions. In this case, the only person to blame for the death of the husband is the person who did it, namely the mugger. No one else has any responsibility for it, at least not in a free society.

Don't be fooled by the false socialist notion that "it takes a village". That concept is based on the notion of "collective security", "collective culture", and "collective guilt". In that version of history, everyone in sight is partly at fault for every crime; thus reducing the culpability of the one criminal actor. The group mentality seeks to reduce individual responsibility, and in doing so, eliminate individual freedom and initiative. Those who advocate for the socialist "one village" mentality are really intent on one thing: to destroy your individual liberty.

One of the common outcomes of this socialist notion of "collective guilt" is to "solve" a problem by taking rights away from everyone. This concept will lead to the steady erosion of individual rights because socialism can be implemented and maintained only when the people have no means to object to the tactics of the ruling elite or reject their actions.

-- § --

Question 46: Music Television

The first music video network, called "Music TV", better known as MTV, was launched in Aug 1981. It began by showing video clips of musical acts, and later expanded to commentary on popular culture, reality shows, satire, and some political activism, mostly concerning the environment and getting young people to vote. There are now several music video networks, among them are VH1 and CMT. What is the underlying purpose of the music video networks?

a) To finally give young people an opportunity to see their favorite musical acts without censorship by the traditional networks.
b) To allow a youth-oriented culture to express itself over the airwaves.
c) To provide an opportunity for up-and-coming musical acts to obtain some exposure.
d) To allow the recording companies to test the potential popularity of their new acts before committing to a full contract.
e) All of the above.

Answer to Question 46

This is a trick question. None of the provided answers address the real purpose of MTV and the other music networks.

The real purpose of these networks is the same as any other network, namely, to get the viewers to watch commercials, because advertising revenue is where the real money is. The music videos are the method used to get you to tune in.

The central goal of any entertainment outlet is to capture the attention and loyalty of a target audience with a lot of disposable income. The more impressionable the audience, the better for the music outlet: it is easier to broadcast propaganda instead of actual music. Those characteristics describe teenagers best: not skilled at critical thinking (hence susceptible to flashy advertising), and with money to spend (from part-time jobs or allowances, with few expenses). You will never see a TV channel devoted to music of the 1940's: most of that target audience is elderly, and most of them do not have sufficient disposable income to attract the attention of advertising industry.

-- § --

Question 47: Presidential Election Results

Suppose, in a U. S. Presidential election, candidate A gets 48% of the popular vote, candidate B gets 46%, and the remaining 6% is divided among various other minor-party candidates as officially reported by the election authorities in all the states. However, candidate B is declared the winner of the election, and takes the oath of office. How could this happen? Between the election and inauguration, neither candidate dies, is convicted of a felony, is found to be ineligible, or refuses the office. Also, none of the 6% gained by other candidates represented a victory in any given State.

a) Candidate B engaged in large-scale election fraud, and was able to get many of candidate A's votes to be rejected. Although 48% voted for candidate A, less than 46% were counted.
b) Candidate A was favored by the mainstream media, and they inflated the vote counts for their favorite, even though he was not as popular.
c) The other minor-party candidates gave their votes to candidate B, so he ended up with 52%, and is clearly the winner.
d) Since neither candidate got a 50% + 1 popular majority, a runoff was held in the U. S. House of Representatives, and candidate B was the winner.
e) A combination of a) and c).

Answer to Question 47

This is a trick question. None of the answers are correct for U. S. Presidential elections.

Answer a) is wrong because the question states that the vote totals were as reported by the election officials; that is, after any electoral fraud.

Answer b) is wrong because the media cannot determine outcomes of elections by inflating pretended vote counts or polls; the votes are what they are per the reported results. In fact, the mainstream media routinely engages in this sort of vote-inflating cheerleading for their favorite, but in the long run, the candidates favored by the media lose most of the time. This indicates that the members of the media are out of step with the voting public, but nothing more.

Answers c) and d) are wrong because neither is permitted in the U. S. electoral system.

The correct answer is that the President is elected by an Electoral College, which is apportioned according to the number of seats in both houses of Congress (sum of the number of House Representatives seats plus one for each Senate seat), plus 3 for the District of Columbia, for a total of 538 electoral votes. The Electoral College is a winner-takes-all system except in Maine and Nebraska, where electoral votes are assigned by congressional district. In the other 48 states, a candidate who wins the popular vote in that state gets all the states' electoral votes, whether he won the popular vote by one vote or if he won with all the votes. Therefore, it is possible for a candidate to win with wide margins in a few large states (thus increasing the popular vote count) and lose in a large number of smaller states, and end up with an insufficient number of Electoral College votes necessary to win the election. This has happened several times in our history, most recently with Bush defeating Gore in 2000 and Trump defeating Clinton in 2016.

Some mental-midget political activists want you to believe that Bush somehow stole the election of 2000 (by legal technicalities in the Supreme Court), and that Trump somehow stole the election of 2016 (by "colluding with Russia"), and that these were the only occasions in which a candidate had won the Presidency with a minority of the popular vote. In fact, it happened twice before Bush vs. Gore: Samuel J. Tilden won the popular vote in 1876, but lost in the Electoral College to Rutherford B. Hayes; and S. Grover Cleveland won the popular vote in 1888, but lost in the Electoral College to Benjamin Harrison. There is one other notable example. In the election of 1824, neither Andrew Jackson nor John Quincy Adams had enough Electoral College votes, so the election was decided by the House of Representatives (per Amendment 12 of the U. S. Constitution), and they chose Adams. But Jackson had won the popular vote.

Another correct answer, not given in the question, is that some electors chose not to cast their vote in the Electoral College per the popular vote. This is permitted by law in some states; electors are not obligated to vote for the person who won the popular vote. This is a good method to prevent people like Hitler or Stalin from being elected, but of course that assumes the electors have the backbone for it.

-- § --

Question 48: Paying First

Which of these should be paid first?
a)   Rent or mortgage.
b)   Car payment.
c)   Credit card bill.
d)   Any utility bill (gas/electric/water).
e)   A bill from a doctor, dentist, chiropractor, or lawyer.

Answer to Question 48

This is a trick question. None of the answers are correct.

The correct answer is "always pay yourself first". This means that you should find a way to live below your means if at all possible, and save or invest a fixed percentage of your income for your future, before you pay any bills. Most experts believe that young people should save or invest between 10% and 15% of their gross pay.

The investment experts advise that a young person should diversify their investments, a certain percentage in high-quality bonds, a certain percentage in U. S. stocks, and a certain percentage in foreign stocks. In these modern times, one does not need to be an expert in finance or investing; many investment companies have developed automatic programs that do it all for you depending on your planned retirement date. Take advantage of investing whenever you can. It is the only way to stay ahead of the planned inflationary policies of the U. S. Federal Reserve and other members of the central banking cartel.

-- § --

Question 49: An Epidemic

A chemical known as dichloro-diphenyl-trichloroethane was accidentally discovered in 1874 by O. Zeidler; and was re-discovered by P. Muller in 1939. It was found to be a very effective pesticide. Its name was abbreviated to DDT, and was produced commercially and used widely from 1943 until it was banned from use in 1972. It was banned due to allegations, since proven to be false, that DDT caused the thinning of bird's eggs, caused cancer in humans, and reduced the populations of eagles, falcons, and pelicans. The main reason it was banned was because the environmental activists wanted to establish a power base, and used the banning of DDT as their test case. The greatest benefit of DDT was in combating the mosquito-borne disease malaria: while it was being used, several million deaths from malaria were prevented [1]. Malaria has always been fairly rare in the U. S.

Since DDT was banned, about 300 to 500 million cases of malaria occur worldwide each year, and about 1 million black people in southern Africa die from it; most of these fatalities are children under 5 years of age. There is at present no vaccine for malaria; and treatment of it must occur rapidly and in the right dosage; otherwise relapses may occur (sometimes decades later) [2].

The best way to prevent an outbreak of malaria is to suppress the population of the mosquito that spreads it. Consider the following scenario. An infestation of the malaria-transmitting mosquito is discovered in Manhattan (part of New York City), and the use of pesticides other than DDT proved ineffective in reducing the mosquito population. Because malaria is so rare in the U. S., Americans have no immunity to the disease (since immunity comes from exposure). Experts therefore predict that about 15% of the population of Manhattan would get malaria, and about 5,000 people living in Manhattan (nearly all children) would be expected to die from the epidemic. What would happen?

a) The people of Manhattan would all temporarily move to their upstate summer homes, and wait for the epidemic to move to Brooklyn, Queens, Staten Island, the Bronx, and New Jersey.

b) The people of Manhattan would sell their homes, quit their jobs, and move elsewhere.

c) The people of Manhattan would stay put, continue their normal activities, and watch 5,000 children die; reasoning that it is only fair that each resident of Manhattan accept the same risks as other people, especially since malaria is a naturally-occurring disease.

d) The people of Manhattan would remain in Manhattan, but would close themselves up in their homes as a self-imposed quarantine, until all the mosquitoes either died or moved elsewhere.

e) Some combination of a) through d). In other words, those who could afford to move would do so; those who could maintain quarantine would do so, and those who could do neither would have to risk their children's lives.

[1] https://junkscience.com/?s=DDT
[2] https://www.cdc.gov/malaria/about/faqs.html

Answer to Question 49

This is a trick question. All of the answers are wrong.

None of the answers are practical, for obvious economic reasons. The people of Manhattan would stage a massive public relations campaign, led by the Manhattan-based mainstream media. They would likely blame the malaria outbreak on a fictional right-wing conspiracy, and demand DDT treatment throughout Manhattan although 99% of those residents oppose DDT use in general.

The correct answer is that they would spray DDT everywhere in all five boroughs and New Jersey until all mosquitoes are confirmed to be dead. This action would be endorsed by every environmental group in the U. S. That is exactly what they should do. It is also what should be done in southern Africa. On the other hand, the environmental activists and their advocates in the Democratic Party are not worried too much about one million black children dying every year. The Democratic Party always has and always will detest black people. They are exceedingly worried if a few hundred children of wealthy white people in Manhattan were to die because of their policy; after all, it is those wealthy white people in Manhattan who can give big contributions to the environmental groups and the Democratic Party.

If malaria actually did break out in Manhattan, you would see first-hand the hypocrisy of the "progressive" and socialist environmental activist do-gooders in the ivory towers when their children are threatened. Their half-baked policies only apply to you, the working person who pays for it all. The evils of socialist policies will never be felt by the socialists or their families.

-- § --

Question 50: Libel and Slander

Suppose a famous nationally-distributed newspaper publishes a news article. This particular story is about a series of arsons and burglaries committed by specific persons, who are named in the story. It is based on information provided to the newspaper by the local police department. This information was provided to the newspaper editors because he is on friendly terms with officials at the police department. Because this newspaper is regarded as the standard for integrity, its story is picked up by other newspapers, and then by various radio and television stations. The broadcast and cable television networks accurately repeat the story in their broadcasts, with full audio and video "dramatic re-creations" of the events described in the story.

A few days later, the truth came out. The police officers who provided the information to the newspaper had lied under orders from their superiors in the police department. The officers knew that the subjects in the story were innocent, but obeyed the chief's order to relay the information to the newspaper. The persons named in the story were in fact completely innocent; the upper echelon of the police department held a personal grudge against them because they were frequent critics of the department. The newspaper editors did not know the people in the story were innocent, but did not investigate to verify the information. They were happy to go ahead and publish it although unverified because the subjects in the story held political views contrary to those of the official position of the newspaper. This story was also widely distributed on the internet, including all of the "social networking" sites. The subjects of the article were libeled, slandered, and publicly vilified until they were completely exonerated by the court. Unfortunately, they experienced considerable loss of income and legal expenses. The Police Chief who created the false allegations and the officers who carried out the politically-motivated orders were subsequently fired. The editors at the newspaper were all subsequently given raises and promotions. But the public was misled and misinformed all along, and some still believe the people mentioned were guilty, since the initiating newspaper never was required to issue a formal retraction or apology. What should be done to prevent this kind of attack upon innocent people and the spreading of false information to the public?

a)   Implement quality controls to prevent inaccurate reporting, such as:

1) All journalists, editors, and commentators shall require a journalism license, to be renewed annually;
2) Persons who are not licensed journalists shall be prohibited from publishing in any format (except for works clearly labeled as fiction).
b) Implement reasonable content controls to prevent political bias, such as:
1) All newspaper, magazine, and printed publications shall be reviewed for news relevance and censored if appropriate, including a prohibition on "editorial opinion";
2) Radio and TV broadcasts shall be subject to the same controls, except for live sporting events (without play-by-play).
c) Implement technological controls in order to reduce the occasions under which this type of crime could occur, such as:
1) Manufacture and possession of high-speed printing presses (above a certain number of pages per hour) shall be prohibited;
2) Manufacture and possession of broadcast equipment, including cameras, microphones, and lighting systems for studios shall be controlled by suitable authorities, to be released to users when required.
3) Social networking sites shall be prohibited from linking to news articles;
4) The internet shall be regulated as a public utility.
d) Implement capacity controls in order to reduce the magnitude of crimes when they do occur, such as:
1) Newspapers shall be restricted to publishing once per month, with a maximum page count based on community population;
2) Magazines shall be published once per year with a page count limit proportional to the number of paid subscribers;
3) Radio and television broadcast talk show hosts shall be restricted to one five-minute segment per month, to make room for greater diversity in broadcasting.
4) Media outlets of all types shall be prohibited form having websites on the public internet (but may create a private internet at their expense).

Answer to Question 50

This is a trick question. All of the provided answers are wrong. Special note: if you chose any of the provided answers, the only thing remaining for you to do is choose your preferred political ideology: communist, socialist, totalitarian dictatorship, or absolute monarchist.

First, let's review the facts. The Police Chief committed a crime and violated his oath of office when he fabricated allegations against his political enemies. The police officers under him violated their oath of office and displayed uncommon cowardice because they knowingly passed false information to the newspaper to placate the Police Chief. The newspaper editor who received the information and then published it without verification demonstrated laziness and journalistic irresponsibility. None of this is good for the public. But, if any of the controls mentioned in the candidate answers were adopted, the situation would be much worse, because the government would ultimately be in control of what information was allowed to the public, either directly or indirectly. Governments do not tolerate competition, and you can be sure that when the government regulates "for the public good", it actually regulates in the interest of acquiring more power.

Most "progressives" and socialists would like to implement some of the suggested answers. As soon as they come into the open with it, their moron co-conspirators in the mainstream media will find they have been backing liars and criminals, and will try to sound the alarm. But it will be too late: the government will have seized power, and the mainstream media will have already lost all credibility. The mainstream media will have fulfilled their role as useful idiots, and then become expendable. Don't be fooled: free speech has worked for a long time, and those with bad ideas eventually get exposed.

-- § --

Question 51: American Political Parties

The political parties in America can be summarized as follows. The Federalists were members of the Founding generation who believed in a strong central government. The Republican-Democrat party was established in the late 1790's, and supported a weaker federal government and stronger State governments. In the 1820's, the Republican-Democrat Party split into the Democratic and Whig parties. The Whig party was the conservative party that favored and aided the western expansion, including many public works such as canals, railroads, and improvement of navigation on the rivers. It became extinct after the election of 1858 and was replaced by the Republican Party. There have been many minor parties in U. S. politics, but none of their candidates have ever become President. The two main parties today are the Democrats, who claim to favor the working people, unions, civil rights, and equality. They are especially critical of the large salaries paid to high-ranking corporate executives. Democrats claim to be altruistic in their motives. The Republicans claim to favor business interests, working people, civil rights, and equal opportunity. Republicans are not bothered by high salaries of top corporate executives, and believe generally that people should be paid what they are entitled to either under the law or by contract.

The Federalists are considered to be a unique party that was short-lived and had no successor. The modern Democratic Party is considered to be the successor to the Republican-Democratic party that split in 1828. The modern Republican Party is considered to be the successor of the Whig party that was disbanded in 1858.

The Presidents belonged to Parties as follows, and the number after their names indicates their order in the line of Presidents. Of all the Presidents, only Washington was not a member of any political party.
a.   None: Washington (1)
b.   Federalist: J. Adams (2)
c.   Republican-Democrat: Jefferson (3), Madison (4), Monroe (5), J. Q. Adams (6)
d.   Democrat: Jackson (7), Van Buren (8), Polk (11), Pierce (14), Buchanan (15), A. Johnson (17), Cleveland (22 and 24), Wilson (28), F. D. Roosevelt (32), Truman (33), Kennedy (35), L. B. Johnson (36), Carter (39), Clinton (42), Obama (44), Biden (46)
e.   Whig: W. H. Harrison (9), Tyler (10), Taylor (12), Fillmore (13)
f.   Republican: Lincoln (16), Grant (18), Hayes (19), Garfield (20), Arthur (21), B. Harrison (23), McKinley (25), T. Roosevelt (26), Taft (27), Harding (29), Coolidge (30), Hoover (31), Eisenhower (34), Nixon (37), Ford (38), Reagan (40), G. H. W. Bush (41), G. W. Bush (43), D. J. Trump (45)

Three Presidents served either for a symbolic salary of $1 per year, at no salary at all, or donated his entire salary to charity. Keep in mind that the President is the nominal leader of his Party, and the most effective leaders lead by example. Based on the above information on party affiliation, and the claimed objectives of each political party, which three Presidents served essentially for free? The letter following their name indicates their political party affiliation.
a)   Van Buren (D), Buchanan (D), and F. D. Roosevelt (D)
b)   Polk (D), Pierce (D), and L. B. Johnson (D)
c)   Wilson (D), Carter (D), and Clinton (D)
d)   J. Adams (F), Nixon (R), and Reagan (R)
e)   It is either a), b), or c).

Answer to Question 51

This is a trick question. None of the choices are correct.

Washington (N) served for $1 per year, Kennedy (D) served at no salary, and Hoover (R) collected his salary but donated all of it to charity. The taxpayers certainly got their money's worth out of Kennedy. The Party platforms and who they claim to advocate for has no bearing on the personal choice of whether or not to accept the official salary. The party affiliation is a very poor indicator in this case. Donald Trump emulated Hoover: he took his salary (now required by law), but donated all of it to charity.

-- § --

Question 52: Hypocrisy in High Places

A certain man was a successful politician for many years. He gradually rose through the ranks from a city council member to state Representative to state Senator to federal Congressman to federal Senator. In all those years, he was a consistent advocate for gun control, including various proposals to ban all guns and ammunition held by private persons. He himself always lived in places with strict gun control, but he also was always in violation of the existing gun laws: he owned many guns that were banned, he failed to register guns he owned, and he bought and sold guns without the legal reporting requirements.

While he was a federal Senator, he was called upon by the President to serve as an under-Secretary of a cabinet-level department by the new administration. As part of the vetting process, he was asked if he had ever violated any gun laws. He lied about his guns, and the administration believed him, since he had a "perfect" voting record promoting and enacting gun control. But once he was confirmed by the Senate, it came to light that he had in fact owned many guns, some of them illegally, and had committed numerous violations of the existing gun laws (some of which he had helped to pass at the state and federal level). What will happen next?
a)   He will be fired by the President.
b)   He will resign in disgrace.
c)   He will be investigated by the federal authorities.
d)   He will be indicted by state and local authorities.
e)   Either a) or b), followed by either c) or d).

Answer to Question 52

This is a trick question. None of the suggested answers will occur.

Examine the facts of the scenario carefully. He voted for laws that were unconstitutional and immoral (as all gun control is), yet he continued to own, possess, buy, and sell guns despite the law. These facts prove that in his view:
1)   Gun control laws take away the rights of regular people, but those laws do not apply to government officials;
2)   That no law required him to give up his rights; and
3)   Violating an unconstitutional law is irrelevant because an unconstitutional law is irrelevant.

Fact 1) is typical of politicians: if your rights mattered, most of the laws on the books would never have been passed. It simply shows that politicians are hypocrites; so what else is new? They were hypocrites when George Washington was President, they were hypocrites when Caesar ruled, and they will always be hypocrites.

Facts 2) and 3) prove that this man is a patriot in his private life, although a hypocrite in his public life. There are many laws that require you to give up your rights; but none of them are legitimate. The fact that he violated laws that he knew were unconstitutional proves that he was in fact, a good citizen. This is a simple example of politicians and bureaucrats believing they are better than you, and the laws restricting your freedom do not apply to them.

But none of the suggested answers can occur. The President will not withdraw an appointment simply because the person exercised his rights and behaved as if he were above the law. There is no reason to resign in disgrace. He is not going to be investigated or indicted for violating the unconstitutional laws because those who would prosecute him are probably also violating them. Besides, he is a protected member of the political elite and has spent his entire professional life increasing the power of the government. No government official will be prosecuted for that.

Most likely the next series of events will go something like this. First, he will endure a week or two of embarrassment for being a hypocrite, but it will be relegated to page 79G in the mainstream press (immediately following the weather report from Zimbabwe). Second, his party propaganda machine will make as many excuses as necessary to make his violations and hypocrisy all seem innocent and well-meaning. Then he will be promoted to Special Advisor to the President with authority over the Bureau of Alcohol, Tobacco, and Firearms, where he can violate your Second Amendment rights full-time (while he retains his rights).

Here is how the "rights" scam works. You, as a citizen have "rights" guaranteed by the Constitution. For the first 150 years or so (until the early 1900's), the federal government did not interfere too often with the rights of free citizens (except during the Civil War). It was around 1910 that the "progressive" movement began to acquire significant power. Since then, government officials have come to believe that legislatures can pass any law they want, executives can issue any decree they want, and judges can issue any ruling they want, and these can contradict or abolish your rights as they see fit. The only way the citizens can regain their rights is to sue the government in the government's courts, but only if the government allows the lawsuit to proceed. The citizen has to defeat the government at every stage up to and including the U. S. Supreme Court, at his expense. Even if he wins, the Supreme Court will issue the narrowest of narrow rulings to reinstate the citizens' rights. This is true of all the rights in the Bill of Rights, although this example used the Second Amendment as an example.

There is a great distinction between Constitutional rights and legal rights. A Constitutional right is one possessed by a citizen, which the government is prohibited from tampering with. These are the ones mentioned in the main body of the Constitution (such as habeas corpus) and in the first ten Amendments (known as the Bill of Rights). A legal right is just the opposite: it is created by a government entity, and can be changed as desired. Examples would include abortion and social welfare (i.e., Roe v. Wade, Social Security, and Medicaid). The rise of governmental power in America is based on equating these two categories of rights. The method is simple: pass laws, issue executive orders, and issue rulings which serve to reduce Constitutional rights down to the level of legal rights (i.e., granted by the government), then narrow the conditions under which said legal rights can be exercised until they are practically non-existent. This constant dilution of the rights of the citizens via criminal violations of their oaths of office by government officials will eventually cause America to descend to an authoritarian dictatorship. It is in fact the favorite tactic of the socialists and "progressives". The only peaceful solution to this problem is to vote against any political candidate who believes that the government has too little power; and vote against any candidate who does not adequately control the natural impulses of bureaucrats and judges to expand their powers. Politicians, bureaucrats, and judges must be disciplined and constrained at every turn. Otherwise, the people will lose their liberties.

-- § --

Question 53: Long-Term Finances

A certain man has a steady job and earns a good income. However, he likes to spend more than he makes. In fact, he has no savings or assets, and he spends about 10% more than he earns every year. At first he financed his excesses by running up large balances on his credit cards. Then, when they were at their maximum, he opened up new accounts, paid off the old accounts, and continued to run up debt on the new accounts. He eventually had to stop paying on the principal he owes, and is now only paying the current monthly interest due (although the principal keeps rising due to his continued spending). Over time, he earns more income, but continues to spend about 10% more than he earns, year in and year out. What is his long-term financial outlook?

a) Gradually, the effect of inflation, in which each new dollar has less buying power, will serve to reduce the true debt and he will then be able to pay it off.

b) In the long run, his real income after inflation will continue to rise, and he will be able to grow his way out of debt.

c) He has purchased a number of things with the debt, and can sell them when he needs to in order to pay off the debt.

d) He will be able to borrow indefinitely, since the creditors realize that they may lose what he already owes them if they force him into bankruptcy.

e) Some combination of two or more of the above.

Answer to Question 53

This is a trick question. In the long run, this man will be bankrupt because he is unable to control his rising debt. He can only avoid bankruptcy by eliminating the overspending, living below his actual means, and paying off what he owes.

Answer (a) is incorrect because it confuses the reduced buying power of an inflated dollar with a reduction of debt. It is true that inflation will serve to reduce the buying power of each new dollar, or, in other words, it will take more dollars to buy the same product. But this man continues to spend 10% more than he earns, so he will spend and go into debt by a larger number of dollars, but that larger number of dollars will still represent 10% of what he earns. A better way to think of it is that if he works 2,000 hours per year, his additional debt grows by 200 hours of his labor every year. So, he owes someone the equivalent of 200 hours of additional work each year (that he is not performing), and it does not matter if those hours are denominated in starting dollars or in inflated dollars. The inflation of the currency only makes the numbers larger, but does not affect the actual debt, so long as he continues to overspend.

Answer (b) is incorrect because although his real income will rise over and above inflation, his real debt increases at the same rate because he continues to overspend at the same 10% rate. Over time, he will become a high wage earner with correspondingly large debt.

Answer (c) is incorrect because all the things he possesses from his overspending are used, and they do not have the value they had when he bought them. There will be an occasional exception in which an object increases in value, but generally, the extra things he buys will decrease in value.

Answer (d) will work for a while, but in the long run, the creditors have to resolve their debts and expenses. Ultimately they will have no choice but to conclude they will never be paid, and cut their losses by refusing to lend this man any more money. When that happens, the man will default (stop paying the interest) on his debts, and he will be bankrupt.

This man can declare bankruptcy and start over with a clean slate. He will be out of debt, but he will not be able to get credit, and if he does, will find it much more difficult to declare bankruptcy again. If he subsequently runs up a debt again, and cannot discharge it, he will be required to work but most of his paycheck will be seized to pay off his creditors. He will in effect become a slave.

Many of the false concepts of the "benefits" of debt are applied at the national level. By doing so, the officers of the government are pretending that these basic economic rules do not apply to nations. Unfortunately, nations are not immune to them, and they will either go bankrupt or will confiscate everything of value to pay off the debt (both of which will impoverish most of the people).

Most government officials at the federal level believe that either answer a) or b) is correct. Democrats seem to believe answer a) will work; Republicans seem to believe that answer b) will work. Note that both parties seem to agree that monetary inflation cures debt, which is why both parties are content with inflation as engineered by the Federal Reserve. When both a) or b) prove to be wrong, politicians will then favor option d). They fail to realize or accept that nations do not actually escape by bankruptcy: every national debt must be paid, and it is possible for a nation to become the servant of another over indebtedness. For example, if one nation is heavily indebted to another, the debtor nation could be ordered to engage in proxy wars to advance the foreign policy of the creditor nation. Or, the creditor nation may exert influence over the spending priorities of the debtor nation, thus controlling it indirectly.

-- § --

Question 54: The Pledge of Allegiance

In 1892, in preparation for the celebration of the 400th anniversary of Columbus' discovery of America, a magazine in Boston called *The Youth's Companion* published a "pledge to the flag" to be recited by schoolchildren. It is believed to have been written either by Francis Bellamy or James Upham. The pledge has undergone several revisions in the years since; it currently reads:

> "I pledge allegiance to the flag of the United States of America, and to the republic for which it stands, one nation under God, indivisible, with justice and liberty for all."

Although it was originally devised for schoolchildren, it was eventually adopted in 1942 as part of the United States Flag Code (U. S. C. Title 36). What is the purpose of such a pledge?
a)   To inspire people to be proud of living in a nation that has liberty and justice for all.
b)   To emphasize that only people who believe in God can be Americans.
c)   To remind people that America cannot be divided.
d)   To confirm that the people are the ultimate sovereign in America.
e)   A combination of a), c), and d).

Answer to Question 54

This is a trick question. All of the answers are false. The correct answer is that the pledge of allegiance is a means to get you, the citizen, to give an oath of loyalty to a flag, which is a mere symbol of the republic.

As a citizen, it is expected that one will be loyal to your fellow-citizens and the government, so long as the government performs its duties to defend your liberties. An oath of loyalty is not necessary; and giving it pre-empts your right with the rest of the people to abolish any government which does not serve their needs. This principle is stated in the Declaration of Independence:

> "We hold these truths to be self-evident, that all men are created equal, that they are endowed by their Creator with certain inalienable rights, that among these are life, liberty, and the pursuit of happiness -- that to secure these rights, governments are instituted among men, deriving their just powers from the consent of the governed, that whenever any form of government becomes destructive of these ends, it is the right of the people to alter or to abolish it, and to institute new government, laying its foundation on such principles, and organizing its powers in such form, as to them shall seem most likely to effect their safety and happiness."

Answer a) is wrong because giving an oath of loyalty is not inspirational; it is an obligation. Furthermore, no nation, no matter how well constituted, can ever secure liberty and justice for all --- there will always be some injustice and some infringements on liberty because it is the nature of people to conduct their affairs imperfectly.

Answer b) is wrong because everyone born to American parents in America is a U. S. citizen, whether they believe in God or not; in fact babies do not believe in anything. The atheist, the devil-worshipper, the born-again Christian, and all the others in between are all equal citizens.

Answer c) is wrong because it is either false (as in the Civil War), or is just an idle sentiment. Of course America can be divided. Many so-called "leaders" have made a fortune doing so: David Duke, Jesse Jackson, George Wallace, Al Sharpton, Bill "Perjurer in Chief" Clinton, Louis Farrakhan (Louis E. Walcott), and Barack "Leading with his behind" Obama, just to name a few.

Answer d) is wrong because, if you are taking an oath of loyalty, then you are in effect giving up your portion of the public sovereignty to an emblem that represents the current government.

Here is a little exercise guaranteed to bring a smile. Imagine John Adams, Thomas Jefferson, George Washington, Alexander Hamilton, Benjamin Franklin, Gouverneur Morris, James Otis, Joseph Warren, James Madison, James Monroe, George Mason, Patrick Henry, John Jay, or John Hancock ever taking an oath of loyalty to the English Union Jack. Even the tyrant George III never demanded it, but we have it in U. S. Code Title 36. Even if the Founders did take oaths of allegiance to the Union Jack or to England or to King George III, it didn't matter much in the long run, did it?

All in all, the pledge of allegiance is OK as a teaching aid to young children, but adults should be careful not to take it too seriously. It was written by a socialist whose main objective is to get you, the citizen, to pledge undying loyalty to a government, even one over which you have no control. There is too much in it that dilutes your citizenship and your rights. Politicians are fond of reciting the pledge on every occasion (if a camera is rolling) but they would serve us better if they took an oath of loyalty to the principles of limited government per the U. S. Constitution.

-- § --

Question 55: Tax Deductions

A man has earned income in a certain year. He took the "standard deduction" on his federal "gross income" tax, and as a result, his "taxable income" is taxed at 25%. If he had made a $100 "tax-deductible" contribution that year, how much would his federal tax have changed?
a) "Tax deductible" refers only to state taxes, so his federal tax would remain unchanged.
b) His tax would have been reduced by $100.
c) The "tax deduction" only applies in the following year, so he would get a reduction next year, not now; his tax for the current year is unchanged.
d) His tax would be 25% of his gross income less the $100, or the amount previously calculated, whichever is less.
e) His total tax is 25% of $100 = $25.

Answer to Question 55

This is a trick question. All of the answers given are incorrect.

Answer a) is incorrect because "tax deductible" contributions are deductible for federal purposes.

Answer b) is wrong because "tax deductible" does not mean that you can deduct the contribution from your taxes; you can deduct it from your income. So, his tax would be reduced by 25% of the $100 contribution ($25) only if the $100 deduction did not lower the "tax bracket" of his "taxable income"; in that case, his tax would be reduced by the tax rate at the lower tax bracket rate. However, if he had any income from rental properties, sales of stock or bonds, farm income or any of the other income sources called out in the Tax Code, there is no way to predict the effect of the donation.

Answer c) is incorrect because contributions can be used a tax deductible usually only in the tax year in which they are made.

Answer d) is wrong because it ignores the "standard deduction".

Answer e) is wrong because the income tax depends on total income less deductions; it is not based on the amount of a deductible contribution.

See how simple the tax code is? The tax code (the regulations of which fill 20 volumes in the U. S. Code of Federal Regulations) is complicated because Congress wants it that way. Here is a bonus question: Why does Congress want a complicated tax code?

a)   In order to make the tax code as fair and equitable as possible.

b)   To ensure that everyone pays their fair share.

c)   To ensure that equal numbers of rich and poor do not have to pay taxes.

d)   Because the tax code must reflect the complexity of the economy, otherwise some people will pay less than they should.

e)   All of the above.

The answer is once again, "none of the above". The tax code is exceedingly complicated because it is a means by which members of Congress can acquire and utilize power to punish their political enemies, reward their allies, and generally coerce people's behavior. If a corporation does something a Congressman doesn't like, he can insert a provision in the code to penalize that corporation; if a corporation gives him a large campaign donation, he can insert a provision to lower that corporation's tax burden. The tax code requires centralized record-keeping of all financial data; any Congressman (in fact any federal legislative, regulatory, or enforcement official) can obtain any and all financial data on any business or person if they give a remotely plausible reason. Complying with the tax code requires an enormous amount of labor and effort. The cost of compliance with the tax code is estimated at $400 billion [1]. Most of that effort is performed for free by taxpayers, or performed by experts who are in turn paid by the taxpayers. Compulsory unpaid labor was once known as slavery (back when words had meaning). A great many hours are expended by professional tax experts; their jobs depend on a complex tax code, hence they are indirectly dependent on Congress for their livelihood. This explains another reason why the tax code never will be simplified --- too many people will become unemployed. The important point to remember is that the tax code is only partly about revenue. It is also about the use and abuse of power, and it partly serves as a make-work jobs program.

Here is an additional note about the complexity of the tax code. In 1927, three economists wrote in their economics book [2]:

> "The [tax] law itself is a lengthy document equivalent to about 100 ordinary printed pages, loaded with technical details and administrative provisions of the utmost complexity. To master all the details of this law, with the mass of administrative rulings and court decisions which has grown up about it, is an ambitious task to be undertaken only by the special student of taxation."

It is good to know that Congress continues to "simplify" the tax code such that we now have only 60,000 pages of tax-related case law to deal with (as of 2016). Don't be fooled by those who say that the code as written by Congress is only about 2,800 pages long. That is true, but you, the taxpayer, are responsible for complying with all the case law that has accumulated from it, now at more than 60,000 pages.

[1]   https://taxfoundation.org/compliance-costs-irs-regulations/

[2]   Fred Rogers Fairchild, Edgar Stevenson Furniss, and Norman Sidney Buck, *Elementary Economics*, New York: The Macmillan Co., 1927, Vol. 2, p. 415

-- § --

Question 56: Roe v. Wade and Dobbs v. Jackson

The Supreme Court legalized abortion nationwide in 1973 in a ruling called the Roe v. Wade decision. Since then, many people who are opposed to abortion have been trying to get either: a) the Supreme Court to reverse itself and overturn Roe v. Wade; or b) have the U. S. Congress pass legislation to supersede the ruling. Now that the Supreme Court overturned the Roe v. Wade decision per the Dobbs v. Jackson decision (24 Jun 2022), what is the net effect?

a)   It is illegal for anyone to be in favor of abortion rights.

b)   Women can be prosecuted under existing federal law for having an abortion.

c)   Doctors who performed abortions can be tried for murder under existing federal law.

d) Women are required to report pregnancy to the federal government so they could be monitored until giving birth.
e) Both b) and c).

Answer to Question 56

This is a trick question. All of the answers are false.

When Roe v. Wade was overturned, the abortion issue returned to legislation in the respective 50 States, as it was before the 1973 decision. Prior to 1973, abortion was legal in some States, illegal in others, and a variety of regulations were in place at the State level. Overturning Roe v. Wade in and of itself did not create new federal crimes as in b) and c). Answer a) is wrong because everyone is free to be in favor of or opposed to anything they choose. This may be proven by the simple fact that abortion was legal due to Roe v. Wade, but no one is being prosecuted for opposing abortion (although some Democrats would prefer it otherwise). No one will be prosecuted for favoring abortion now that Roe v. Wade is overturned. Answer d) is wrong because reporting of pregnancy was never required in any State, and will not be required under the Dobbs decision (and unlikely in any State).

The important point here is to consider the factual chain of events that would occur if a law or ruling were overturned, instead of relying on what propagandists claim might happen. With no other modifiers, the situation would return to what was before the law or ruling was passed. In the case of Roe v. Wade, the States have resumes regulation of abortion, as it was before. Likewise, if the federal narcotics laws were repealed, the States would be free to regulate them as they did before.

How did we get into this mess with the abortion debate? As usual, the federal government arrogated to itself the power to regulate medical procedures, a power never granted in the Constitution. The federal government would be wiser to avoid entering into areas where the Constitution is silent, and allow the States and local entities pass laws suitable for their own needs.

Don't fall for the false claim that overturning Roe v. Wade changed anything at the federal level; abortions are not a federal crime. As stated above, the power of regulating abortions, if any, is now returned back to each State.

-- § --

Question 57: TV Interviews

You are watching a talk show on TV. The host is conducting an interview with three guests. Each of them, including the host, gives their view on the topic at hand. You are trying to determine which of the four people on the show is most likely to be correct about the issue being discussed. Which is the most efficient method to determine who is correct?
a) The host is correct because it's their show, and they are not allowed to lie on TV.
b) The person who looks most like a nerd is probably the smartest of the four, so they are most likely to be correct.
c) The most attractive person is probably correct because people like attractive people, and they likely were told the correct answer in advance.
d) If a government official is part of the discussion, then they are likely to be correct.
e) If a member of the clergy is part of the discussion, then they are most likely to be correct.

Answer to Question 57

This is trick question. There is no way to judge the accuracy of the guest's opinions based on the information given.

Answer a) is incorrect because a talk-show host is not responsible for anything said on the air, unless it is specifically libelous or defamatory. If a host were to make a conclusion based on outright lies, there is still no direct penalty to the host.

Answers b) and c) are incorrect because appearance is a very poor determinant of anything other than appearance.

Answers d) and e) are incorrect because one's profession is not necessarily a good indicator of accuracy.

The important point to remember is that the person who is most likely to be correct is the one who provides the greatest amount of relevant and verifiable facts coupled with a conclusion based on sound logic that considers the relevant facts. Such a situation rarely occurs in television, since most "discourse" and "debate" consists of either five-second "sound bites", political party "talking points", or self-righteous socialists telling you that you are evil unless you agree with them. In television, the emphasis is nearly always on drama over substance.

-- § --

Question 58: Unequal Credit

Credit is a situation in which a person or institution lends money to another person or institution upon a written promise to repay the loan. The loan is usually repaid at an agreed-upon interest rate. This additional amount paid by the borrower to the lender is the fee to the lender for the use of his (or the lending institution's) money. In other words, the lender gives his money temporarily to the borrower; the borrower repays the amount borrowed plus a certain percentage per year at a certain rate. The additional amount repaid is income to the lender for the borrower's use of his money.

Normally individuals borrow from banks or credit card companies, but not every person is allowed to borrow the same amount. Some people are allowed to borrow more than others. Why do banks and credit card companies give credit unequally?

a) Most banks prefer to deal with people they know, and are more likely to be more liberal with those people in the amount of credit they give --- in other words, those who know bankers and those who work at credit card companies have an advantage.

b) People who are given less credit are victims of some bias or prejudice by the banks and credit card companies; in fact offering different credit levels is a violation of the Fair Lending Act.

c) Banks and credit card companies give credit based on what is necessary to maintain their lifestyle. Therefore, wealthy people are given more credit than the middle class people, and middle class people are given more credit than poor people because the wealthy have more day-to-day needs than the middle class, and the middle class likewise has greater needs than the poor.

d) Banks and credit card companies prefer to give more credit to those who are desperate, because they can squeeze a higher interest rate out of them.

e) Some combination of the above, depending on state regulations.

Answer to Question 58

This is a trick question. All of the answers provided are wrong because neither banks nor credit card companies "give credit".

Credit is something each individual has (or not). Your creditworthiness is based on the lenders' estimate of the risk taken by the lender when lending you money. In other words, the issue is whether or not you are able and willing to repay the loan. If the lender has reason to believe that you will fail to repay, then you are considered a higher risk than someone else, and your credit is low compared to another person. If you have a steady income and pay your bills on time, the risk of lending to you is low and your creditworthiness is high. In both cases, the amount of credit you have depends on your situation and your past behavior, along with normal market forces, since credit is like any other commodity. Remember that you, as the individual, possess a certain amount of credit; it is not "given" to you by banks, credit card companies, or another person. The amount of money you can borrow and upon what terms is a consequence of your creditworthiness, which is to say, the amount of risk you represent to the lender.

-- § --

Question 59: Witness Protection

One evening, a local tavern was invaded by a large number of motorcycle gang members. Their main mission was to intimidate the bar owner over some previous incident, but some of the members of the gang decided to have a little "fun" and assault the customers, including people who had no stake in the previous incident, and were only having a few beers after work. Some of the bar patrons were injured seriously enough to require hospitalization. The police were called, and they were able to make a few arrests, although most of the gang members dispersed before the police came.

Because so many innocent people were injured, the case became a local sensation. Usually the gang members were able to buy off certain officials to reduce charges, but were unable to do so in this case because of public outrage at the scale and severity of the attack. As the prosecutor was preparing his case against the gang members who had been arrested, a reliable informant reported that the other members of the gang intended to kill anyone they believed would testify against the defendants. This particular gang operated nation-wide according to a strict organized crime discipline. They had a long-established reputation for carrying out their threats; they have promised "to finish the job" if any of the victims testify. But there is little chance of a conviction if the victims do not testify. The prosecutor was faced with a choice of: a) dropping the cases; b) watering the charges down to a laughable set of misdemeanors, or c) proceeding with the case, and offering each victim entry into the Witness Protection Program. The victims are asked to consider the third prosecutorial option. What are the benefits of the Witness Protection Program for the victims who testify?
a)   They are given a new identity.
b)   They are relocated out of the area.
c)   They receive special police protection at public expense.
d)   They receive monthly payments in return for standing up to the criminals in the interest of justice.
e)   All of the above.

Answer to Question 59

This is a trick question. All of the answers are false.

Answers c) and d) do not actually occur, and are patently false.

Although a) and b) actually occur, they are not "benefits" to the Witness Protection Program. The Witness Protection program was set up to provide aid, comfort, and protection to professional criminals who wished to avoid a long prison sentence by testifying against their fellow gang members (known as "turning state's evidence"). An innocent person who enters the program has to give up everything: their good name, home, friends, family, job, and church. They lose nearly everything that matters to regular people. Admittedly, these are not quite so problematic for professional criminals, since they do not have a good name, friends, a job, or a church. At least the professional criminal stays alive to commit some more crimes when the heat dies down. But for a regular person, there is no "benefit" to the Witness Protection Program. In this particular case, since the gang operates nationwide, most likely with moles in local police departments, a victim who enters the program would always have to be careful, looking over his shoulder as if he were the criminal. It is actually worse than that: if you do testify, you will most likely be prohibited from owning a gun to protect yourself after entering the program.

What should you do if you become a victim of organized crime and are faced with a choice of either refusing to testify or entering Witness Protection? You should refuse to testify. Why should you be penalized the rest of your life for the government's failure? It is bad enough that you were victimized the first time. The prosecutor will certainly have contempt for you, and may even call you a coward, especially if the case is sensational enough to have earned him a chance to run for Governor. Don't worry --- he'll get over it.

How is organized crime the government's failure? Because most organized crime is based on providing goods that are prohibited or inordinately taxed. Common examples include the importation and distribution of alcohol during Prohibition, and importing and distributing illegal narcotics at the present time (drug prohibition began in 1919). With cigarette taxes rising so high, we may in the future hear of "tobacco cartel kingpins" who smuggle in cigarettes and sell them for only $6.00 per pack.

Another case where organized crime represents governmental failure is through passive aiding and abetting of organized criminal activity. The prime example is J. Edgar Hoover. As the first director of the FBI and the one of the nation's top law-enforcement officers, he spent nearly four decades (1930's to 1970's) denying the existence of the Italian mafia. It first came to power during Prohibition, at the same time J. Edgar Hoover came to power. It seems like J. Edgar Hoover was either the nation's highest ranking pathologically incompetent law enforcement ignoramus, or was on the mafia's payroll. I guess we'll never know (but the latter seems more likely).

-- § --

Question 60: Causes of Death

The U. S. Government published a report [1] summarizing the causes of death among Americans in 2004. A total of 2,397,615 deaths occurred in that year, broken down by cause as follows. The text in parentheses appears in the original; that in square brackets is editorial explanation.

a. Diseases of the heart: 652,486
b. Malignant neoplasm [cancers]: 553,486
c. Cerebrovascular diseases [stroke]: 150,074
d. Chronic lower respiratory diseases: 121,987
e. Accidents (unintentional injuries): 112,012
f. Diabetes mellitus: 73,138
g. Alzheimer's disease: 65,965
h. Influenza and pneumonia: 59,664
i. Nephritis, nephritic syndrome, and nephrosis [kidney diseases]: 42,480
j. Septicemia [blood poisoning]: 33,373
k. Intentional self-harm (suicide): 32,439
l. Chronic liver disease and cirrhosis: 27,013
m. Essential hypertension [high blood pressure] and hypertensive renal [kidney] disease: 23,076
n. Parkinson's disease: 17,989
o. Assault (homicide): 17,357
p. All other causes: 414,674

Consuming too much salt (also known as dietary sodium) is known to cause an increase in blood pressure (hypertension). Increased blood pressure is known to be a contributing cause of strokes, kidney disease, and some heart attacks. There is a sub-category of "Accidents" that deals with poisoning, but none of those deaths are listed as sodium or salt poisoning. None of the 414,674 residual deaths from accidents are related to stroke, heart disease, or kidney disease. Also, none of the 414,674 residual deaths are called out as being due specifically to salt intake. Based on these facts and statistics, how many of these deaths can be attributed directly or indirectly to the intake of salt?

a. The sum of those due to stroke (150,074) and nephritis/nephritic syndrome/nephrosis (42,480), which totals to 192,554.

b. The sum of those due to stroke (150,074) and essential hypertension/renal disease (23,076), which total to 173,150.

c. The sum of those due to stroke (150,074), nephritis/nephritic syndrome/nephrosis (42,480), and essential hypertension/renal disease (23,076), which totals to 215,630.

d. The sum of those due to stroke (150,074), nephritis/nephritic syndrome/nephrosis (42,480), and essential hypertension/renal disease (23,076), plus some unknown portion of those due to heart disease (652,486), in which the total is somewhere between 215,630 and 868,116.

e. All 2,397,615 (except the 414,674 residual deaths) were caused by salt because: a) all of them are dead; and b) all of them had to have eaten some salt at some point in their life.

[1] A. M. Minino, M. P. Heron, S. L. Murphy, K. D. Kochanek, *National Vital Statistics Report*, Vol. 55, No. 19 (21 Aug 2007), p. 8; Hyattsville, MD: National Center for Health Statistics (U. S. Department of Health & Human Services); available at: https://www.cdc.gov/nchs/data/nvsr/nvsr55/nvsr55_19.pdf

Answer to Question 60

This is a trick question. The correct answer is none of the above: since the report does not list salt intake as a cause of death, the number of deaths due to salt is zero.

It is true that salt intake may be a contributing factor to a number of health issues such as kidney failure, but it would be impossible, except in the case of salt poisoning, to claim that salt per se was the primary cause of any deaths from those causes. The most that can be said is excessive salt may increase the risk of some health hazards, which in turn may be a contributing factor to death. This does not mean that salt caused any deaths. Be careful, therefore, when an activist claims that "trans-fats are the fourth leading cause of death", or "smoking cigarettes kills over a million Americans per year". To make such claims, the activist would have to attribute some fraction of categories of death unambiguously to these particular causes. But, there are exactly zero death certificates that read "Died of excessive intake of fatty acids". Keep in mind that a large number of people die of "old age", which means they lived so long that the body degraded and a cancer developed, or the heart gave out. The primary cause of those deaths is actually old age, and the heart attack or cancer was simply the consequence of old age.

Be careful of those activists who also claim that "guns kill more people than ..." The same report mentions (Table 10, p. 33) that there were 649 deaths due to accidental discharge of firearms, 16,750 deaths by suicide by self-inflicted firearms discharge, and 11,624 homicides by discharge of firearms. There were 15,689 suicides by other means, and 5,783 homicides by other means. How dangerous is America due to the presence of guns? Note that the number of suicides with and without firearms is nearly the same, which suggests that a person determined to commit suicide is going to find a way. The absence of guns would have little effect on the suicide rate. It is interesting to note also that the suicide rate in South Korea, a nation in which privately-owned firearms are exceedingly rare, is more than three times higher than the suicide rate in the U. S [1, 2]. This proves that suicide is a societal and cultural problem, not a gun problem.

It has been estimated that a significant fraction of homicides are professional criminals killing other professional criminals (in Chicago, about 65%). (There would be a net gain to society if professional criminals killed even more professional criminals.) If even half fall into this category (which would be easy to track), the number of firearm-related homicides that matter (i.e., those in which the victim is not a criminal) is down to 5,812. Combined with the 649 deaths due to accidental discharge, the actual number of relevant deaths involving firearms is down to 6,461; or put another way, constitutes 0.000215 of the cited population of the U. S. This fraction is equivalent to 0.0215%. It is odd that no statistics are kept on how many criminals are killed by citizens, or how many crimes are prevented or pre-empted by citizens with guns.

[1]   Small Arms Survey 2007 Part 2, Aug 2007, available at:
       https://smallarmssurvey.org/resource/small-arms-survey-2007-guns-and-city
       and summarized at: http://en.wikipedia.org/w/index.php?oldid=547789057
[2]   http://en.wikipedia.org/w/index.php?oldid=547795916

-- § --

Question 61: Leasing Cars

A certain car could be purchased for $18,500 from any of four dealers at 7% interest for 4 years with $1,850 down ($398.70 per month = $19,137.82 total). Including the down payment, the average monthly cost is $437.25. The exact same car is available for lease at the same four local car dealers. The terms of the leases being offered are shown in the following table:

Dealer	Amount Down ($)	Length of Lease (months)	Monthly Payment ($)	Annual Mileage Allowance	Total Mileage Allowance	Cost per Mile Over Limit ($)
Abbott	2,470	36	180	10,500	31,500	0.30
Baker	2,060	42	224	11,000	38,500	0.35
Canton	1,650	48	258	11,500	46,000	0.40
Drury	1,500	54	276	12,000	54,000	0.50

Figure 61-1: Data for Car Leases

For example, at the Baker dealership, you would pay $2,060 down, and pay $224 per month for 42 months, at which time you would give the car back to the dealer. If you drive more than 11,000 miles annually, you are required to pay 35 cents per mile. In the Baker example, if you drove 12,000 per year over the 42 months (42,000 miles), you would owe $0.35 for each mile above 38,500, which comes to $1,225, payable at the end of the lease. In all leases, you are responsible for insurance, registration, and maintenance costs.

Suppose you drive an average of 13,000 miles per year. If you desire to do what makes the most sense financially over the long run, which lease should you enter into?
a)   Abbott
b)   Baker
c)   Canton
d)   Drury
e)   Either Canton or Drury, because they have the longest term leases.

Answer to Question 61

This is a trick question. The correct answer is that all leases are a bad deal in the long run. Leasing is a basic trick in which the chump gets to pay insurance on the leasing company's car, maintain the leasing company's car, and pay taxes and fees on the leasing company's car, while never owning anything. It is nearly always better to buy a car, maintain it well, and keep it for a long time. Most modern cars will last 10 to 15 years or 250,000 miles.

Here is how the comparison numbers work out. The costs of insurance and maintenance incurred during a lease period do not enter into the calculation, since they have to be paid under all lease and purchase circumstances. The average monthly cost for any lease is calculated as follows. Multiply the lease cost times the number of months to get the total payments. Multiply the total number of miles driven during the lease term and subtract from it the annual limit times the number of years in the lease. Add these two numbers to the down payment, and then divide by the number of months in the lease. In the case of the Abbott lease, we have $180 x 36 = $6,480. Driving an average of 13,000 miles per year means $0.30 times 2,500 miles per year times 3 years = $2,250 in excess mileage charges. Adding these two numbers with the down payment, obtain $2,470 + $6,480 + $2,250 = $11,200. Dividing by 36 months, we obtain $311.11 average cost per month. Here is the complete table, including the corresponding costs for purchase:

Dealer	Amount Down ($)	Length of Lease (months)	Monthly Payment ($)	Total Mileage Allowance	Mileage Driven During Lease [1]	Miles Above Limit	Mileage Surcharge	Total Payments	Total Cost [2]	Average Monthly Cost ($)
Abbott	2,470	36	180	31,500	39,000	7,500	2,250	6,480	11,200	311.11
Baker	2,060	42	224	38,500	45,500	7,000	2,450	9,408	13,918	331.38
Canton	1,650	48	258	46,000	52,000	6,000	2,400	12,384	16,434	342.38
Drury	1,500	54	276	54,000	58,500	4,500	2,250	14,904	18,654	345.44
(Purchase)	1,850		399					19,138	20,988	437.25
1. The total miles driven during the lease is based on 13,000 per year average										
2. Total cost is the sum of lease payments, mileage surcharge, and the down payment.										

Figure 61-2: Results for Car Leases

The average cost for purchasing the car is higher than any of the lease options. Why then is purchasing better? The answer is that under a lease, one never stops paying; with a purchase, there comes a time when you own it and only have to pay maintenance, insurance, and registration. The calculation to be made here is: for each candidate lease, how long would it take for the total payout to be equal to the total payout on the purchase? Once that time is known, how likely is it that the car will provide reliable service? It is easy to find the break-even point by dividing the purchase option total ($20,988) by each of the monthly average lease costs; this will be the number of months for the leasing costs to equal the purchase cost. We obtain 67.5, 63.3, 61.3, and 60.8 months for the Abbott, Baker, Canton, and Drury leases respectively. In other words, if the car will last longer than 67 months, buying is the best way to go in the long run. At 13,000 miles per year, most new cars will last at least 12 years (144 months); if so, the long-term cost of purchasing the car is less than half the lease costs.

Here is how to reduce long-term expenses on cars: buy either a new car or a high-quality late-model used car, maintain it per the manufacturer's specifications, and drive it until the monthly maintenance costs equal the lease costs then prevailing at that later time. At that point, even leasing is better than hanging onto the old car. That will prove that it is time to buy another new or high-quality used car and repeat the cost-saving process.

There is one exception to the general rule of not leasing a car. If you receive a notice from your doctor that you are terminally ill with less than a year to live, then you should lease the finest car you can find and enjoy your last year on earth riding in style. Do not worry about the leasing company being cheated by your early death prior to the lease termination: they watch the obituary notices, and their car will be removed from your driveway before your body is cold.

-- § --

Question 62: Anti-Christian Activists

A certain city has experienced a large influx of people who have embraced a hatred of Christianity. They claim to be atheists who reject the concept of God and all religions, but in practice, only seek to offend

Christians, and to a lesser extent Judaism. They never have an unkind word for Moslems, Buddhists, Sikhs, Wiccans, or Hindus. The atheists have distributed leaflets against "all religion", but only single out Christian traditions as being evidence of evil, hypocrisy, or ignorance. The Christians in the community are subjected to the tirades of atheists in many public places, and even on public property.

The atheist groups have become increasingly aggressive, up to the point of calling Christians names on the streets, demonstrating in front of churches during services, and occasionally disrupting a service by physical intrusion. What should the Christians of this community do in response?

a) Appeal to the American Civil Liberties Union (ACLU) for their help in opposing the atheists, or hire lawyers and sue the city directly in order force the city to enact an ordinance that restrains the activities of the atheist groups.
b) Close all the churches.
c) Organize and stage counter-demonstrations whenever they find a group of atheists.
d) Appeal to the Civil Rights Commission or other federal government agencies for help against the atheists (since they are violating the rights of Christians).
e) Both a) and d) are viable options.

Answer to Question 62

This is a trick question; all of the answers are wrong.

Answer a) is wrong because hiring lawyers to sue the city, if successful, would force the city to enact an ordinance against one religion (atheism) to the benefit of Christianity; anything the city did would be regarded as either promoting or restraining religion, contrary to the First Amendment. Don't be fooled: atheism is a religion like any other, except it does not have a deity with power over people. It is a religion in which a few "enlightened" people have absolute power over other people. Appealing to the ACLU is a waste of time because the ACLU favors any activity that is regarded as opposing Christianity.

Answer b) is wrong because doing so would give the atheists what they want; it would be tantamount to Christians voluntarily giving up their rights.

Answer c) is wrong because it would give the atheist groups some free publicity, while at the same time, draining Christians of time and money that could be put to better uses.

Answer d) is wrong because government agencies have been sensitized by numerous lawsuits to never be seen as favoring Christianity (although it acceptable to favor the Moslem religion now). It would open the government agencies to a claim of choosing sides in what the universities and the mainstream media (ABC, CBS, NBC, MSNBC, CNN, and PBS) will call a "battle between rationality and those ignorant inbred Bible readers".

The correct answer is to remember what Jesus Christ said [John 15:18-20]:

"If the world hates you [Christians], keep in mind that it hated me first. If you belonged to the world, it would love you as its own. As it is, you [believers] do not belong to the world, but I have chosen you out of the world. That is why the world hates you. Remember the words I spoke to you: 'no man is greater than his master.' If they persecuted me, they will persecute you also."

And so it is; sooner or later, Christianity is rejected and Christians become the object of scorn and ridicule. The only practical recourse for the Christian community is to take comfort that Jesus' prediction is true, and to laugh it off. If they are confronted in public by the atheists, laugh them off. If the atheists put up signs ridiculing Easter or mocking Christmas, laugh it off. But if the atheists go beyond verbal taunts, and start violent confrontations, then each Christian should send a few of them over to the coroner a little sooner than they expected. Self defense is legitimate and it takes over when free speech crosses over into intimidation.

Jesus also had made these other statements, which greatly offended the high and mighty religious and political leaders of His day:

a. [John 6:40] "For my Father's will is that everyone who looks to the Son and believes in Him [i.e., personal faith in Christ as the Savior] shall have eternal life, and I will raise him up at the last day."
b. [John 14:6] "I am the way, the truth, and the life. No one comes to the Father except through Me."
c. [Luke 22:36] He [Jesus Christ] said to them [disciples]: "But now if you have a purse, take it, and also a bag; and if you don't have a sword, sell your cloak and buy one" [i.e., be prepared for the problems of this world, especially persecution].
d. [Matthew 26:11] "The poor you will always have with you, but you will not always have Me." [predicting His crucifixion].

You can see that all of these statements are in direct conflict with the notions of the "progressives" and socialists. Those types want you to believe that this life is all there is, and that it is the government's duty to create paradise on earth. They also believe that you should be dependent on a wise and benevolent government for everything.

Christianity is one of the things that socialists fear the most. Why is that? It is because a few of the foundations of Christianity are:

a) The grace of God, not the legalism of government;
b) The confidence of eternal life in heaven, not just the temporary pleasures of this life; and
c) The importance of individual initiative in freedom; not the tyranny of one-size fits all regimentation.

-- § --

Question 63: Impeachment Timeline

State legislatures have a power to impeach (convict) a State Governor and to remove him from office. Suppose a Governor of a State has been implicated in a wide variety of corrupt activities, and federal investigators have videotapes, emails, and wiretapped phone calls in which the Governor is observed engaging in numerous criminal conspiracies to commit fraud and bribery. The evidence is provided to the State legislature by the investigating authorities. The Governor refuses to resign his office. How soon will the State legislature impeach the Governor and remove him from office?
a) Within a few hours
b) Within a few days
c) Within a few weeks
d) Within a few months
e) As soon as possible, consistent with the procedures called out in the state constitution.

Answer to Question 63

This is a trick question. It is highly unlikely that the legislature will impeach him (although it does happen on occasion). The reason he is not likely to be impeached by the legislature is that the corrupt Governor knows about a lot of the corruption being practiced by the members of the legislature. He will intimidate them into abandoning impeachment by threatening to rat all of them out for their illegal activities.

Members of the legislature are not disturbed by revelations of corruption by Governors. They are not usually bothered by the fact that the people continue to suffer under a government staffed by professional criminals. Their main concern is whether or not they appear on the tapes, phone calls, or emails; i.e., to what extent they can be implicated in the Governor's crimes, and whether the public suspects that they benefitted.

If a State legislator fails to impeach, and the State prosecutor fails to act, a Governor can be only be removed by indictment and conviction by the federal government (thus forcing a resignation). A rare exception may occur when the Governor is already unpopular enough that he will have a negative impact on the re-election chances for members of his party. In that case, the members of his party in the legislature may go along with impeachment in order to save their own reputations and re-election chances, not because they care about corruption in State politics. The opposing party will be happy to impeach the Governor, and they will drag the whole process out as long as possible for political gain.

The Governor's party will spend a great amount of time and energy attempting to avoid this kind of negative press by putting forward a sufficient number of plausible excuses for the Governor's behavior. The hope is that they can buy enough time until some other scandal or bigger problem causes it all to fade into the background.

Any members of the legislature that are found by the federal investigators to be co-conspirators with the Governor will most likely immediately cut a deal with the federal government and rat out the Governor to save themselves.

-- § --

Question 64: Breaking Glass

A local neighborhood gang threw a party, and in the course of having a good time, smashed 1000 beer bottles all over a residential street. The gang members all left the area before the police showed up, and none were arrested or charged. The beer had been purchased at a local store, and the gang members all paid a deposit to the store on the beer bottles that they subsequently broke. No matter what you think about parties, or beer, or about gangs in general, consider this action in the economic sense. In what economic sense did the gang members indirectly perform the most useful economic service?

a)   The store that was paid the deposit on the beer bottles gets to keep the deposit paid by the gang members.

b)   It is possible that some people will make money when they are paid to clean up the broken beer bottles.

c)   Broken beer bottles are a true sign of urban life, and will probably increase the partying type of tourism in that area.

d)   Some people will run over the beer bottles and get flat tires, which have to be replaced, which will those who manufacture, sell, and install tires will indirectly benefit from increased sales.

e)   Some combination of a) and d).

Answer to Question 64

This is a trick question. The breaking of the beer bottles has no economic benefit; in fact it reduces the general benefit of past economic activity.

Answer a) is wrong because although it's true that the store gets to keep the deposit, the store owner gains nothing because he had to pay the deposit to the beer bottler. The gang members lost money because they could have returned the bottles and received back their deposit, which would have allowed them to buy something else (maybe more beer, which would have benefited the brewer). Also, the price of the deposit may be less than the replacement cost, because the bottler expects to get nearly all his bottles back. So the bottler incurs a loss by having to pay more than the deposit to replace the broken bottles.

Answer b) is wrong because although it's true that someone may be paid to clean up the mess, the money to pay the cleanup crew will come out of someone else's pocket (the neighbors), which they would otherwise have spent on something else.

Answers c) and d) are wrong for the same reasons. If people run over the bottles and get flat tires, the tire dealer will make money, but the people with the flat tires will have to do without something else they planned to buy instead of the now necessary tires. Responsible partying tourists do not want to go to a place that is dirty and dangerous, and the gangs that like to make a mess like this will cause this area to experience more broken bottles and more losses.

The main point here is to consider the full effects of economic questions. It is not sufficient to consider who is next in line to make a few dollars, but remember to consider all the alternatives that did not happen because of the broken beer bottles. For example, suppose one of the neighbors was going to buy a new garden hose. That hose cannot purchased with the money in hand because that money now has to be paid as part of the contribution toward cleaning up the broken bottles. The neighbor now has to work another hour to get the money for the hose he could have had if the bottles hadn't been broken. Likewise, the people who replaced their tires could have bought many other things. Those things now cannot be bought with the money then in hand, and those people now have to work more hours to get what they could have bought if the bottles hadn't been broken by the gang members. The gang members thus indirectly caused money to be wasted in some form (the beer bottler, or the neighbors who had to pay for the cleanup, or those who need new tires). It pre-empts productive activities that would have occurred had the bottles not been broken.

When all the secondary and tertiary effects are considered, it is obvious this seemingly minor incident has no economic benefit and in fact has a negative impact. Don't be fooled by those who try to convince you otherwise. This is in fact the most important rule in economic analysis: be sure to consider all the consequences of a policy or action, not just what is immediately obvious [1].

[1]   Henry Hazlitt, *Economics in One Lesson*, NY: Harper and Brothers, 1946 (second edition 1979)

-- § --

Question 65: Mattress Warranties

Joe is at a furniture store to buy a mattress. He tested them all out by lying on them briefly. He found four mattresses that were comfortable, they are all priced about the same, and all are made by known manufacturers of good reputation. The only real difference between them is the nature of the manufacturer's warranty. He can buy a warranty on Mattress A that consists of a one-year warranty against workmanship flaws; it costs $21.00. He can buy a warranty on Mattress B that offers a three-year warranty against workmanship flaws which also includes replacement of any broken springs; it costs $74.00. The manufacturer of Mattress C offers a lifetime warranty against workmanship defects plus a warranty against tears in the fabric and replacement of springs; it costs $91.00. The manufacturer of Mattress D offers a lifetime warranty on all problems and defects except if the mattress is used for commercial purposes (does not apply to Joe, since he will use his at home); the Mattress D warranty costs $125.00. Which is the best warranty to buy?
a)   Mattress A, because it is the cheapest.
b)   Mattress B, because it lasts three years, and most problems occur between one and three years, so is better than Mattress A's warranty.
c)   Mattress C, because it is for the life of the mattress and covers the most common mattress problems.
d)   Mattress D, because it covers everything for life, and for the few dollars more, offers the best overall protection.
e)   In general, it won't matter which one he gets, because there are a wide variety of problems with mattresses. The important thing is to get at least the protection offered by Mattress A, but the other ones are worth considering.

Answer to Question 65

This is a trick question. The correct answer is that you should never pay for a warranty on a mattress. Why? Because the terms and conditions imposed on the buyer means that the warranty can never be enforced. For example, in many warranties, any stain on the mattress (even from a Kool-Aid spill) invalidates them. Also, any kind of discoloration of the cover invalidates most mattress warranties. Sometimes additional warranties require that the mattress be packed and shipped to the manufacturer's location in the original cardboard box and the original plastic lining, at the buyer's expense. So, additional mattress warranties are just a money-making gimmick that can never be enforced, and you should never waste your money on one. Buy the best quality mattress you can afford and live with the default warranty that is included in the price.

The general point to be made here is that additional warranties are of value only if they can be enforced without too much time and expense on your part. It applies equally to any warranty on cars, homes, electronics, and everything else for which an extended warranty can be purchased. An extended warranty on a car is of little value if the work can only be done by one repair shop. A warranty on a computer is useless if it has to be shipped to the manufacturer in the original box (in which case the cost of shipping may be more than the cost of the repair). Make sure you understand all the fine points of how a warranty can be enforced before you pay for one.

-- § --

Question 66: Evolutionary Probability

Charles Darwin (1809 - 1882) was an English "naturalist", that is, a scientist who studies nature and the workings of nature. He is highly regarded as an honest, patient worker who sifted through the facts available to him, testing various hypotheses per the scientific method, until he obtained some measure of consistency that allowed him to propose theories. His most famous theories have been combined under a general concept of "the theory of evolution". He presented his work on "evolution" in two books, *The Origin of the Species By Means of Natural Selection* (1859) and *The Descent of Man and Selection In Relation to Sex* (1871). Consider the following passages from Charles Darwin's original work; the italicized portions in square brackets are explanatory notes that I have added.

"As species have generally diverged in character during their long course of descent and modification, we can understand why it is that the more ancient forms, or early progenitors of each group, so often occupy a position in some degree intermediate between existing groups. Recent forms are generally looked upon as being, on the whole, higher in the scale of organization than ancient forms; and they must be higher in so far as the later and more improved forms have conquered the older and less improved forms in the struggle for life; they have also generally had their organs more specialized for different functions. This fact is perfectly compatible with numerous beings still retaining simple and but little improved structures, fitted for simple conditions of life; it is likewise compatible with some forms having retrograded in organization, by having at each stage of descent better fitted for new and degraded habits of life." [1]

"The similar framework of bones in the hand of a man, wing of a bat, fin of a porpoise, and leg of the horse, -- the same number of vertebrae forming the neck of the giraffe and of the elephant, -- and innumerable other such facts, at once explain themselves on the theory of descent with slow and slight successive modifications. ... On the principle of successive variations not always supervening at an early age, and being inherited at a corresponding not early period of life, we clearly see why the embryos of mammals, birds, reptiles, and fishes should be so closely similar, and so unlike the adult forms." [2]

"Throughout whole classes various structures are formed on the same pattern, and at a very early age the embryos closely resemble each other. Therefore I cannot doubt that the theory of descent with modifications embraces all the members of the same great class or kingdom. I believe that animals are descended from at most only four or five progenitors [ancestors], and plants from an equal or lesser number." [3]

[Note: Apparently "class" and "kingdom" in this context are synonymous, and refer to mammals, reptiles, birds, fish, and insects. I have inferred this from two sources. The first is a glossary in The Origin of the Species, in which "mammalia" are called the "highest class of animals". The second is a section in Chapter 21 of The Descent of Man (paragraph 19) in which Darwin states: "In the several great classes of the animal kingdom,--in mammals, birds, reptiles, fishes, insects, and even crustaceans..."]

"The main conclusion here arrived at, and now held by many naturalists who are well competent to form a sound judgment is that man is descended from some less highly organized form. The grounds upon which this conclusion rests will never be shaken, for the close similarity between man and the lower animals in embryonic development, as well as in innumerable points of structure and constitution, both of high and of the most trifling importance, -- the rudiments which he retains, and the abnormal reversions to which he is occasionally liable, -- are facts which cannot be disputed." [4]

From the preceding statements, which is most likely within the kingdom of mammals, considered over the entire course of earth's history?
a)   That birds are descended from dinosaurs.
b)   That humans are descended from monkeys.
c)   That monkeys are descended from tigers.
d)   That elephants are descended from rabbits.
e)   That cats are descended from dogs.

[1]   Charles Darwin, *The Origin of the Species By Means of Natural Selection*, Chapter 15 "Recapitulation and Conclusion", paragraph 30.
[2]   Charles Darwin, *The Origin of the Species By Means of Natural Selection*, Chapter 15 "Recapitulation and Conclusion", paragraph 35.
[3]   Charles Darwin, *The Origin of the Species By Means of Natural Selection*, Chapter 15 "Recapitulation and Conclusion", paragraph 46.
[4]   Charles Darwin, *The Descent of Man and Selection In Relation to Sex*, Chapter 21 "General Summary and Conclusion", paragraph 2.

Answer to Question 66

This is a trick question. None of the answers are correct.

Answer a) is incorrect because birds and dinosaurs are not mammals (or at least the scientists currently estimate that dinosaurs were not mammals). Darwin's theory is that the kingdoms remain separate; since birds are of their own kingdom, and experts have claimed that dinosaurs are of the reptile kingdom, neither can be descended from the other. The reason why answers b) through e) are wrong is that none of them can be more likely than the others. Darwin's theory is based on natural selection arising out of chance changes to the animal; therefore the entire system is random and each is equally likely.

In the first three quoted passages, Darwin allows for trends toward both higher-organized forms and lesser-organized forms ("retrograded"). Therefore, in Darwin's original theory, any mammal is equally likely to have "descended" from any other mammal; any reptile is equally likely to have descended from any other reptile, etc. In other words, Darwin's basic claim is that the evolution of species within a kingdom is entirely random over the long run, but there is no transmigration of kingdoms. Notice that Darwin never claimed that all animal life on earth started from some single-cell critter floating in the ocean that somehow adapted to life on land, then somehow evolved into various animal types, and finally evolved into humanity. If that were so, why did evolution stop with humanity?

In passage four, Darwin concluded that man "descended" from a "lesser organized form". Wouldn't it be more accurate to say that man "ascended" from a "lesser-organized form"? Judging from his exposition of the general theory, it is equally likely that man "descended" from a "more highly organized form". Each of the answers b) through e) should have an "or vice-versa" appended to it.

Darwin claims in passage four that man is descended from a less-organized form; he is confident enough to assert that it cannot be refuted. His first justification for his proof, as he states, is that there is a close similarity between man and the lower animals, and secondly because of the numerous similarities in structure between man and the animal kingdom. But his reasons do not provide the proof. The features of similarity may be due to the fact that both man and animals are optimized for conditions on earth. Such are more likely to be the results of creation than random-chance evolution. He also does not attempt to answer why evolution does not continue today. Why are honeybees unable to see the color red? Certainly they would be attracted to more flowers if they could see red, and would be able to produce more honey to feed more hives and expand their species. But they have not evolved in that direction, and Darwin's theory offers no evidence as to why not. Maybe there is a valid reason (unknown to us) as to why bees should not see red, which would imply that the conditions found in nature are the result of an intelligent design beyond random chance.

Scientists claim that humans first appeared about a million years ago. If so, why has evolution stopped? Why can humans only hear to 20 kHz? Why can humans only see in the waveband between 380 and 770 nm? Why aren't human infants self-sufficient soon after birth, as are many in the animal kingdom? Darwin's theory has no hope of answering any of these questions.

When considering whether to believe in any theory or not, it is useful to go back and read what the original developer said about his theory. Darwin's observations are also explainable by creation. Do not be content with reading what others or later workers claim was intended. If you read Darwin's original work, you will find it is different than what modern writers claim Darwin intended.

-- § --

Question 67: Successful Acting Off-Screen

An actor is anyone who pretends to be someone they're not. If an actor works hard and persistently studies to become skillful at his profession, he can sometimes achieve great fame and earn a lot of money (that is, he becomes a celebrity, which is defined as being someone who is famous for being famous). When such an actor subsequently endorses a political proposition or supports some cause, he is often able to persuade many other people to adopt his views. Why are actors so successful in political causes?

a) Acting skill is extremely rare, and those who have been blessed with it generally have a higher intellectual capacity. The general public is smart enough to recognize superior intellect, and is therefore inclined to trust the opinions of actors.

b) Acting skill requires an unusual amount of insight into the character of people, which enables the actor to acquire a very keen sense of morality. The general public is smart enough to recognize superior moral perception, and is therefore inclined to imitate the actor and adopt his views.

c) Achieving success as an actor requires an inordinate amount of hard work that most people cannot even imagine. Those who have put in this kind of effort demonstrate their total commitment to something; therefore, their endorsement of a political cause indicates a true level of commitment not observed among ordinary people. The general public is smart enough to recognize the virtue of sincere commitment, and is therefore inclined to imitate the actor.

d) Being a famous and wealthy actor affords him the luxury of leisure time which he can use to increase his knowledge on subjects of interest to society. This is aided by his access to people of greater knowledge and he is then able to acquire true wisdom on important issues. The general public is smart enough to recognize true wisdom, and is therefore inclined to defer to the actor for guidance.

e) It is generally one of the above, although the motivation to trust actors' judgment may vary from person to person and with the importance of the political cause.

Answer to Question 67

This is a trick question; none of the answers are correct. It is true that an actor is a person who pretends to be someone he is not, in other words, he makes a living by being a professional phony.

Answer a) is wrong because although it is true that acting skill is rare, it does not follow that actors are smarter than anyone else. If acting skill and intelligence were so highly correlated, certainly Albert Einstein would have received an Academy Award.

Answer b) is wrong because although it is true that actors acquire insight into men's habits and motives, it does not increase their morality; they are the same person they always were. Survey the behavior exhibited by Hollywood personalities and see where they rank on a morality scale. They are no different than the general public (sometimes they are on the lower end of the scale).

Answer c) is wrong because although some actors work hard, some don't; the same as any other line of work. But there is no evidence that acting is the hardest kind of work; if it were, there would not be so many people trying to be actors.

Answer d) is wrong because having wealth and leisure does not lead to wisdom; if it did, a logical conclusion would be that poverty and hard work lead to stupidity. No one is dumb enough to believe that, not even a professional actor.

The truth is that people with common sense recognize that an actor is just another workman, no better or smarter or more moral or more of anything than anyone else, and that the endorsement of a political cause by an actor is usually nothing more than shameless self-promotion in order to keep the actor in the public eye (upon which his entire career depends). Makes you wonder why the media reports the opinions of actors, doesn't it? The media reports the opinions of actors for two reasons: a) it is easier than researching and reporting relevant facts; and b) using the name of a famous person may increase viewership. Both contribute to filling airtime and column space with little effort by reporters and editors.

-- § --

Question 68: Home Ownership

Why is owning your own home a good investment?
a) In the long run, values of houses tend to go up, thus owning a home causes a person's net worth to increase over time.
b) The federal government and most state governments give homeowners an income tax deduction for interest payments made on a house (if it's a primary residence).
c) It is easier to customize and decorate one's own house to one's own tastes, which is not normally permitted when leasing or renting.
d) One will be able to live very cheaply after the house is paid off, whereas one never stops paying rent.
e) It is a combination of a), b), and d).

Answer to Question 68

This is a trick question. All of the answers are false.

Answer a) is false because although the value of the house does increase, the price of all the other houses is also increasing. Therefore, to benefit from the increase of the value of your house, you would have to sell it and buy another house whose price did not similarly inflate. There are significant costs associated with selling and buying another house: making repairs per the inspection, realtor fees and commissions, loan origination fees, title insurance, etc. It is often better for most people to rent or lease, especially if their occupations require them to relocate often. It is better to own a home only if you intend to stay in that house permanently, which in modern times, is more difficult than it used to be.

Answer b) is wrong because the deduction from income is not an additional deduction; it is in lieu of the standard deduction. It is true that the deduction for interest paid is sometimes greater than the standard deduction, but the homeowner also has additional expenses, such as property taxes and fire insurance.

Answer c) is false: it is a true statement, but it is not relevant because it has nothing to do with the financial aspect of owning a house.

Answer d) is false because the maintenance costs associated with owning a house continue to increase as the house ages. Also, there is rarely any limit to the amount of property taxes that can be assessed on a home; often property tax increases nearly replace the mortgage payment if the house is in a good location and the surrounding area is prosperous. For most working people, there is little economic benefit to owning a home (unless you stay in it for a long time); most of the benefits are intangible. There can be a significant benefit for retired persons, for whom owning a home can improve their monthly cash flow. But in general homes are a poor investment because they require maintenance; whereas true investments do not require a constant input of wealth to prop them up.

-- § --

Question 69: The Gang Problem

A certain community has been plagued by many years of violence by criminal gangs. These gangsters have engaged in street battles in which innocent people, sometimes even small children, were killed in the cross-fire. They have burned peoples' houses down, ruined the schools and parks, and hold loud parties that reduce the quality of life in the neighborhood. Children are afraid to go to school, and people in general are afraid to go outside after dark. Over the past ten years, 92 innocent people (24 of them children under the age of 10) have been killed by the gangs, with 264 others injured seriously enough to warrant hospitalization. The local police force has done the best they could with limited resources. They do manage to arrest a few gangsters after especially infamous crimes, but overall the neighborhood is becoming increasingly dangerous. Criminal activity by the gangs shows no signs of abating, despite the fact that the members of the gangs are well-known to the police and residents alike. The residents have found that complaining to City Hall is a waste of time, as the politicians say they are doing the best they can.

A group of residents decides to act in their own interests. They hold a secret meeting and develop a plan to take up arms, patrol the neighborhood, and attack and kill as many known gang members as they can find. A local informant finds out about the plan, and reports the residents to the police. What will happen next?
a)   The Chief of Police will arrange a meeting with the residents, and offers to share all the information about the gangs possessed by the police, so that the gangs can be eliminated more efficiently.
b)   The Chief of Police will order his men to assist the residents in any way they can.
c)   The Mayor intervenes and convinces the residents to abort the plan and also orders the police not to aid the residents. He arranges for representatives of the residents and the various gangs to sit down and discuss the issues in the neighborhood, with the idea that a negotiated settlement can be worked out.
d)   The Mayor tries to convince the State to fund a jobs-training program for the gang members. At the same time, he convinces the residents to hold off on their plan until the jobs program takes effect.
e)   Some combination of the above.

Answer to Question 69

This is a trick question. The correct answer is that: a) the Chief of Police will notify the Mayor of an impending action by the residents; b) the Mayor and Chief of Police will agree henceforth to call the planned citizen action an "insurrection"; c) the Mayor will notify the Governor; and d) the Governor will call out the National Guard to round up and arrest all the residents who were alleged to be involved in the plan.

Those who resist arrest are to be executed on the spot. Those who are arrested will be tried for participation in a terrorist conspiracy. They will also be charged with hate crimes if any of the targeted gang members are either illegal aliens or belong to a racial group different than a majority of the residents involved in the plan.

The Mayor will then call a press conference and brag about the efficiency of his administration when it comes to dealing with "impending terrorist threats by crazed vigilantes". The Mayor will then re-iterate his call for control of all weapons in the hands of citizens, especially guns, knives with blades longer than 2", baseball bats, tire irons, chains, bricks, rocks larger than 3" in diameter, and rope in lengths exceeding 4 feet. He will then declare a state of emergency and send the police door-to-door to confiscate all these items, excepting of course, from: a) known members of organized crime syndicates; and b) government employees.

Note that the city administration is not the least bit concerned about the deaths of the innocent people over the past ten years; it is greatly concerned about the armed conspiracy to eliminate the criminals. The child who is murdered on the way to kindergarten is not a problem for the city administration. After all, the parents can always make another one, right? But the prospect of professional criminals turning up dead is a serious matter indeed.

The fact that the residents are forced to hide in their homes after dark is acceptable, but the city government simply will not tolerate any situation in which criminals are impeded in their activities. The city will exert powers to regulate the ability of law-abiding residents to exercise self-defense, and will promptly prosecute all "extremists", defined as anyone who believes their life has value. Therefore, the amount of criminal violence in any given neighborhood is based on what the politicians and the Police Chief will tolerate. On the other hand, residents are required to tolerate an infinite amount of violence against themselves and their children. Politicians like any situation that keeps the people in fear because people in fear do what they are told.

The only remedy for this situation is to move out of the neighborhood, because politicians and Police Chiefs are generally afraid of organized crime. There is little point in fighting back against criminals and being rewarded with life without parole in a maximum security facility. It is better to give up your home, change jobs if necessary, and move to a safer neighborhood until the gangs take that one over too.

Just don't forget to pay your local taxes to support your ever-efficient justice system and the politicians who are always bragging about their promises to protect you and your family.

-- § --

Question 70: Charitable Foundations

A famous person decides to set up a tax-exempt Foundation. He names the Foundation after himself (like the Ford, Carnegie, and Rockefeller Foundations), files all the necessary paperwork, and begins to solicit tax-deductible contributions from the public. Although the Foundation has zero assets at the beginning, the Foundation receives a great deal of money from the public owing to the founder's personal popularity. After withholding a small percentage for administrative costs, he bundles all the contributions received from the public into large amounts and gives the money away to various causes, such as AIDS research, literacy, etc. All of the donations are made in the name of the Foundation. What is the main benefit of this arrangement?

a) People get to take a tax deduction for their contributions.
b) The money contributed, except for administrative costs, goes to good causes that help the less fortunate.
c) Enough money can be concentrated in each of the charitable areas to make a real difference.
d) People feel better about themselves by helping others.
e) All of the above.

Answer to Question 70

This is a trick question. The main benefit accrues to the person who established the Foundation, because he gets to put his name on the charitable contributions, despite the fact that the money really came from contributions he received. Note that the Foundation had zero assets before he started receiving contributions; that is, he did not put any of his own money into it. The big difference between this scam and the Ford Foundation is that the Ford Foundation was funded by money actually contributed by Henry Ford.

All of the given answers are true to some extent, but they are equally true for all charitable giving. They are false in the context of this question because none of the answers address the reason why the Foundation was established. He established the Foundation to magnify his name and reputation at the expense of all the chumps who donate to it. He is using their money as if he were the generous one, despite the fact that not a dime of what goes out in his name actually came out of his pocket.

If you donate to such a Foundation established by a famous person, be sure to inquire as to how much of their money goes into it.

-- § --

Question 71: Risky Foods

Popular foods consumed by millions of people have been discovered to have a process involving a dangerous chemical in the manufacture of those food items. Upon investigation, it was discovered that manufacturers used a process in which a quantity of carbonic acid gas was dissolved in hydroxic acid, which then forms what the manufacturer claims is a safe, edible compound although it contains known levels of carbonic and hydroxic acids. Consider the following facts regarding carbonic acid gas and hydroxic acid.

Item: Carbonic acid gas, although naturally occurring, is a known asphyxiant. It is odorless and colorless. It is dangerous because in concentrations of 15% in air, carbonic acid gas causes unconsciousness, coma, and death. However, the carbonic acid gas used in the manufacture of the "edible" compound is 100% pure, that is, at more than seven times the lethal concentration.

Item: Hydroxic acid is an odorless, colorless liquid at room temperature. It is known to cause death in humans if too much of it penetrates into the lungs, which can occur in the process of ingesting the manufacturers' "edible compound". It is particularly deadly in children. In 2004, statistics show that children under the age of 14 died from this cause 14.73 times more frequently than adults over the age of 85.

Item: The "edible" compound containing these materials has no known health benefits, but has not been studied to determine if it poses any health risks. It is used merely for aesthetic reasons in the production of some foods.

With these facts in mind, what would be the most prudent course for regulation of these materials?
a)   A study should be done to determine if anyone has been poisoned, and if so,
      1) The manufacturers should be prosecuted, and then
      2) These substances should be regulated the same as other poisons.
b)   Manufacturers should require a license, be subject to periodic government inspections, and warning labels should be placed on all containers until the risk level has been determined.
c)   Prohibition on sale to minors should be enacted to protect children.
d)   An excise tax should be levied to discourage production and consumption since it has no known health benefits.
e)   Manufacture, importation, possession, and consumption should all be prohibited, with an exemption for those entities specifically licensed to handle this material, due to the danger to children.

Answer to Question 71

This is a trick question. The process described in the question is that of manufacturing an "edible" compound known as carbonated water. "Carbonic acid gas" is an old-fashioned name for carbon dioxide (CO_2), and hydroxic acid is a technically correct chemical name for water. It is true that water can be dangerous if it penetrates into the lungs (known as drowning). In 2004, 943 children under the age of 15 drowned accidentally, and so did 64 people over the age of 85. Of all other ages, 2,835 people also died of accidental drowning. Carbon dioxide is a known asphyxiant (usually found in mines), and 100% pure CO_2 is used in the manufacture of carbonated water. But the carbonated water is ingested into the stomach, not into the lungs, and therefore is safe to drink, as we all know from drinking soda, mineral water, and other things.

This is an example of a scare tactic that relies on using obscure names for common materials in an effort to promote more regulation. Instead of stating the true facts, it camouflages the real topics at hand. This type of scare tactic is common among those who want to control your life, but don't have any logical justification for it. It has been particularly effective in the "man-made climate change" debate. The basic claim of the "climate advocates" is that humans have been burning carbon-based fuels, which increases the nominal level of CO_2 in the atmosphere. The claim is that the increased level of CO_2 leads to a "greenhouse effect" in which heat cannot escape into space; then the earth warms up, the oceans rise, the weather becomes worse, and all life on earth will become extinct within 50 years. But they never mention two scientific facts. First, from a purely historical perspective, we do not know what the long-term nominal CO_2 in the atmosphere has been, since we have been able to make measurements only for about 100 years. Secondly, CO_2 is to plant life what oxygen is to animal life; if you want to reduce CO_2, plant more trees.

-- § --

Question 72: Congressional Workload

Consider the following chart, which contains data on the salaries of members of Congress [1] and the number of days Congress (House) was in session [2]. The solid line shows the annual salary of House members for each year, normalized to 2008 dollars (the salary value is read from the vertical axis at left). The long-dashed line shows the number of calendar days the House was in session for each year; the value is read on the vertical axis at right. The short-dashed line shows the salary per working day (annual salary divided by the number of days in session); the value is read on the vertical axis at right. Finally, the thin dotted line shows a linear fit to the salary per day (value read at right); it indicates the general trend. What conclusions can be drawn from this data?
a) The annual salary has leveled off in the past two years, and the number of days worked has increased, driving the salary per day down. This trend will continue.
b) The salary per day is becoming too large compared to what ordinary people make. Eventually, Congress will either reduce the Congressional salary or work more days in order to bring their compensation more in line with ordinary people.
c) The salary per day is increasing only because the number of days worked is steadily decreasing. This shows that Congress is becoming more efficient. Therefore, the salary per day will increase, but that is a positive trend because it reflects increased Congressional productivity.
d) The salary per day line shows that Congress took pay cuts in 1979, 1983, 1987, 1989, 1993, 1995, 1997, 1999, 2001, 2003, 2005, and 2007. Therefore, it is only fair that the long-term trend of salary per day be upward to compensate for those cuts.
e) Either b) or c).

[1] Ida A. Brudnik, "Salaries of Members of Congress: A List of Payable Rates and Effective Dates, 1789-2008"; Congressional Research Service, The Library of Congress, 21 Feb 2008

[2] https://history.house.gov/Institution/Session-Dates/All/

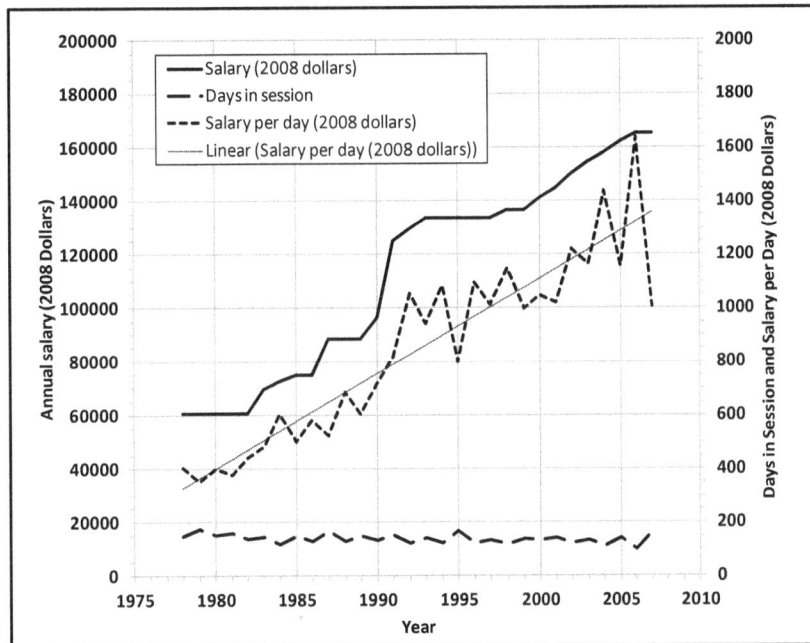

Figure 72-1: Congressional Salaries and Work Days

Answer to Question 72

This is a trick question. All of the answers are false, but are the type of claims you might hear from members of Congress as they attempt to justify the low number of workdays.

Answer a) is wrong because it is contrary to the thirty-year trend shown in the chart; there is no evidence to believe that salaries will level out.

Answer b) is wrong because the data shows that Congress has never taken a salary cut, and the number of days worked continues to decline, although ordinary people have to work more days (or hours) over time to maintain the same standard of living. It is reasonable to conclude that the members of Congress do not believe their compensation should be related in any way to the compensation of ordinary people.

Answer c) is wrong because the quality of work done by Congress continues to worsen every year; if anything, useful productivity is going down.

Answer d) is wrong because the salary per day is the wrong metric to use in evaluating whether or not they took a pay cut. The solid line shows that Congress has never taken a pay cut.

Given the poor quality of Congressional work (they weaken the nation every time they take a vote), we would be better off if they were paid multi-million dollar salaries plus were allowed to keep all the campaign donations for personal use, so long as they were constrained to work only three weeks per year.

It is true that the members of Congress work relatively few days in session, but they do usually put in a lot of hours on the other days, mostly meeting with constituents, attending strategy meetings, speaking at various events, and fundraising. Although the members of Congress work very few workdays, they have large staffs which are constantly churning out new legislative proposals. Most of those proposals are submitted to the Committees for consideration without having been read by a Member beforehand. The growth of regulation follows the growth of legislation, and thus the growth of power and control. "Progressives" never tire of promoting more and more legislation, all in an effort to control everything about a person's life. That is all the "progressives" and socialists want: a bureaucracy with arbitrary power over every aspect of your life. Then you will be a slave, just like the Russian people were in the good old days of the Soviet Union, and as the serfs were during the Middle Ages. Contrary to some claims, socialism is not the least bit scientific. It is a series of good-sounding slogans designed to return civilization back to a primitive system of kings and entrenched ruling-class nobility with absolute power over the other 99.5%.

-- § --

Question 73: Basketball and NASCAR

Two men, one white and one black, are being interviewed on TV. The two men are successful engineers being honored for their inventions and contributions to technology. The interviewer, who (as usual) understands nothing of the technology and inventions made by the two men, decides to spend most of the interview on subjects not related to the two engineers' expertise, focusing instead on two sports: basketball and NASCAR racing.

It turns out that the white engineer hates both basketball and NASCAR racing; he hates basketball because it finds it monotonous, and also hates car racing because he thinks there are too many phony rich people involved in the sport.

The black engineer also hates both basketball and NASCAR racing; he hates basketball because he thinks there are too many phony rich people involved in the sport, and he finds NASCAR racing to be monotonous.

Suppose the interviewer asks both about basketball and NASCAR racing. What responses should the two engineers give? This is a family-oriented show.
a)   Everyone knows that engineers are nerds who should not waste our time giving opinions on anything. Both should simply lie, and say "I don't know anything about either one" and hope that the interviewer finally asks a relevant question.
b)   The black engineer should give his honest opinion on basketball, since it won't offend either whites or blacks. But he should not give an opinion on NASCAR racing because whites might find it offensive. The white engineer should give his honest opinion on NASCAR racing, because that won't offend anyone, but should not give his opinion of basketball so as not to offend black people. In other words, they can comment on the sport they dislike so long as it is played primarily by people of their own race, but each should refrain from commenting on the sport they dislike if it is played mostly by people of the opposite race.
c)   The black engineer can say anything he wants about basketball, and can mention that he doesn't like NASCAR racing so long as he compliments a famous white race car driver (preferably a deceased one) for being a good role model. The white engineer can say what he wants about NASCAR racing, and can mention that he doesn't like basketball, so long as he compliments a famous black basketball player (preferably a deceased one) for being a good role model.
d)   The question is illogical because it is inconceivable that a black person could dislike basketball, or that a white person could dislike NASCAR racing.
e)   Any of (a), (b), or (c) is acceptable.

Answer to Question 73

This is a trick question. All of the given choices are wrong. The correct answer is that they should say what they want about the two sports because no one in their right mind gives a crap anyway. In this case, the opinions are benign, and reflect the personal preferences of the engineers. On the other hand, if the engineers actually do hold negative opinions based on some unwarranted racial bias, then they have a problem and it would be better to keep silent and be suspected a fool than to speak up and remove all doubt.

Answer a) contains a preconceived notion about engineers; so those who chose it should not be offended if engineers (and members of any other occupation) have preconceived notions about them based on their profession. Note: pocket protectors are good.

Answer b) contains the premise that the audience would actually be offended by a private opinion on sports. If in fact the audience would be offended by an opinion about whether basketball or racing is boring (or that sports figures are paid too much), then the audience obviously consists of the type of morons who will find a way to be offended by something, no matter what. The engineers can't do anything about that level of ignorance on the part of the audience, nor should they cater to it.

Answer c) is based on a level of pandering suitable for a career in politics. It assumes that a statement about sports equates to a statement about the predominant race of those who play the sport. It promotes the moronic notion that not appreciating the sport is the same as being prejudiced against the race of people who play that sport. But on the other hand, it's OK to paper over a negative opinion on the sport and/or race with a suitably nauseating and insincere compliment.

Answer d) is based on false stereotypes suitable for a career at any of the Marxist mainstream media outlets, where efficient projection of false stereotypes puts a person the fast track to success.

Do not be conned or coerced into believing that every difference of opinion reflects some political issue that must be resolved by intimidation or ostracism. It turns out that I don't like jazz music. I think it meanders aimlessly; it has no continuity; it emphasizes technical skill at the expense of musical interest. Are you willing to assume or speculate that I am therefore either an Uncle Tom or a Klansman?

-- § --

Question 74: Public Harassment

A certain homosexual man is consistently being harassed and intimidated by people who are opposed to the "gay lifestyle". He has been assaulted several times (requiring hospitalization), lives in fear for his life, and is thinking of buying a gun for self-defense. However, it is illegal to own, possess, or carry a gun in his city. The city is economically distressed, and he is unable to sell his house and move away. What should he do?
a)   File complaints with the police, and depend on them for protection.
b)   Turn "straight".
c)   Get a gang of gays together, go out and administer a beating one of his assailants; that will send a message to his abusers and solve the problem.
d)   Hire some lawyers and attempt to sue his antagonists for harassment and violations of his civil rights.
e)   A combination of a) and c).

Answer to Question 74

This is a trick question. All of the answers are wrong.

Answer a) is wrong because the police are not legally required to provide protection to anyone. The police are far too busy answering calls to spend much time protecting one person or a group. (They are not legally required to respond to a call for help, either.)

Answer b) might work, it might not, but why should a person change their personal habits because someone doesn't like them?

Answer c) is wrong, even if it were possible, because the gays would then be committing the same crime as their harassers.

Answer d) is wrong because it is too late for paper shuffling by lawyers.

The homosexual's opinion of the value of his own life is far more important than the opinion of some "legislator" who passed laws to prohibit gun ownership (in effect, outlawing self defense). The homosexual should get a gun regardless of how many laws he violates. If even 20% of gays armed themselves for self defense, and if even two or three of their abusers turned up dead or in the operating rooms, there will soon be far fewer incidents, because people who are offended by the gay lifestyle are not offended enough to die over it.

In fact, this is how Jim Crow ended. Contrary to some political views, Jim Crow was not abolished because some legislators passed some "equal voting rights" laws, or formally ended legal segregation. Those laws were passed in the 1960's, after Jim Crow was already on his deathbed, so to speak. Jim Crow was nearly dead because black people got guns and started shooting back at the Klan. The Klan was mightily offended by black people asserting their right to life and liberty, but not offended enough to die over it.

Gun control does not work and those who favor it know it. Here's the proof. Require any police chief, Mayor, Governor, or legislator who favors gun control to sign the following statement:

> "I do hereby solemnly swear under penalty of perjury that the gun control laws in effect during my previous tenure in office guaranteed, and during my future tenure will guarantee, that no member of any criminal gang or any independent criminal had, or will have, any access to any firearm at any time for any reason."

No official will ever sign such a statement because they know full well that "gun control" has no effect on the criminal element. It certainly has no effect on government employees (who are generally exempted from the law anyway). It only affects the citizens, making them weaker and both the government and the criminals stronger. Care to guess why most governments (and criminals) favor gun control?

This is a general principle: your life and safety, and that of your family and your property take precedence over the whims of all politicians, the regulations of all bureaucrats, and all the laws. If you are any type of patriot, and you need a gun to defend yourself, your family, and your property, then get one, no matter who in the government doesn't like it or what the law is.

-- § --

Question 75: Responsibility

If a married couple makes a decision about something, and the decision turns out to be wrong, which is the best method to determine who takes the responsibility for it?
a) Whoever yells the loudest gets to blame the other one.
b) The one who feels the least guilty about it has to take the blame.
c) Neither should have to take responsibility for it.
d) The couple should agree to blame someone else.
e) The couple should discuss the situation rationally and mutually agree on who should take the responsibility.

Answer to Question 75

This is a trick question; all of the answers are wrong.

It turns out that the responsibility for an incorrect decision in a marriage always falls upon the husband; there is no need to debate it. The husband is designated per the Bible as having the final say on decisions affecting the family. Since he has the final authority (whether he uses it or not), he gets the final responsibility (whether he is willing to accept it or not).

So, does that sound like a good deal, ladies? You get to blame him for everything? You get to screech and whine because he has to take the responsibility? Not so fast. The reason he takes responsibility is because he gets to make the final decision when the two cannot come to consensus. That means, ladies, your husband has the final word on every important issue (except abortion). Not prepared to defer to his judgment? Well, then ladies, you will make a lousy wife, and everyone will know it. Therefore, choose for a husband a man you respect as a leader and can trust to make good decisions (even if you are smarter), and who owns up to his mistakes. If you don't trust his judgment, wait until he matures or find someone else.

How about you, gentlemen? Do you like the idea of getting the final say, thinking you can yell louder and intimidate her into taking the blame when things go wrong? Being the husband means being the leader of the family. Leaders take responsibility for their mistakes; they do not go around blaming their subordinates, or in this case, their partner/wives. So if you think you can do as you please and be as irresponsible as you like, then you will be a lousy husband and everyone will know it. Therefore, choose for a wife a woman who has confidence in and will respect your judgment, and not spend all her time second-guessing you (even if she is smarter).

-- § --

Question 76: Using Realtors

When buying a house, many people use the services of realtors, who are licensed specialists in handling real-estate transactions. Usually they operate in "territories", and acquire an extensive knowledge of the neighborhoods and school systems. Normally they will assist the buyers in helping them get around, and "showing" the houses for sale. Their fee for this service is normally 7% of the selling price of the house, which is paid by the seller out of the proceeds of the sale. What are the benefits of using a realtor if you are buying a house?

a) The realtor provides protection for the buyer against unscrupulous sellers, since they work directly with and therefore, have a vested interest in satisfying the buyer.
b) The services rendered by the realtor are paid by the seller, so whatever the realtor does is ultimately free to the buyer.
c) The realtor can provide legal advice on the complexities of real-estate law and regulations governing these transactions.
d) Since the realtors are licensed, the buyer can be confident that every property listed for sale is listed accurately with regard to age, conditions, known defects, and any existing liens against the property.
e) All of the above.

Answer to Question 76

This is a trick question. All of the answers are false.

Answer a) is false because the realtor has a contract with the seller in regard to showing the house and acting as the seller's agent, but is not responsible for protecting anyone from anyone. The realtor is an agent who provides certain services, but insurance against unscrupulous sellers is not one of them. If the seller claims something about the property is true, the realtor accepts it as true except for patently obvious things like incorrect addresses and the like. Realtors cannot be held liable for crooked sellers' actions unless they were actually in on the conspiracy.

Answer b) is false because although the realtor has a contract with the seller, and the seller writes the check covering the fee to the realtor, where do you think the seller gets the money for the fee from? He builds it into the selling price of the house! So the seller does not really pay the realtors' fees, the buyer does; note that the buyer indirectly pays the fees for a contract in which the payee is working for the seller. Nice work if you can get it.

Answer c) is false because realtors are prohibited from giving legal advice on transactions to which they are an intermediary, other than obvious things like which form is to be filled out when making an offer. Besides, realtors are not qualified to give real-estate advice unless they have passed the state bar exam (real-estate law being a specialty in most states); if they were lawyers, why would they be realtors?

Answer d) is wrong because the licensing of realtors has nothing to do with the items mentioned. Buyers are responsible for hiring other specialists to conduct investigations on each of these topics: the buyer must pay for a physical inspection of the property and report on defects; the buyer must hire an investigator to verify the accuracy of the title (or buy title insurance); the buyer must hire a specialist to investigate the legal condition of the property and any remedies.

There is nothing wrong with using a realtor to buy a house. Certainly there are some conveniences: a) the realtor has access to the home and can negotiate convenient showing times; b) the realtor has access to listings of other realtors, and can act as a "one-stop shop" for all the homes in the area; and c) the realtor can pre-screen homes for sale in your price range or by type (ranch vs. two-story) or your particular desires (number of bedrooms, etc.). But you should know that realtors do nothing more than this, and ultimately they work for the seller.

-- § --

Question 77: Short-Term Sacrifices

A certain man has a full-time job. Every work day (Monday through Friday), he spends an average of $7.00 for lunch. His wife has offered to make him a lunch every day (which would cost about $2.00 per day). Suppose the man took his wife up on her offer, and invested the $5.00 per day in mutual funds that received an average annual return of 8%. Will saving these small amounts make any economic difference over the long run, say 20 or 30 years? To assess this question, the formula for calculating the value of an investment with a fixed annual return is (neglecting inflation):

$$A = P(1.0 + r)^n$$

where P is the amount invested, r is the rate of return expressed as a decimal (8% = 0.08), n is the number of years the money is invested, and A is the value of the investment after n years. In this case, P would be the amount saved in a year. Inflation is ignored here because we are interested in the buying power, not the number of dollars. (Including inflation makes the calculation more difficult, and increases the number of dollars the investment is worth, but those dollars have less buying power). The effect of inflation does not change the general answer to this question.
a)   It is not worth it because "brown-bagging" is not cool, especially if one is a white-collar worker. In our image-conscious society, people think "brown-bagging" is a sign of cheapness, and appearing cheap may impede one's chances of getting ahead.
b)   "Brown-bagging" over long periods of time is bad for the environment because several trees will probably have to be sacrificed to manufacture the bags, so it is not worthwhile.
c)   It may be worthwhile for short periods when money is tight, or if one's workplace is far away from restaurants, but is otherwise socially degrading.
d)   It is not worth it; the amount accumulated will be so small that he would have been better off to enjoy buying his lunch every day.
e)   It is not worth it in general, for a combination of the above reasons, and possibly some others.

Answer to Question 77

This is a trick question. None of the answers are correct.

Answer a) is incorrect because the question was not about what is "cool"; it was about the economic effect of a certain action. If you are one of those who care about what others think, then you, by definition, are not cool. The truly cool people don't care what people think, which is why people respect them.

Answer b) is incorrect because the question pertains to economics, not the environment. But speaking of the environment, even if one consumed a "brown bag" every day for 40 years, only a small amount of wood would be consumed. So, the "environmental effect" of brown-bagging is a virtually a non-issue (it might make you feel virtuous, but only if you also refrain from using charcoal fires at barbecues).

Answer c) is incorrect because history demonstrates otherwise: a very large number of people spent their entire lives brown-bagging. Are they to be despised? Well, aren't we hoity-toity?

Answer d) is also incorrect because the total that can be accumulated through investing small amounts is surprisingly large, due to the effect of "compounding". "Compounding" is a fancy word that means the growth of a certain sum of money over one year does the same thing for every succeeding year, except in each succeeding year, the amount grows on the basis of the gains made in all the previous years. For example, if one invests $500 in one year and it grows by 10%, one will have $550 the next year. If that $550 grows by 10%, the new total is $605, and so on. After 10 years, the total is $1,296.87. This is considerably more than one might expect.

In the example given in the problem, the person saves $5 per day, which is $25 per week, which is $1,300 per year. At the end of the first year, he has accumulated $1,300 to invest. Now let us use the formula given in the problem for a 20-year period. It took the first year to get the first $1,300, so we want to know how much that grows for the next 19 years. Here P = 1,300, n = 19, and r = 0.08. Thus, the first $1,300 grows to $5,610.41 at the end of the 20-year period. But that is not the end of the story. What about the $5 per day he saves and invests during the second year? That $1,300 will accumulate for 18 years, which will grow to $5,194.82; the results of two years savings over 20 years is 5,610.41 + 5,194.82 = $10,805.23. The same behavior occurs for all the other years that he saves and invests. As you can see, it is the time that makes all the difference. As a concrete example, this $1,300 per year, invested with an average return of 8% for 20 years, returns $59,490. After 30 years, it grows to $147,268; after 40 years, is $336,773. Now these may not seem like enormous sums. But if you are now 20 years old, think about where you will be 20 years from now. Would you like to have an extra $59,000 in your pocket then, or would you rather fritter that kind of money away at $5 per day? It's up to you. You can either patronize restaurants in the near-term by wasting small amounts on soda and tacos, or you can make yourself rich in the long-term. When you consider the long term costs of buying lunch, they are not as cheap as they appear.

The important point here is to watch out for the little things that you spend money on. No one wants to live like a termite, but restraining the little things, and having the discipline to invest it, will pay off in the long run. Incidentally, this is one of the positive changes from the administration of President Ronald Reagan. It was during his administration that the rules were changed such that people of modest means could save and invest in small amounts, thus building up considerable wealth over the long run.

-- § --

Question 78: Marginal Income Tax Rates

The U. S. has a graduated personal income tax system. This means that income levels are divided into several levels, and those income divisions are taxed at different rates. The tax rates increase as the amount of income increases. The tax rate of the lowest division of income is called the "base rate", and all the other tax rates at the higher income levels are called "marginal rates". As a person's income increases, the marginal rates become higher; hence the name "graduated tax". For example, in tax year 2014, the income level divisions and marginal rates for single persons and married couples were:
a)   10% rate for incomes between $0 and $9,075 (single person), $0 to $18,150 (married)

b)   15% rate for incomes between $9,075 and $36,900 (single), $18,150 to $73,800 (married)
c)   25% rate for incomes between $36,900 and $89,350 (single); $73,800 to $148,850 (married)
d)   28% rate for incomes between $89,350 and 186,350 (single); $148,850 to $226,850 (married)
e)   33% rate for incomes between $186,350 and $405,100 (single); $226,850 to $405,100 (married)
f)   35% rate for incomes between $405,100 and $406,750 (single); $405,100 to $457,600 (married)
g)   39.6% rate for incomes above $406,750 (single); and above $457,600 (married)

There are slightly different marginal rates for "heads of household", but those are not relevant for this topic.

The overall size of the federal government depends on how much tax revenue it can obtain. It is clear from the tax schedule above that those who earn more must generally pay more in taxes. Some activists desire to reduce the size of the government by using a tactic they call "starving the beast". The idea is that if marginal tax rates are reduced, the government will receive less income tax revenue, and thus will ultimately force the government to reduce its budget targets. The claim is that in the long run, steadily declining revenue will require the government to reduce its spending and therefore its size. In other words, nearly all taxpayers would have more money left over from their paycheck. In what ways could this policy "starve the beast"?

a)   Money that would otherwise go to the government can be spent on appliances, cars, etc; the benefit accrues to selfish individuals and deprives the government of some revenue.
b)   Money that would otherwise go to the government can be spent on furthering one's education; the benefit accrues to selfish individuals and deprives the government of some revenue.
c)   Money that would otherwise go to the government can be spent on charitable causes. The benefit accrues to the less fortunate, but deprives the government of some revenue.
d)   Money that would otherwise go to the government can be spent on vacations or saved for the future; either way, the benefit accrues to selfish individuals and deprives the government of some revenue.
e)   All of the above to varying degrees, depending on individual preferences.

Answer to Question 78

This is a trick question; all the answers are false, because they are all based on the false assumption that the total economy would remain fixed if the marginal tax rates are changed. Generally (but not always), a reduction in marginal tax rates causes the people to have more money in their pocket, which they desire to either save or spend. Spending it means increased demand for goods and services, which is met by suppliers that expand their businesses, which they do by buying equipment and hiring more people. These are financed by the portion of money retained by the taxpayers that is saved and invested rather than being spent. The net result is that although marginal rates are lower, the overall economy is larger by an amount that offsets the lower marginal rates, and the revenue to the government actually goes up. The "beast" is "fed", not "starved". (A similar problem occurs if marginal rates are increased on the argument that it will increase government revenue. Normally doing so will contract the overall economy due to a reduction in incentive, and less overall profit potential to businesses. The net result is that government revenue usually goes down, even though the tax rates are higher.) Reducing marginal rates is a good policy because it enhances freedom and allows the people to enjoy more of what they earn, but it does not usually decrease the government's revenue, and does not decrease the government's size. No economic policy established by the government will reduce the size of the government; governments can be restrained only by political means.

The error in each of the answers lies in the phrase "deprives the government of revenue". The benefit in answer a) accrues both to the individual and anyone who builds, designs, or sells the cars and appliances; but it is not selfish to provide for oneself.

In answer b) the benefit accrues both to the individual and those who supply education; but it is not selfish to provide for oneself.

In answer c), the benefit accrues both to others who are aided and to the individual, since he can reduce his income tax liability by deducting the charitable contribution. Even though he can deduct his contribution, the overall expansion of the economy does not deprive the government of revenue.

In answer d) the benefit accrues both to the individual who receives a return on his savings and investment, as well as those who borrowed it to expand production. The same thing applies to vacations: those in the tourism industry benefit from increased business. But again, it is not selfish to provide for oneself. The thing to remember is that while individuals will benefit, the overall expansion of the economy causes the government to collect more revenue.

Here is an extreme example of how marginal tax rates affect an economy. Suppose Congress was dumb enough to pass a law which taxed incomes up to $60,000 at 10%, but raised the marginal rate to 98% on any income over $60,000. In such a scenario, a person would keep 90% of the first $60,000, or $54,000. But he would keep only 2% of all the income above $60,000. Figure 78-1 shows net income after taxes.

Gross Income ($)	Net on First $60,000 of Income	Net on Income above $60,000	Total net Income ($)	Effective Tax Rate (%)
30,000	27,000	0	27,000	10.00
40,000	36,000	0	36,000	10.00
50,000	45,000	0	45,000	10.00
60,000	54,000	0	54,000	10.00
70,000	54,000	200	54,200	22.57
80,000	54,000	400	54,400	32.00
90,000	54,000	600	54,600	39.33
100,000	54,000	800	54,800	45.20
150,000	54,000	1,800	55,800	62.80
250,000	54,000	3,800	57,800	76.88
500,000	54,000	8,800	62,800	87.44
750,000	54,000	13,800	67,800	90.96
1,000,000	54,000	18,800	72,800	92.72
2,000,000	54,000	38,800	92,800	95.36
5,000,000	54,000	98,800	152,800	96.94
10,000,000	54,000	198,800	252,800	97.47

Figure 78-1: Net Income and Total Tax Rates for 98% Marginal Tax Rate above $60,000

If your job pays less than $60,000 per year, you will not have to pay the 98% rate, and your effective tax rate is only 10%. But suppose you had the opportunity to earn $70,000 by working some overtime. Would you do it? Of course not --- why would you, as a rational person, work to earn $10,000 extra if you only got to keep $200 of it? It is a waste of your time. You would refuse the overtime, and your employer would either forego the additional production you could provide, or incur the overhead expenses of employing other workers to so the same work. In either case, overall productivity would decrease.

But it is worse than that. Consider a person already making $100,000. He would only get to keep $800 of the last $40,000 he earned, which is clearly not worth his while. He will do the logical thing and reduce his work to a little over part-time; that is, limit his income to around $60,000, and enjoy the rest of his time off. Meanwhile, productivity goes down. What if the person currently earning $100,000 is the only doctor in a certain town? That town will suffer a reduction of available medical services, due solely to the doctor making a rational choice over tax rates. As the Figure shows, the situation gets increasingly worse as income increases. The net result is that nearly everyone will work up until they make $60,000 and then take the rest of the year off. The overall result will be a loss of national income, stagnation of the economy, and widespread shortages because not enough is being produced; all due to the 98% marginal tax rate. The cause is traceable back to a lack of incentive caused by confiscatory tax rates; in fact overall revenue to the government would also decrease.

But Congress would never admit an error after passing such an idiotic law. Rather than repeal the 98% tax rate, Congress would then pass another law prohibiting vacations and sick time, and force everyone to work a full 2000 hours per year no matter how much or little they kept from their income. Such a policy was once known as slavery; it would now be known as "progressive economics".

Congratulations if you understand Figure 78-1 and the overall effects on the economy of an extreme marginal tax rate. You are smarter than most members of Congress.

-- § --

Question 79: Crooked Presidents

Which of the following are crooks?
a)   A U. S. President who covered up a burglary of the opposing political Party's headquarters that was engineered by a group of his subordinates.
b)   A U. S. President who committed perjury for the purpose of obstructing justice in order to deprive a citizen of their legal rights in a civil case in which the President was a defendant.
c)   A U. S. President who authorized and enforced a mandatory confiscation of all gold possessed by Americans.
d)   A U. S. president who knowingly used questionable evidence to entice Congress into authorizing a foreign war.
e)   All of the above.

Answer to Question 79

This is a trick question. None of them are crooks.

In answer a), considerable evidence came to light that Richard M. "I am not a crook" Nixon had, at minimum, covered up the illegal activities of his subordinates, which constituted obstruction of justice (a felony). But he was never required to answer for it in court; in fact he resigned the office of the Presidency and was subsequently pardoned by President Gerald R. Ford before he faced removal by Congress. He was never prosecuted in a legal court.

In answer b), William J. "Perjurer in Chief" Clinton was tried in a political venue (the House of Representatives), but was never charged in a legal venue for his on-video perjury (a felony) in a civil suit while conducting a policy of obstructing justice (a felony) in a sexual harassment case (a felony) filed against him. He was never prosecuted in a legal court.

In answer c), Franklin D. Roosevelt simply decided that common Americans could not be trusted to possess gold, so he had it confiscated and replaced with paper money. Soon after, he conspired with the Federal Reserve to devalue the paper money, thus robbing the people of about 40% of their wealth that was held in gold. But he was never charged with grand larceny (a felony); in defiance of all logic, he is widely regarded as America's savior, although it was his moronic policies that caused the Great Depression to last a full decade. He died in office, but would probably never have been prosecuted had he lived since he was so successful at portraying himself as the messiah.

In answer d), Harry S. Truman, Lyndon B. Johnson, Ronald W. Reagan, George H. W. Bush, William J. "Perjurer in Chief" Clinton, and George W. Bush did not commit any crimes per se in the course of pursuing foreign wars (Truman in Korea, Johnson in Vietnam, Reagan in Grenada, G. H. W. Bush in Iraq and Panama, Clinton in Yugoslavia and Haiti, and G. W. Bush in Iraq and Afghanistan). (I have omitted the other minor foreign conflicts and interventions). History has shown that at minimum, the wars in Korea, Vietnam, Panama, Yugoslavia, Haiti, and the second Iraq war were unnecessary. The decision to go to war is inherently a political one, and is not covered by statute.

Incidentally, George W. Bush did not lie about the presence of "weapons of mass destruction" (WMD) in Iraq. We do not know if Saddam Hussein had WMDs at the time but: a) removed them to Syria; or b) had disposed of them after the First Gulf War of 1991. We do know that most intelligence services believed Hussein had WMDs. At minimum, Hussein pretended to have them as a way of manipulating and deceiving his enemies. All the members of Congress of both parties who voted for the Iraq War authorization did so based on the intelligence assessment believed Hussein had WMDs (including Hillary Clinton). Bush, relying on the intelligence assessment, also believed Hussein had them; therefore Bush was not lying about the evidence as it then stood (lying means to make a statement that you know to be false). However, Bush did lie about the need to invade Iraq: the lie was that somehow the U. S. was responsible for enforcing U. N. resolutions.

Therefore, none of them are crooks, showing that every crime is legal and every lie is respected if a person gets elected to a high enough office. Don't forget to vote.

-- § --

Question 80: Secret Codes

A certain foreign group is in the business of smuggling heroin into the U. S. They are aware that the FBI and DEA have tapped their phones and are monitoring their emails. They wish to communicate to their allies in the U. S. that: a) a shipment of 40 kg of heroin is available; b) it will brought into New Orleans, LA on the 14th of April; and c) they will meet their co-conspirators at the pre-arranged safe-house at noon. It is decided send this message by posting it on a blog using a pre-arranged user name, and using an encryption method developed by the group and their allies. Thus, even though the blog is being monitored by the FBI and the DEA, they believe a sufficiently strong code will prevent the police from figuring out what is going on.

Here are the candidate codes they have developed, each of which sends the message above:
1) XCV TY YORE BNY EDT WSAAAW PLLU GJJ GYEWQ
2) B9X42 N83 FGJPT 6HOGD 9JNU 49 BPO954E VB6 R5 4E3F GA 78HB
3) 83927 83261 90943 74835 12772 81934 61732 91846 91034 17283 81926 88225
4) #7(*^ %^#ED *(K 7H 9JH6& FgR^N GhE$4 GH*dE H&%%B &()UH eRbVG

Which is the most effective way for the drug dealers to send their secret message?
a) Code #1, because it is the shortest, and hence the most efficient.
b) Code #2, because it uses numbers and letters and has no repeating sequences.
c) Code #3, because it consists only of numbers in a uniform sequence of 5 characters, which does not give any hint about what words are being represented.
d) Code #4, because it uses all the upper and lower case letters plus the special characters on the keyboard, and therefore is more difficult to break.
e) The group should use commercial encryption software.

Answer to Question 80

This is a trick question. All the answers are false. The problem with the codes developed by the drug dealers is that each of them appears to be an encrypted text. If it appears to be an encrypted text, especially a simple one that could be developed by non-experts, it will be easily broken.

As for answer e), it is likely that some government agency already has the keys for all commercial software, or has already broken it. Even if they haven't broken it, the government could get a court order to have the blog posting decrypted by the software developer. It is likely that all data that you store in the "cloud" is: a) for sale by the corporation that owns the "cloud" servers; and b) already available to most government agencies at their discretion. Don't fall for the ruse that "encrypted" data on the "cloud" is magically safe from prying eyes. If you want to keep your private data private, store it on a media that you keep in your house. The best method of protecting your data is to disconnect that media from your computer whenever you access the internet, so it does not become encrypted or downloaded by the criminal element.

The most effective code is the code that does not appear to be a code. The best way to communicate a secret message is to convey it in such a way that camouflages the fact that it contains a secret message at all.

-- § --

Question 81: Buying a New Car

A person went to a new car dealer to buy a new car. He found one that he was interested in, and the dealer offered to let him take a test drive, but required that the prospective buyer first provide his drivers license so the dealer could make a copy of it before the test drive. Why did the dealer want to see the license and make a copy?

a) To check with the police to see if the prospective buyer has any outstanding arrest warrants and report him to the local police.
b) To make sure the prospective buyer is legally allowed to buy a car.
c) To see if the prospective buyer has any unpaid parking tickets, and report him to the local parking violation bureau.
d) To verify that the prospective buyer has adequate automobile insurance, in case of an accident during the test drive.
e) Some combination of the above, which varies from state to state depending on the state and local laws.

Answer to Question 81

This is a trick question. None of the answers are correct.

Answer b) is incorrect because licenses are not required to buy a car.

Answers a) and c) are incorrect because car dealers are not required to enforce traffic laws or assist in the apprehension of wanted persons, but it is possible that some enterprising politician will introduce legislation to require it.

Answer d) is incorrect because car dealers maintain considerable insurance on all their unsold vehicles, since those vehicles are their stock and source of revenue.

The real reason the dealer wants the license has nothing to do with driving skill or insurance. The purpose of the "license check" is to access the prospective buyer's financial history and credit score, so they will know what kind of interest rate to offer the buyer on a car loan, or whether to offer the buyer a loan at all.

Therefore, when shopping for a car that you intend to finance, be sure to know your credit score. Then you can just tell the dealer what it is as you hand him your license. Better yet, obtain financing from your bank or credit bureau first, which will allow you to choose the better deal when the car dealer makes you a financial offer on the loan agreement.

-- § --

Question 82: The Penny

There has been some discussion in recent years about the utility of small-denomination U. S. coins such as the penny and the nickel. Some people have concluded that we would be better off to abolish these coins. What is the most plausible reason for abolishing the penny?
a)   The buying power of the penny is so low as to not be worth continuing; for example, there is no such thing as "penny candy" any more.
b)   The penny is too heavy to justify carrying around, when considered with regard to its buying power.
c)   The effect of monetary inflation has made penny nearly worthless. People don't even collect change if it is only a few cents; people won't stop to pick up a penny on the street.
d)   It has always been an inconvenience, since it is nearly the same size as a dime.
e)   It is some combination of a), b), and c).

Answer to Question 82

This is trick question. All of the answers are false.

Answers a), b), and c) all mention monetary inflation. It is true that monetary inflation has reduced the purchasing power of the penny, but that is not why the coin itself will be abolished. The real reason is the opposite: the metal has become too valuable relative to its purchasing power.

Answer d) is wrong because convenience has never been an issue.

The penny was once made of copper, but when the currency was inflated to the point that the cost of making the penny became greater than its face value, the formula was revised to use cheaper metals. Here are the dates of minting along with weights and relative compositions from 1783 [1]:
1783 - 1837: 3.1 g copper, total = 3.1 g
1837 - 1857: 2.945 g copper plus 0.155 g tin/zinc; total = 3.1 g
1857 - 1863: 2.728 g copper plus 0.372 g nickel; total = 3.1 g
1864 - 1942: 2.945 g copper plus 0.155 g tin/zinc; total = 3.1 g
1943: 3.1 g steel, coated with zinc (due to shortage of copper for the WW II war effort)
1943 - 1961: 2.945 g copper plus 0.155 g tin/zinc; total = 3.1 g
1962 - 1981: 2.945 g copper plus 0.155 g zinc; total = 3.1 g
1982 - present: 2.4375 g zinc plus 0.0625 g copper; 2.5 g total

So, because of inflation of the currency, the dollar prices of copper and zinc rose until the amount needed to mint a penny cost more than $0.01 dollar; i.e., it costs more to make a penny than its resulting face value.

For example, the price of copper today (10 May 2019) is $2.77/lb, which is $6.094 per kg. If the coin were made of copper per the original specification (1783-1837), it would cost (3.1 grams/1000 grams per kg) = $0.0188 per coin, just for the material. Zinc now sells for $1.27 per lb, which is $2.794 per kg. With the current formula (1982-present), the material costs of a penny are (2.4375/1000)*$2.794 + (0.0625/1000)*$6.094 = $0.0071, or just over seven-tenths of a penny.

In other words, the metals in the penny are too valuable (in dollar terms) to be wasted making units of currency that have the buying power of $0.01 dollar. That is why the penny will be abolished, and the nickel and dime shortly thereafter. It is interesting to note that the value of the metal in the current penny is 70% of its face value; that makes the penny the closest thing we have to real money as a store of value.

Here is a recent example of this trend. The Turkish lira was subdivided into 100 kurush, much as a dollar is divided into 100 pennies. Over time, the Turkish lira became so heavily inflated that the government began to make coins out of aluminum, including coins of having a face value of several lira. (Aluminum usually sells for about 60 to 65% of the price of zinc.) The Turkish government also began making coins out of steel. But the inflation of the currency progressed so quickly that the cost of minting even aluminum coins was far in excess of their face value in lira/kurush; and the aluminum coins were abolished in 1980.

[1]   https://www.livescience.com/32401-whats-a-penny-made-of.html

-- § --

Question 83: Rat Sightings

There are 8.143 million (8,143,000) people and an estimated 25 million (25,000,000) rats in the New York City metropolitan area. Suppose that the estimated rat population is accurate. The area of the metropolitan area is 322 square miles (8,976,844,800 square feet). Therefore, the population density of rats is 25,000,000/8,976,844,800 = 0.002784 rats per square foot, or one rat for every 359 square feet. Likewise, the density of people is 8,143,000/8,976,844,000 = .000907 persons per square foot, or one person per 1102.4 square feet. Since the density of rats is higher, and an area of 359 sq. ft. is a square with sides 18.9 ft long, and since the distance from the center of such a square to any corner (where a person could be) is 13.4 ft, a researcher has concluded (to a first approximation) that a person in New York City is at most (on average) 13.4 ft. from a rat.

On the other hand, another researcher conducted a survey about how often rats are observed in New York City. Some people reported seeing rats every day, while others could not recall the last time they saw one, even for protracted periods. A survey was taken in 2002. In the survey, people were asked if they had seen rats or evidence of rats in their homes in the previous 90 days. On the upper end, 43% of Hispanic people with income less than $25,000 had seen rats or evidence of them, while only 10% of white people making over $50,000 saw them [1]. Other income levels among whites and Hispanics fell between these two extremes, as did the data for black people of all income levels.

How can these two sets of facts about rats be reconciled?

a)   They can be reconciled if one recalls that white people and some upper-class black people have high rates of baseball bat ownership, which rats fear the most.

b)   They can be reconciled if one realizes that some people in New York live in expensive neighborhoods and others live in slums because they are victims of the rich. Since rats prefer to live in the poorer neighborhoods because the rodent controls are not as effective, it is logical that some (the poor) see rats every day while others (the rich) never see them.

c)   They can be reconciled if one recalls that averages do not apply here because rats prefer to live near people of Hispanic descent because Hispanics throw out a lot of unused vegetables, which are the favorite food of rats.

d)   The data can be reconciled because most blacks and nearly all whites will deny or minimize any rat problems in their homes, whereas Hispanics are much more honest.

e)   The data can be reconciled because most Hispanics will exaggerate any rat problems in their homes.

[1]   A. Karpati, B. Kerker, F. Mostashari, T. Singh, A. Hajat, L. Thorpe, M. Bassett, K, Henning, T. Frieden, *Health Disparities in New York City*, NY: New York City Department of Health and Mental Hygiene, 2004, p. 23

Answer to Question 83

This is a trick question. None of the answers are correct because the method of analysis is not consistent with the way rats live.

Most rats live underground, and most are nocturnal. The method of analysis assumed that all the people and all the rats are on the surface at the same time. But most people in New York City spend some of their time well above ground in high-rise buildings, whereas most rats spend most of their time underground. It is also true that neither the people nor the rats are evenly distributed. Therefore, the mean distance between any person and any rat cannot be reliably calculated. If anything, the 13 ft. figure is low because the distance below ground is not accounted for. The data about rat sightings is not material because the question relates to distance, not necessarily clear-sight distances.

The choices given are wrong for the following reasons. Choice a) is wrong because rats are not smart enough to perceive the threat from a baseball bat; nor are they smart enough to figure out who owns them. Choice b) is wrong because it assumes that rats know or care about the income level of people; in reality, rats will go wherever there is food and a place to nest. Choice c) is partly true in the sense that averages do not apply, but there is no evidence other than prejudice that rats prefer Hispanic company. There is no evidence that choices d) or e) are true.

-- § --

Question 84: The Cabinet Officer

Article 2, Section 2 of the U. S. Constitution states, regarding the office of the President:

"He shall have power, by and with the consent of the Senate, to make treaties, provided two-thirds of the Senators present concur; and he shall nominate, and by and with the advice and consent of the Senate, shall appoint ambassadors, other public ministers and consuls, judges of the Supreme Court, and all other officers of the United States, whose appointments are not herein otherwise provided for, and which shall be established by law; but the Congress may by law vest the appointments of such inferior officers, as they think proper, in the President alone, in courts of law, or in heads of departments."

The President's Cabinet members fall under the category of "officers of the United States", and require confirmation by the Senate. A member of the U. S. Senate once voted against the creation of a federal Department of Education (although it passed). But now, many years later, he has been nominated by the President to be the Secretary (head) of the Department of Education. On what grounds should the Senate confirm or not confirm him?

a) His original opposition to the creation of any federal Department proves that he cannot be trusted to lead any department. Therefore the Senate should not confirm him.

b) The Senate should not confirm him. The fact that he voted against the creation of the Department proves he is opposed to education, so schools will get worse under his "leadership".

c) The Senate should not confirm him. If he voted against the creation of the Department, then it is likely that he has contempt for teachers, teachers unions, Department of Education workers, and children in general. Such a person would not command respect within the department.

d) The Senate should confirm him only in the interest of getting him out of the Senate. True, his original vote proves he is unqualified, but he will do less harm overall as a member of the bureaucracy than as a member of the Senate.

e) The Senate should confirm him only if he promises not to change current policy and promises to recuse himself from budget debates; that way, his biases against education will have no practical effect.

Answer to Question 84

This is a trick question. All of the answers are false. He should be confirmed by the Senate if the President wants him to be the Secretary of Education, and there is no evidence that he is incompetent or unqualified for the job. (It's an appointed position over a federal bureaucracy; most departments are on automatic pilot anyway.)

Answers a), b), and c) are false because his original vote against the Department does not "prove" that he is opposed to education, teachers unions, teachers, or children; he voted against it because he believed it was bad policy at the time. His vote had nothing to do with being untrustworthy for the position as head of the department.

Answer d) is wrong because his original vote does not prove he is unqualified.

Answer e) is wrong because Congress cannot impose these conditions on a Secretary (to do so would strip the office of its powers, which Congress can do only by legislation). Also, no self-respecting department head would make such a concession, as the office would not be worth having.

It is unwise to assume that a person is unfit or unqualified to head a department simply because he voted against its creation in the past. Each case must be considered on its own merits; i.e., is the candidate willing and able to perform the required duties. For example, James Monroe, the 5th President of the United States, voted against ratification of the U. S. Constitution in the Virginia ratification debates [1]. Monroe voted against ratification because it originally lacked a bill of rights. He wanted a conditional ratification which would not be effective until a bill of rights was established. In the Virginia debate, he stated [2] (square brackets are explanatory notes):

> "Adopt it [Constitution] now, and it will never be amended [with a bill of rights], not even when experience shall have proved its defects. An alteration will be a diminution of their power, and there will be great exertions made to prevent it. I have no dread that they will immediately infringe the dearest rights of the people, but that the operation of the government will be oppressive in operation of time."

Here was a man who believed that the federal government would encroach upon the rights of the people. Imagine that! He was wrong however about his prediction that Congress and the States would never propose and ratify a Bill of Rights; they constitute the first ten amendments to the Constitution, and were ratified on 15 Dec 1791. The Bill of Rights should be considered as part of the original Constitution [3]. He was right about the federal government infringing on the rights of the people; it does so now even with the Bill of Rights. Governments never cease in a quest to acquire more power.

Clearly, Monroe's vote against ratification of the original Constitution did not subsequently disqualify him for the office of President, nor did he prove to be unfit. As President, he established the only viable foreign policy the U. S. has ever had. It is known as the Monroe Doctrine, in which foreign powers are to stay out of the Western hemisphere. Incidentally, this policy was established by Monroe, but it was written by John Quincy Adams, who served as Monroe's Secretary of State. J. Q. Adams succeeded Monroe as President, and was probably our best President overall.

[1] The ratification vote in Virginia was 89 to 79; future 4th President James Madison was among those who voted for ratification; James Monroe, George Mason, and Patrick Henry were among those who voted against it. See Jonathan Elliott, *Elliott's Debates*, Philadelphia; J. B. Lippincott, 1881, Vol. 3, pp. 654, 655

[2] Jonathan Elliott, *Elliott's Debates*, Philadelphia; J. B. Lippincott, 1881, Vol. 3, p. 630

[3] *The Congressional Record*, Volume 44, part 4, (61st Congress, first session), 1909, pp. 4407; available at: https://www.govinfo.gov/app/collection/crecb/_crecb/Volume%20044%20(1909)

-- § --

Question 85: Energy-Efficient Commuting

Four people commute to work in the following ways. Person A drives a very fuel efficient car that gets 50 miles to the gallon; he drives alone 75 miles each way to work. Person B drives alone in an old inefficient pickup truck that gets 12 miles to the gallon; he drives 12 miles each way. Person C drives a car that gets 25 miles to the gallon. He drives it alone 5 miles each way to a light-rail station. There he gets on public light-speed rail; each train consists of 4 cars, and each car holds up to 30 people. The train is electric, but its energy usage is the equivalent of 2 miles to the gallon, and his commute on the train is 20 miles each way. Person D takes the city bus 16 miles each way; the bus gets 4 miles per gallon, and holds up to 60 people. Figure 85-1 shows a summary for each person.

Person	Total Miles Alone	MPG Traveling Alone	Total Miles, Mass Transit	MPG, Mass Transit	Maximum Number of Passengers, Mass Transit
A	150	50	0	N/A	N/A
B	24	12	0	N/A	N/A
C	10	25	40	2	120
D	0	N/A	32	4	60

Figure 85-1: Data for Energy Usage in Commuting

Assume that all the mileages are calibrated to the same blend of gasoline (although they may actually use different fuels). Which person uses the most efficient means of energy expenditure in the course of getting back and forth to work?
a) Person A
b) Person B
c) Person C
d) Person D
e) Indeterminate exactly, but it is either Person A or D.

Answer to Question 85

This is a trick question because there was not enough data provided to solve it. To figure out who is the most efficient in their energy usage, it is necessary to calculate how many equivalent gallons of gas are used by each one. The total equivalent amount of gas consumed per person is given by the formula:

$$\frac{gallons}{person} = \frac{total\ miles}{miles\ per\ gallon} \frac{1}{number\ of\ people\ carried}$$

Figure 85-2 shows the results; there are two extremes for Person C and D, depending on the number of riders on the mass transit system.

Person A travels by himself 150 total miles in a car that gets 50 MPG, so he uses 3 gallons per day. Person B travels by himself a total of 24 miles in a car that gets 12 MPG, so he uses 2 gallons per day. Right away, this shows the need to beware of the euphemisms about relative energy efficiency. In this case, Person B, who drives a "gas-guzzler", is actually more fuel-efficient than Person A, who drives a "gas-sipper".

Person C drives by himself 10 miles total in a car that gets 25 miles to the gallon, so this portion of his trips uses 0.4 gallons. Then he travels 40 total miles on the rail line. If the train is full the entire distance both ways (the maximum case), then the average number of gallons used by person C for this portion is (40/2)*(1/120) = 40/240 = 0.1666. But if Person C is the only one on the train for the entire distance both ways (the minimum case), the number of gallons used for this portion alone is (40/2)*(1/1) = 20 gallons. For the two extremes, person C uses either 20.4 or 0.5666 gallons per day. Person C's real average usage is somewhere between these, but there is not enough data provided to calculate it.

Person D travels 32 total miles entirely on a city bus that carries 60 people and gets 4 MPG. If the bus is full both ways (maximum case), then the average number of gallons used by Person D is (32/4)*(1/60) = 0.133. But if he is the only one on the bus both ways (minimum case), then his average energy usage is the equivalent of $(32/4)*(1/1) = 8$ gallons. Again, his average consumption is somewhere between 0.133 and 8, but there is insufficient data to calculate his real average usage.

Person	Gallons Used, Alone	Mass Transit Actual Riders		Total Gallons Used	
		Case 1: Minimum	Case 2: Maximum	Minimum Mass Transit	Maximum Mass Transit
A	3.0	N/A	N/A	3.000	3.000
B	2.0	N/A	N/A	2.000	2.000
C	0.4	1	120	20.400	0.566
D	0.0	1	60	8.000	0.133

Figure 85-2: Results for Energy Usage in Commuting

Unless the average number of people riding on the public transportation at all times is known, it is impossible to determine which is the most efficient. Many times one can see city buses and commuter trains traveling nearly empty, and yet they are consuming energy. Also, those public facilities require additional energy to light the parking lots; plus heating, cooling, and lighting the centralized maintenance terminals, etc. The main point here is that when evaluating energy usage, one should reduce it down to either total costs or total energy usage with all these other factors included. One of the most important factors is the average number of riders per trip on public facilities.

In fact, the better argument for public transportation is congestion relief, not energy efficiency. There are some places, like New York City, where the subway is clearly better than cars from both an energy usage and congestion standpoint. It works because there are a lot of riders going from many stops on the line to many other stops on the line. But such a system may be inefficient in a place like Albuquerque, where the large number of riders per trip cannot be assured.

-- § --

Question 86: Identity Theft

An insurance company offers insurance against identity theft. It covers you for all losses you incur due to the fraudulent use of your identity, should it be stolen. On average, identity theft cases result in losses of about $3,500. The insurance company offers various types of coverage at various costs described below. What is the best value for the money, considering the risk?
a) For $10 per month, there is a $750 deductible, after which the insurance company will cover all losses up to $5,000, and will cover 50% of losses above $5,000 up to $10,000. The insured is responsible for half the losses between $5,000 and $10,000, and all the losses above $10,000.
b) For $15 per month, there is a $1,000 deductible, after which the insurance company will cover all losses up to $50,000. The insured is responsible for losses above $50,000.
c) For $25 per month, there is a $3,000 deductible, after which the insurance company will cover all losses up to $100,000. The insured is responsible for losses above $100,000.
d) For $35 per month, there is no deductible, and the insurance company will cover all losses up to $75,000, and 80% of all losses thereafter up to $250,000. The insured is responsible for losses above $250,000.
e) For $50 per month, there is no deductible, and the insurance company will cover all losses up to $1,000,000.

Answer to Question 86

This is a trick question. Identity theft insurance is actually "identity theft protection" insurance, and generally does not compensate you for actual money lost by the fraud. It only covers incidental expenses necessary to "recover" your identity, but it usually does cover lost wages in the course of doing so. In other words, it covers fees and expenses, but not the actual losses. The insurance policies implement measures to warn you about attempted fraud or identity theft by monitoring transactions, checking credit scores, and tracking new applications. But these services do not prevent fraud or identity theft directly; they alert to attempts to commit fraud using your (stolen) identity.

You are not responsible to a bank or credit card company for any losses incurred due to fraud (except possibly $50). All insurance of advertised a compensating for direct losses is a rip-off, designed to get you, the chump, to pay some of the losses incurred by banks, credit card companies and other institutions due to fraud, which usually occurs because said institutions are careless with their records of your financial and personal information. "Insurance" of this type is itself a form of fraud.

-- § --

Question 87: Athletic Statistics

On a football team, a "cornerback" is a defensive player whose main job is "pass defense". His job is to "cover" the other teams' pass receivers. His duties include preventing the receiver from catching a pass from the quarterback, intercepting the pass if he can, and tackling the receiver if he does catch a pass from the quarterback. He also has other defensive duties related to defending against running plays and blocking.

What would be the best way to determine, based on statistics collected over player's careers, of which cornerbacks were the most highly skilled at pass defense?
a) Total number of interceptions of passes.
b) Total number of tackles made against receivers who caught passes.
c) Sum of total number of interceptions and number of passes broken up.
d) Sum of total number of interceptions and fumbles forced (i.e., total "turnovers").
e) Some weighted combination of all of the above.

Answer to Question 87

This is a trick question. None of the answers are correct.

The answers do not necessarily relate to the issue of how well he covers his man, because they deal partly with actions against men he was not covering. Second, all of the answers pertain to events that occurred after the receiver he was covering either attempted a catch or made a catch. They do not indicate, however, the total number of times a covered receiver caught the ball, or how many touchdowns the receiver made afterwards, or a host of other relevant data. What about a cornerback that was so good that the opposing quarterback never attempted to pass to the receiver being covered? That cornerback has perfect pass defense because the receiver he is covering is essentially out of the game. Yet, such a cornerback would have no statistics recorded: if no passes were ever thrown to the man he was covering, there would be no opportunity for an interception, breaking up the pass, a tackle after the catch, or forced fumbles. Statistically, would be no record that he had never played, although he may well have been the very best at his position (see Robert James, who played for the Buffalo Bills in the 1960's).

The important point here is to make sure that any statistics being collected are relevant to the question at hand. It is quite possible that stacks of numbers have little meaning to a player's value in each individual game; and a statistical evaluation alone is not a sufficiently accurate measure of true ability. This same principle applies to all other questions in which statistics are used a source material. It is usually much more important to evaluate both the relevance and completeness of the statistics than to utilize them, since utilizing the wrong statistics in a correct manner still gives the wrong answer.

For example, suppose there is a rapid increase in the number of part-time minimum wage jobs available, and they are all filled, some by people who are already working full-time, and some by people who were not working before. That would be a good trend: more people have a little more money in their pocket, and they are probably a little more optimistic in general. But it would be wrong to assume from this data that there will be a surge in the sales of new cars. The reason is that the additional income is still insufficient to finance a new car. In this case, the person who predicts an increase in car sales ignored the relevance of the improved part-time minimum wage job market to the car industry.

-- § --

Question 88: Social Security and Your Estate

A man graduated from high school in January of 1972, and went to work in an office immediately afterwards. His initial salary was $10,500 per year. Over time, he received raises and promotions. His income rose on average 3.5% per year. He never married, never had children, and died suddenly in 2006 at age 52. During his working life, he paid in the required percentage of his income in Social Security payroll taxes, and his employer paid in an equal amount. Both types are required by law, with certain exception for agricultural workers, which did not apply to this man. At the time of his death at the end of 2006, his equivalent hourly wage was $16.57 (annual salary = $33,819.03).

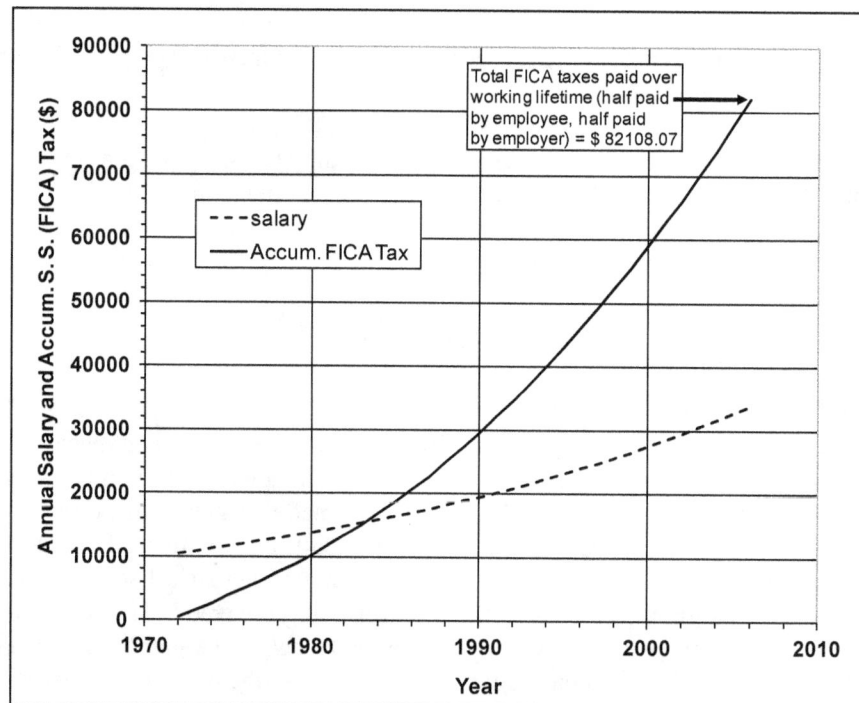

Figure 88-1: Income and Social Security Taxes Withheld

Figure 88-1 shows his income by year (dashed line), and the total Social Security taxes paid in over his working lifetime (solid line). The total FICA Social Security tax paid during his lifetime was $82,108.07; half was paid by the man, and half was paid by his employer. The earliest age at which Social Security retirement benefits can be paid is 62. Since he did not live long enough to collect any Social Security retirement benefits, how much did his estate receive from the Social Security Administration after his death?

a) His estate received a total slightly more than $82,108.07, since FICA contributions are invested in U. S. Treasury bonds, which earn a small amount of interest. It is difficult to calculate exactly because of the bond maturation schedule. No taxes are due.

b) His estate received exactly $82,108.07 (the total paid in by the man and on his behalf by his employer) since Social Security benefits are not invested, and do not earn interest. No taxes are due.

c) His estate received $41,054.04, which is the amount the man contributed. It would not be fair for him to receive contributions made by his employer. No interest is paid, but no taxes are due.

d) His estate received $34,895.93, which is his contribution without interest ($41,054.04), but with income taxes taken out (15% marginal rate).

e) His estate received an amount equal to the last 40 quarters (10 years) of his contribution, less 15% income taxes. In the last 10 years of his working life, his contributions totaled $18,048.43; this amount less 15% comes to $15,341.16, which was paid to his estate.

Answer to Question 88

This is a trick question. All of the answers are incorrect.

The man's estate received zero from the Social Security Administration, since he had no widow or descendant survivors. Pretty good investment, don't you think? This will also help some of his insurance beneficiaries and relatives get out of debt and pay for a good education for their children, don't you think?

So where did the all the money he and his employer paid in all those years end up? In reality, it is already gone; it was given out to people who were already retired when the man was working. Had this man lived to retirement, he would receive his benefits from those still working. Had he lived to retirement, his retirement benefit over his retired lifetime would probably be less than he would have if he had been allowed to keep the tax money and invest it. The younger you are, the more likely it is that Social Security will result in an overall loss compared to what could have been accumulated by investing the taxes you paid in over your working lifetime. Aren't you glad Congress is looking out for you by forcing you to pay into a system that will, in the long run, have a decreasing benefit compared to the amount paid in?

Some critics have called Social Security a "Ponzi scheme". A Ponzi scheme is designed to defraud investors by paying high returns to those who get in early; they are paid by those who begin investing later. Usually the so-called money manager is simply robbing most of the investors, and there comes a time when he cannot attract enough new investors to fulfill the withdrawal promises he made to the existing investors. The scheme then collapses. That said, Social Security is not a Ponzi scheme, since first, no claim is made that anything is being invested, and secondly, there is no means to withdraw from the system.

Social Security is often advertised as "old age insurance", but it is not insurance, because there is no formal contract between you and the Social Security Administration specifying the legally binding terms of payments and benefits. It does not function like an annuity that has a specified death benefit directly related to what you put into it.

Social Security is not a savings program, since although you pay in throughout your working life, you do not have any control of any account, and if you die before reaching the retirement age, everything you paid in is lost (unless a spouse or children are eligible for "survivors benefits").

Social Security is a transfer-of-payments scheme in which people now working pay benefits indirectly to those who are retired, with the U. S. government acting as intermediary. The initial idea was to mitigate poverty in old age as a supplement to normal savings, but has since been transformed into a politically untouchable "entitlement". It behaves like every other well-intentioned government program: the government makes promises it cannot keep in order to buy votes, and over time if finds that it cannot raise sufficient taxes to fulfill those promises, so it simply reduces the benefits accordingly. In the long run, the taxes paid in will increase, and the benefits paid out will decrease when considered on an individual basis. The "progressives" and socialists naturally believe the entire economic system should function like Social Security: that everyone should be dependent on the promises of politicians and bureaucrats. The newest false claim is that the government can run the entire health care system more efficiently than it operates now. These are the same people who cannot get potholes filled or streetlights timed correctly.

The important point to remember is that the Social Security system is purely political: the entire system could be abolished if the economic situation of the nation required it. The people who then lose their payments will have no legal recourse because there is no legally enforceable contract between the recipients and the Social Security Administration. That is why you should do the best you can to provide for your own retirement, and if Social Security is still around, it will be a small extra benefit.

-- § --

Question 89: Public Disclosure

The Governor of a certain State desired to appoint a certain man to a position in his Cabinet. It is very important that this person be confirmed by the State senate because giving this particular person the appointment will serve to unite their political party. The prospective appointee has worked as a lobbyist and used his connections within the State government to influence policy. He also operates a political action committee (PAC), taking in donations from contributors and distributing them to other activist groups so they will have funds to pursue their agendas. He is rumored to have many connections to foreign interests, to some domestic corporations, and activist groups that routinely seek special favors from the State government. Some in the media and many citizens have claimed that the candidate cannot be impartial in carrying out his duties if appointed. In order to avoid the negative publicity, the Governor and candidate held a joint news conference wherein the candidate promised full disclosure of his financial and political ties. What is likely to happen next?

a) The candidate will set up a public-access website and list all the contacts, working relationships, and financial transactions of his PAC over the past twenty years.

b) The candidate will provide a list of all the contacts, working relationships, and financial transactions of his PAC over the past twenty years to the media that has been most vocal in demanding it, which they may review and publish as desired.

c) The candidate will hold a series of "town meetings" with all the relevant data on contacts, working relationships, and financial transactions of his PAC for the past twenty years, and answer any questions the public may have.

d) The candidate will send full documentation to all interested parties, which will contain all the relevant data on contacts, working relationships, and financial transactions of the PAC over the past twenty years.

e) The candidate will do at least two of the options cited in a) through d) in the interest of honest government.

Answer to Question 89

This is a trick question. None of the suggested answers will occur.

"Full disclosure" in this context means that the candidate will provide only as much information as is necessary to secure the confirmation by the Senate. The Governor and Senate leaders will first count the number of votes the candidate already will receive without disclosing anything. Then, they will decide what information will satisfy whatever number of Senators whose votes they need; they will pick and choose the least amount to be disclosed in order to get those votes. The data will then be disclosed secretly only to those Senate members. Those Senate members will state that they are satisfied with the information provided, and the candidate will then be confirmed.

Did you actually think a candidate for an appointed office would actually provide the public (taxpayers) with this kind of information? That is not in their interest, and they will do whatever is necessary to avoid it. The candidate will forego the office and withdraw his nomination before he allows any of this kind of data to be released publicly.

-- § --

Question 90: Speeding Ticket Probability

A certain district lies along 25 miles of Highway U. S. 193, where the speed limit is 55 MPH throughout. The police force in this district issues speeding tickets based only on radar readings, and the department regularly calibrates its equipment to make sure the readings are accurate. It is also department policy to issue tickets only if the driver is more than 7 MPH over the speed limit (i.e., is considered speeding only if going more than 62 MPH). Over the long run, the probability of getting a speeding ticket in this locality is 0.2 (meaning that over a long period of observations, 20% of people who were going faster than 62 MPH got tickets).

Consider the following situation. It is a Tuesday morning, after the rush hour. The weather is clear and traffic is light in this locality on Hwy U. S. 193. The police officers on duty at this time checking for speeders are 30% black male, 40% white male, 20% black female, and 10% white female, which is approximately the racial makeup of the police force at most times. A black woman in a foreign sports car was going 73 MPH in the 55 MPH zone. What is the likelihood that she will get a speeding ticket?

a)   50%, because half the officers on duty are white.
b)   100%, because she is driving a foreign car.
c)   Greater than 50%, because more than half the officers on duty are men.
d)   Either zero or 100%, depending on the race of the officer who sees her first.
e)   This question is illogical because everyone knows that black women never exceed the speed limit.

Answer to Question 90

This is a trick question. The correct answer is 20%, consistent with the given fact that the probability of getting a ticket in this area when speeding is 0.2. In the question, it was stated that the long-term probability is 0.2; this data is independent of race, sex, or make of vehicles in a particular case. If the local police force has biases with respect to race, sex, or make of cars, those biases are already built into the 0.2 number since it is a composite from a large number of incidences over a long period of time. Barring any additional information about behavior in particular cases, there is no logical basis for assessing the probability of a ticket in this particular case at anything other than 0.2.

There will be many times when people, especially the progressives and socialists, will attempt to influence your opinion by adding extraneous or irrelevant information into a discussion. Their objective is usually to get you to jump to an incorrect conclusion based on your biases, while implying that someone else's biases are at work. Be careful not to be conned with so-called "facts" that are not pertinent to the question at hand. They are background noise designed to either confuse you or trick you into accepting a false conclusion.

-- § --

Question 91: Legal Exemptions

A Bill was introduced in House of Representatives during the 111th Congress (2009-2010) called H. R. 45 (6 Jan 2009), named "The Blair Holt's Firearm Licensing and Record of Sale Act of 2009". The bill, if passed into law, would require:

1) Every person is to obtain a federal license to buy, sell, or possess any firearm;
2) All persons who owned a firearm prior to enactment of the law to obtain a license for those firearms;
3) Each person would have to apply for renewal of the license every five years;
4) Each person would have to pay a fee to obtain the license;
5) All firearm sales would be permanently recorded in a federal database;
6) All persons seeking to buy or possess a firearm would be required to submit to a background check;
7) A licensee would be required to report theft or loss of a firearm to federal authorities within 72 hours;
8) Licensees would be required to maintain secure storage of all firearms such that persons under age 18 cannot access them;
9) Firearms owners would be required to permit the federal government to search without warrants any facility where firearms are stored, manufactured, or held;
10) Persons seeking a license would be required to pass an examination on handling, use, and storage of firearms; and
11) Imposition of various penalties for violations of any of the foregoing.

However, Section 801, called "Inapplicability to Governmental Authorities", states:

"This Act and the amendments made by this Act shall not apply to any department or agency of the United States, of a State, or of a political subdivision of a State, or to any official conduct of any officer or employee of such a department or agency".

One of the stated justifications for the bill is "to protect the public against unreasonable risk of injury and death associated with the unrecorded sale or transfer of qualifying firearms to criminals and youth".

Why is it necessary to exempt every level of the government and their employees from this Act?
a) Requiring government agencies and their employees to comply with this Act would reduce their efficiency.
b) Requiring government agencies and their employees to comply with this Act would cost too much money that could be devoted to more important objectives.
c) Requiring government agencies and their employees to comply with this Act would cause unnecessary confusion over which agency is to defer to which other agency.
d) Requiring government agencies and their employees to comply with this Act would interfere with the powers of the governments under the respective Constitutions.
e) All of the above.

Answer to Question 91

This is a trick question. All of the given answers are false. The correct answer is that requiring government agencies and their employees to comply with this Act would: a) force governments and their employees to obey the same laws as non-government employees; b) refute the notion that regulatory and enforcement government employees are the first class citizens they believe themselves to be; and c) impede the quest by some government employees for the absolute arbitrary power that they so desperately crave. Exempting governments from obeying the law is fairly common.

Answer a) is false because governments excel at bureaucracy above all else. Manufacture and exploitation of bureaucratic "red tape" is the primary product of government regulators. Far from reducing their efficiency, it would demonstrate their efficiency.

Answer b) is false because the amount of money spent on regulation is immaterial; all the money comes from the taxpayer anyway. While many government officials will make this excuse, note that you, the person, have to pay for the license. There is no concern on the government's part about you having to divert resources from other more important things.

Answer c) is false because precedence is well-established among the U. S.: federal, State, county, and local agencies; but that is true only in cases where powers have been granted per the Constitution.

Answer d) is false because this would not reduce the powers of the government; it would enhance them. This Act would grant an unlimited power to destroy the individual right to keep and bear arms under the Second Amendment. Remember, if you have to get a license for something, you are in effect getting permission to do something. If you have to get permission, you are not exercising a "right"; you are begging for a privilege, like the serf in medieval Europe. Do not think that licenses will be "renewed"; there is no penalty spelled out if the federal government declines to renew any license. This is a confiscation scheme; the very same tactic was used by Hitler in 1930's Germany.

But we will never hear the end of excuses about why government employees are above the law. Many government employees are confirmed to high-ranking posts even though they violated a law that would get you put in jail: failing to pay income taxes, hiring illegal immigrants, giving and taking bribes, etc. But these excesses of power are all done in good-natured fun. The auditors at the IRS are always happy because they can't stop laughing at taxpayers, who have to sign forms under penalty of perjury and submit to random arbitrary searches and audits. The clerks at the Motor Vehicle Bureau are always happy because they can't stop laughing at car buyers, who have to take time off from work to stand in line for the privilege of paying a tax to "register" their car. The inspectors at OSHA are always happy because they can't stop laughing at small business owners who must submit to warrantless searches of their property and comply with the arbitrary demands of the inspector to "fix" whatever they decide needs "fixing". The people on the parole boards are happy because they can place thousands of convicted child molesters back onto the streets. Never forget who they are laughing at – they are laughing at you.

They are laughing at you because you are a funny person. You actually believe that the government should exercise only those powers that the people have granted it per the Constitution, and that anyone who exceeds that power should be immediately removed and prosecuted. Ho, ho, ho --- now you really are a funny person --- so funny that you may be on some government list somewhere.

The only solution to this basic problem is to force the various levels of government to return back to obeying the most basic laws, the respective Constitutions. But this will prove impossible to do, because the common people do not have the means to force governments to do anything, especially if it conflicts with the governments' desire for power.

James Madison already addressed this problem in a section from *The Federalist Papers*, #57. Here he reminds his readers that any government that exempts itself from its own laws has degenerated into a tyranny, and the people who tolerate it have become slaves. It worth quoting in full:

> "I will add, as a fifth circumstance in the situation of the House of Representatives, restraining them from oppressive measures, that they can make no law which will not have its full operation on themselves and their friends, as well as on the great mass of the society. This has always been deemed one of the strongest bonds by which human policy can connect the rulers and the people together. It creates between them that communion of interests and sympathy of sentiments, of which few governments have furnished examples; but without which every government degenerates into tyranny. If it be asked, what is to restrain the House of Representatives from making legal discriminations in favor of themselves and a particular class of the society? I answer: the genius of the whole system; the nature of just and constitutional laws; and above all, the vigilant and manly spirit which actuates the people of America -- a spirit which nourishes freedom, and in return is nourished by it."

> "If this spirit shall ever be so far debased as to tolerate a law not obligatory on the legislature, as well as on the people, the people will be prepared to tolerate anything but liberty."

The important point here is that any law that exempts any government employee from compliance is unconstitutional on its very face, regardless of the excuses and decrees from politicians, bureaucrats, lawyers, legislators, and judges.

-- § --

Question 92: Overall Government Policies

Which of the following general government policies will contribute to general happiness and prosperity of the people?

a)   An economic policy that eliminates profiteering by the business community.
b)   A political policy by which the government itself will gradually give up power because everyone will be equal.
c)   A foreign policy of assisting all the people of the world in their desire to pursue freedom.
d)   A policy of public decision-making based on scientific facts and advances.
e)   All of the above would be beneficial policies.

Answer to Question 92

This is a trick question. All of the answers are false, because all of these policies were implemented by the Bolshevik Socialists (headed by Vladimir Lenin) who founded the Soviet Union in 1917. History has shown how well that worked --- the Russian people now believe with good cause that they are socialism's first victims.

Regarding answer a), here is how Vladimir Lenin (real name: Vladimir Ulyanov) described the actual policy of eliminating profiteering [1]:

> "Clearly, in a small-peasant country, the petty-bourgeois element predominates and it must predominate, for the great majority of those working the land are small commodity producers. The shell of our state capitalism (grain monopoly, state-controlled entrepreneurs and traders, bourgeois co-operators) is pierced now in one place, now in another by profiteers, the chief object of profiteering being grain."

> "We know that the million tentacles of this petty-bourgeois hydra now and again encircle various sections of the workers, that instead of state monopoly, profiteering forces it way into every pore of our social and economic organism."

First we must understand the definitions of his terms. The petty-bourgeois and profiteers are any business owners who believe they should earn a salary or keep some reward for taking the risk and managing the enterprise. "State capitalism" means the government owns or controls every entity that produces goods or performs a service. Here is the translation. The small business owners and farmers are the enemy, and must be liquidated because they are competing with the state-owned and operated industries. Lenin mentions the production of grain as the main occupation of the profiteers. He solved this problem by killing all the "kulaks". The kulaks were the small farmers who had run their farms successfully. They were able to employ other workers, and invest in the latest technology to improve output. Once they were dead, the Russian people went hungry for 70 years because the state-owned agricultural collectives were too corrupt and incompetent.

Regarding answer b), here is how Lenin described the actual policy of a socialist government giving up power [2]:

> "The state will be able to wither away completely when society adopts the rule: 'from each according to his ability, to each according to his needs', i.e., when people have become so accustomed to observing the fundamental rules of social intercourse and when their labor has become so productive that they will voluntarily work according to their ability."

But later he wrote [3]:

> "The dictatorship of the proletariat, the proletarian state, which is a machine for the suppression of the bourgeois by the proletariat, is not a 'form of governing', but a state of a different type. Suppression is necessary because the bourgeoisie will always furiously resist being expropriated."

First we must understand the definitions of his terms. The bourgeoisie consists of all who believe in freedom and private property. The proletariat is supposedly the non-property owning workers, but in fact is the socialist ruling elite. Here is the translation: the state can cease to exist when mankind establishes utopia on earth, where everything is so easy to come by that no one will mind a few hours of work here and there, and there will of course be no need for the government since there will be universal peace and happiness. This is to occur because the proletariat (ruling socialist elite) has successfully overthrown the tyranny of business owners and others who believe in private property. But, the people who believe in freedom will resist having everything stolen from them by the socialist elite and therefore must be persecuted and eliminated. Therefore, the state must continue to get more and more powerful, and become an absolute tyranny in order to protect the common people from those who believe in freedom. The government of the Soviet Union exercised absolute power over the Russian people.

Regarding answer c), here is how Lenin described the correct socialist foreign policy [4]:

> [Discussing socialist revolutions in Eastern Asia] "The peoples of the East are becoming alive to the need for practical action, the need for every nation to take part in shaping the destiny of the world. That is why I think that in the history of the development of the world revolution -- which, judging by its beginning, will continue for many years and will demand much effort -- that in the revolutionary struggle, in the revolutionary movement you will be called upon to play a big part and to merge with our struggle in the international imperialism."

First we must understand the definitions of his terms. The "destiny of the world" is one-world government headed by the socialist ruling elite. "International imperialism" is any system of government in which the people are not ruled by the iron fist of conformance-demanding bureaucrats and socialist enforcers. Here is the translation. The socialist foreign policy therefore consists of provoking revolutions all over the world in order to impose upon everyone the socialist system. Anyone who believes in freedom or free enterprise must be destroyed; and you will be required to lend your support to the world-wide revolution.

Regarding answer d), here is how Lenin described scientific decision-making policy [5]:

> "It should be remembered that the sharp upheaval which modern science is undergoing very often gives rise to reactionary philosophical schools and minor schools, trends and minor trends. Unless, therefore, the problems raised by the recent revolution in natural science are followed, and unless natural scientists are enlisted in the work of a philosophical journal, militant materialism can neither be militant nor materialism."

First we must understand the definitions of his terms. A reactionary is anyone who opposes socialism; a philosophical journal is the socialist-approved orthodoxy on any given subject. Militant materialism is the active promotion of atheism and suppression of all religions except socialism in order to free the people from the influence of the clergy. Here is the translation. You can have all the scientific advances you want, so long as they are only used to advance the cause of socialist atheism, where man is required to worship only the state. The policy of scientific decision-making involves distorting science as required to promote socialist control over the people.

It is easy to see even from these few fragments that Lenin, the Great Socialist Messiah, was nothing more than a power-mad babbling moron. There is nothing in socialism that contributes to peace or prosperity, nor is there anything scientific about it. It is brainwashing by sloganeering. Power is conferred not on the knowledgeable or experienced, but on those who have managed to memorize a few dozen half-baked socialist slogans from the writings of Karl Marx and Vladimir Lenin. If you vote for socialism, this is what you will get because every socialist traces his policies back to Marx and Lenin.

[1]   V. I. Lenin, "Left-Wing Childishness and Petty-Bourgeois Mentality", Section 3, *Collected Works*, Vol. 27 (originally published in *Pravda*, May 1918)
[2]   V. I. Lenin, "The State and Revolution", Chapter 4, *Collected Works*, Vol. 25
[3]   V. I. Lenin, "The Proletarian Revolution and Renegade Kautsky", *Collected Works*, Vol. 28 (originally published in *Pravda*, 11 Oct 1918)

[4] V. I. Lenin, "Address to the Second All-Russia Congress of Communist Organizations of the Peoples of the East", 22 Nov 1919

[5] V. I. Lenin, "On the Significance of Militant Materialism", *Collected Works*, Vol. 33

-- § --

Question 93: Actors and Dictators

A wealthy American-born celebrity Hollywood actor routinely visits a nation that is ruled by a ruthless dictator. Although the dictator uses populist rhetoric, the economy and political system is actually run as a closely-held corrupt oligarchy, and the poor continue to be worse off each year. Also, the people have no civil liberties to speak of (and in fact are prohibited from immigrating out of the nation). However, the actor consistently praises the dictator as a man of the people, a champion of the poor, a defender of the rights of the common man, and as a model of what every government leader should be. The actor and dictator are not related by blood or marriage, nor does the actor have business or family ties to this nation. Why would a famous American actor bother to make any comments about the internal politics and economics of a nation run by a dictator?

a) The actor recognizes that poverty can only be alleviated if the government steps in and guides each person's work, ensuring that each person is assigned the work for which he is best suited.

b) The actor thinks it important to give dictators some positive publicity in the interest of fairness; the actor knows how it feels to be rejected since he had many unsuccessful auditions early in his career.

c) The actor wants to help the poor people of the foreign nation by giving the dictator sufficient publicity so that the people can understand why the dictator's programs are good for them.

d) The actor admires the orderliness of the dictator's nation, in contrast to the usual chaos on a movie set.

e) Some combination of the above.

Answer to Question 93

This is a trick question. None of the answers are correct.

Answer a) is incorrect because no actor could be dumb enough to believe that his success was outside of government influence, yet other people require the government to control their lives. There are a total of zero actors who became wealthy celebrities by acting in government-produced movies.

Answer b) is incorrect because dictators have no use for fairness (otherwise they would not be holding power), and have no fear of rejection (since the people have been deprived of any means to reject him). Actors know full well that the amount of publicity given is unrelated to talent.

Answer c) is incorrect because dictators do not have any problems getting their propaganda distributed to the people; in fact, it is likely the only thing the people ever hear. Actors do not like competition from other actors or other movie productions, just like dictators.

Answer d) is incorrect because it is the actors themselves that cause most of the chaos on movie sets.

The reason wealthy Hollywood actors support dictators is because they believe that artists like themselves have suffered greatly for their art and for the sake of humanity. Artists always have and always will (in their own mind) live in poverty for the sake of their art and the advancement of society. Hence, they favor any dictator who claims to support the poor and downtrodden in the hopes that the same kind of government will come to exist in America, so that the actor can finally be lifted out of his destitution and misery and get the recognition he deserves. In other words, the typical Hollywood actor is so divorced from reality that he actually believes: a) actors and movies are indispensible to society; and b) it is people like him that the dictators refer to in their phony populist rhetoric.

-- § --

Question 94: Helpful Welfare

In the 1960's the federal government instituted a program of assisting young women who had illegitimate children. This aid came in the form of cash payments, housing at low rents, and assistance for food and medicine via government-issued stamps that could be used as cash for most grocery and medical items. In what ways were these programs beneficial to the recipient?

a) It allowed the young women to provide for their children in a safe and secure environment, without the violations of privacy and crowding that would prevail if she had continued to live with her parents.

b) It allowed them sufficient spare time to pursue education or other career training.

c) It allowed them to live independently, and although they were initially poor, they would eventually be able to rise to the middle class.

d) It provided them with an additional income if she chose to get married, even if her husband was working.

e) All of the above.

Answer to Question 94

This is a trick question. All the answers are false.

The welfare programs accomplished none of these because the result of these policies, whether intended or not, was to subsidize irresponsibility, laziness, and dependence. When something is subsidized, more of it occurs.

Answer a) is wrong because these "welfare" programs kept the recipients in poverty, usually in dangerous public housing projects, or locked into poor neighborhoods, and nearly always in areas with poor public schools.

Answer b) is wrong because the people who accepted the payments found it easier to stay on welfare rather than pursue education or a career. They made a logical economic decision: why work when one can be paid simply for existing?

Answer c) is wrong because the welfare payments were gradually increased just enough to keep the recipients slightly above the poverty line. But, being locked into poor neighborhoods with deficient school systems, they and their children found it more difficult to rise to the middle class. The net result was that a fairly large segment of the population in some cities became completely dependent on the government, which is to say, the taxpayers.

Answer d) is wrong because these people lose their benefits if they marry someone who is working (unless they scam the system, which happens sometimes). That keeps them unmarried and dependent, exactly where the government wants them. Women made another logical choice: who needs husbands if marriage leads to a loss of benefits? Thus there was built into the system a great disincentive to maintain the traditional family unit.

The money paid by the government to these women came out of taxes paid by those who worked. The welfare recipients were in fact sending their bills to other people; they themselves became part of a permanent "underclass" locked into poverty, distress, dependence, and low self-esteem. Guess who they vote for? They vote for anyone who will give them more out of your pocket (if you are working). Don't expect to receive any thanks. After all, these payments are now "entitlements".

-- § --

Question 95: Presidential Debates

Why is it important for the voters to watch the Presidential debates?
a)   Because it is one of the few times that the voter gets to hear both candidates explain their policies.
b)   Because the candidates receive sufficient time to show how their policies will work, which is more effective than the usual 30 second commercial.
c)   Because the debates are sponsored by the League of Women Voters, which ensures that the debate is conducted in a non-partisan way.
d)   The debates allow all the candidates equal time.
e)   All of the above.

Answer to Question 95

This is a trick question. All the answers are false. The format of the so-called "Presidential Debates" is either a joint press conference with questions posed by moderators, or a series of call-in questions screened by a moderator.

Answer a) is wrong because politicians thrive on avoiding answering questions, and will often repeat their standard rhetoric regardless of the question. The last thing a politician wants to do is explain their policies, since most of them are either: a) so convoluted that no one can understand them; or b) full of optimistic assumptions as to be unrealistic on their face.

Answer b) is wrong because many of the questions do not pertain to policy. Secondly, when the question is about policy, the candidates are typically required to answer within 30 or 60 seconds. How can anyone expect a candidate to explain a complete Middle East policy in 30 seconds? No serious candidate would even try, which is why we get very few serious candidates.

Answer c) is wrong because the moderator(s) choose the questions, regardless of who the sponsor is. The moderator has every opportunity to ask easy or innocuous questions of their favorite, while reserving the hard or impossible ones for the other. Also, moderators rarely ask both candidates the same exact question, so the public does not get to compare answers one-to-one.

Answer d) is wrong because only the candidates of the two main parties are allowed to participate, unless an independent or minor-party candidate is polling at 15% or better among likely voters (a very high threshold). The independents and minor-party candidates are generally shut out of the debates altogether in most races for all offices, not just the Presidency.

These so-called debates are nothing more than opportunities for politicians to present their standard stump speeches to a larger audience, while seeking a chance to come up with a memorable one-liner that will be repeated incessantly until the election. It is also an opportunity for each candidate to reinforce a negative image of his opponent, while carefully avoiding any specific policy discussion or review of his own record. So, why would any intelligent voter waste their precious time listening to what one lying, divorced-from-reality politician says about another lying, divorced-from-reality politician? Intelligent voters don't --- an intelligent voter researches what the candidates voted for in the past and the policies that they directly enacted. It doesn't matter what a candidate says. The only thing that matters is what they do, and what they have done in the past is the best indicator of what they will do in the future.

-- § --

Question 96: News Coverage

Consider these two fictional newspaper stories.

Ex-County Executive Gets Jail Time for Multiple Felonies

David S. Ramsey, former Republican County Executive of Hamilton County, Arkansas, received an unusually light sentence of 8 years and 2 months in a federal prison for many sensational crimes, among which are (unsurprisingly) witness intimidation, mail fraud, and bribery.

Ramsey's defense team presented a bizarre argument for probation, claiming that Ramsey had spent many years as a public official, and was known as "a good husband and father that had made some serious mistakes but was sincerely repentant for his actions". Prosecutors had demanded that Ramsey be sentenced to the maximum 30 years as allowed for these three convictions. But U. S. District Judge Paula Wilson, who willfully ignored the guidelines, sentenced the former Republican politician to a shorter term that is in fact less than one-third of the maximum. Ramsey will also have to pay a $100,000 fine, less than one year's pay from his former $110,000 salary, and will also have to pay a paltry $250,000 in restitution.

Ramsey, 65, had been a state representative for the township of Richmond. When Democratic County Executive Sheila Watson was killed in a tragic automobile accident, Republican Ramsey seized the opportunity presented by the vacancy, and took over her office in a special election in 1993. He was accepted by the voters during a few of his early years in office, winning elections in 1994 and 1998 with about two-thirds of the vote. Due to a curious quirk in the law, even though he will be in jail for multiple felony convictions, Ramsey will continue to receive his $75,000 annual pension throughout his prison term. Wilson was appointed to the bench by Republican President Richard Nixon.

Ex-County Executive Receives Sentence

Former Delaware County Executive George F. Dunaway was sentenced to ninety-eight months in federal prison in a questionable corruption case.

Prosecutors had demanded that Mr. Dunaway be sentenced to 30 years, technically the maximum allowable for convictions of this type. Dunaway's defense team respectfully petitioned the judge for probation. U. S. District Court Judge Sandra McMillan rejected the plea for leniency from the public servant's legal team, ordering Mr. Dunaway to pay a heavy $100,000 fine and imposed an additional harsh requirement to pay a quarter of a million dollars in restitution, in addition to the long prison sentence.

Mr. Dunaway was convicted last year of mail fraud, bribery, and witness intimidation in a trial of questionable legitimacy. His defense team noted that Dunaway had been a long-time public servant who was "a good husband and father … who was sincerely repentant for his actions". Tragically, Mr. Dunaway will be 73 years old by the time he is released from custody.

Dunaway (D) was a well-known state representative from Marlboro Heights who ran successfully for County Executive in a 1993 special election upon the death of then-Executive Thomas P. Randolph (R) in a car accident. He became wildly popular public official, winning re-elections in 1994 and 1998 by overwhelming 66% majorities in both races. As County Executive, Mr. Dunaway's annual salary was $110,000 per year, and he will justly continue to receive a $75,000 annual pension for his service. Judge McMillan was appointed to the U. S. District Court by Democratic President Jimmy Carter.

Which of the following is true, based on these two stories:
a) Judges appointed by Democratic Presidents tend to give higher sentences because they are tough on crime.
b) Republican judges find a way to help other Republicans convicted of crimes.
c) Ramsey should have received the full 30 years because he took advantage of someone's death.

d) Prosecutors in the Dunaway case attempted to trick Judge McMillan by citing technicalities, which could have resulted in an unfair sentence for Dunaway. Fortunately, McMillan was smart enough not to fall for the tricks.

e) Dunaway did not have the benefit of an adequate defense.

Answer to Question 96

This is a trick question. If both stories are read carefully, all of the following are true:

a) Both defendants came to office on the untimely death of another official of the opposite political party

b) Both of the defendants committed the same number of the same crimes

c) Both received the same sentence (same prison term, same fine, and same restitution)

d) Neither judge is bound by the sentencing guidelines

e) Both defendants are now 65 years old, and will be 73 at the end of their sentences

f) Both prosecutors asked for the maximum sentence

g) Both defense teams entered the same request for leniency

h) Both of the defendants will continue to receive their pensions as convicted felons

The only difference in these two cases is that the defendants are from different political parties (Ramsey is a Republican, and Dunaway is a Democrat). Although the basic facts in both stories are the same, they were written in such a way as to offer different views on the same subject:

a) Republican Ramsey got a light sentence of 8 years and two months (98 months), while Democrat Dunaway has to suffer for a whole 98 months.

b) Republican Ramsey was convicted of "many sensational crimes", while Democrat Dunaway was convicted in a "questionable corruption case".

c) Republican Ramsey's defense team made a "bizarre argument" for probation; Democrat Dunaway's defense team "respectfully petitioned" the judge.

d) Republican Ramsey got his sentence because the judge willfully ignored the higher sentencing maximums, but Democratic Dunaway got the same sentence because the judge unfairly rejected a legitimate leniency request.

e) Republican Ramsey obtained his office because he was an opportunist who "took over" after a tragic accident, Democrat Dunaway got his by "running successfully in a special election".

f) Republican Ramsey has to pay $100,000 fine, Democrat Dunaway has to pay a "heavy" $100,000 fine

g) Republican Ramsey has to pay a lousy $250,000 in restitution, but Democrat Dunaway has to pay an entire quarter-million ($250,000) due to harsh treatment by the judge.

h) Republican Ramsey was accepted by the voters for a few years, whereas Democrat Dunaway was wildly popular (both won their elections by the same margins (two-thirds = 66%)).

i) Republican Ramsey gets his pension in jail through a "quirk in the law"; Democrat Dunaway gets his pension in jail for his "public service".

j) Republican Ramsey is going to jail and prison; Democrat Dunaway is only in custody.

k) Both will be 73 on their release, but it is tragic only in the case of Democrat Dunaway.

This is the nature of some types of bias in the media. In this instance, the two stories used different words in different contexts to paint different images, even though the two cases are essentially identical. This is what the media calls "setting the stage" --- slanting the story to promote the interests of their political favorites.

-- § --

Question 97: NSA Leaks

Consider the following sequence of events. On 11 Sep 2001, adherents of Osama bin Laden hijacked U. S. airliners and flew them into the World Trade Center Buildings in New York and the Pentagon in Washington DC. All of the following information was taken from newspaper and magazine articles, but, for the sake of argument, assume all of what follows is true. Once the federal government figured out who was behind the attacks, it engaged in a series of actions to combat terrorism. One of those actions was that President George W. Bush, in 2002, signed a secret directive authorizing the National Security Agency (NSA) to conduct email searches and make recordings of phone calls within the U. S. without a warrant, so long as one end of the party was overseas. Normally a warrant to conduct this kind of surveillance is required under the 1978 Federal Intelligence Surveillance Act (FISA). Some government officials were concerned about the legality of the program (since it was authorized by Presidential order instead of by Congress), and secretly provided information about the secret program to reporters working for the New York Times. Because of the sensitive nature of the program, the New York Times agreed not to disclose its sources. The administration learned about the disclosure of the program, and asked the New York Times not to publish the story. The New York Times held off for about a year, but then went public with the information on 16 Dec 2005 [1]. The revelation led to debates in Congress, and a law was subsequently passed in Aug 2007 allowing the NSA to continue to perform this function. Prior to the passage of the new law, the President withdrew the authorization for it, according to a letter by Attorney General Alberto Gonzales, 17 Jan 2007. It was later learned that Thomas M. Tamm, an employee of the Justice Department, was one of the people who revealed the NSA program to the New York Times reporters in 2004, although he was not directly involved in its execution (he was never "read into" the NSA program) [2]. Apparently he learned about it indirectly while working on unrelated programs in and around the same offices where the NSA surveillance was being conducted. Mr. Tamm subsequently lost his job at the Justice Department, apparently due to an unrelated issue. Although his house was searched, Mr. Tamm has not been arrested. Assuming all of the preceding is true, what is likely to happen next?

a) James Risen and Eric Lichtblau, the reporters for the New York Times, will be arrested and tried for endangering national security.

b) The New York Times will be shut down for publishing a story that endangered national security.

c) Michael Isikoff, the columnist for Newsweek, who revealed the identity of the leaker, will be prosecuted for interfering in an investigation.

d) Thomas M. Tamm, the person who leaked the program to the New York Times, will be prosecuted for revealing the classified methods used by NSA to conduct domestic surveillance.

e) Both a) and d).

[1] James Risen and Eric Lichtblau, "Bush Lets U.S. Spy on Callers Without Warrants", The New York Times, 16 Dec 2005: available at:
https://www.nytimes.com/2005/12/16/politics/bush-lets-us-spy-on-callers-without-courts.html

[2] Michael Isikoff, "The Fed Who Blew the Whistle"; Newsweek, 13 Dec 2008, available at:
https://www.newsweek.com/whistleblower-who-exposed-warrantless-wiretaps-82805

Answer to Question 97

This is a trick question. All of the answers are wrong.

Answers a) and b) are wrong because the U. S. Supreme Court ruled in Bartnicki vs. Vopper (532 U.S. 514 (2001)) that it is legal to publish information that was illegally obtained unless the reporters or news organization did something illegal to obtain the information [1, 2]. The same reasoning applies to answer c).

Answer d) is wrong because (if the news articles are correct), Mr. Tamm never worked on the surveillance activity directly, and therefore technically does not know, and therefore could not reveal, how NSA operated.

What is likely to happen is an investigation into the multiple levels of leaks on this matter:

a) If it was an NSA program, and Mr. Tamm was not "read into" it, how did he learn enough about it to provide accurate data for the *New York Times* to publish? Either there was a large breakdown of security among those actually working for NSA, or there were other, far more important leakers than Mr. Tamm.

b) How did the government learn about the disclosure to the *New York Times* a year before the newspaper went public in December of 2005? Did they find out at that time who leaked it?

c) How did *Newsweek* find out that Mr. Tamm was one of the leakers, if Mr. Tamm had been promised anonymity by Mr. Risen and Mr. Lichtblau (both of whom declined to confirm to *Newsweek* that Mr. Tamm was one of their sources)?

But make no mistake about one thing. None of the people mentioned, whether government employees or not, will ever be prosecuted for any of this. The reason is -- they are fully paid-up members of the ruling elite.

There are two things we do not know, and probably will never know. First, we will never find out what the NSA is actually doing. The second is why the big tough guys in Congress (you know, the ones who are always claiming that they work 24 hours a day protecting your rights) did not lift a finger when they found out about a domestic surveillance activity being conducted by NSA that is not publicly authorized by Congress. What were the members of Congress doing during all of 2006 and the first half of 2007? There must have been a lot of fund-raisers in those years.

[1] https://mtsu.edu/first-amendment/article/575/bartnicki-v-vopper
[2] L. Levine, N. E. Siegel, J. M. Bead, "Handcuffing the Press: First Amendment Limitations on the Reach of Criminal Statutes as Applied to the Media", New York law School Law Review, Vol. 55, Issue 4, Article 4, Jan 2011; available at:
     https://core.ac.uk/download/pdf/322560272.pdf

-- § --

Question 98: L. B. Johnson and G. W. Bush

What are the main differences between Democratic President Lyndon B. Johnson (36) and Republican President George W. Bush (43)?

a) Bush got the nation involved in foreign war in Iraq which some claim was justified on false pretenses, whereas Johnson responded properly to the attacks made by the North Vietnamese in the Tonkin Gulf Incident.

b) Johnson helped poor and middle class people by encouraging Congress to pass Medicare, while Bush cut taxes for the rich.

c) Johnson became President by defeating Goldwater in a landslide in 1964; whereas Bush defeated Gore by a very narrow margin, which required an extensive recount in Florida and ultimately a decision by the Supreme Court.

d) Bush was born and raised in Texas; in fact he served as Governor of Texas before being elected President. Johnson spent nearly his entire life in Washington, DC, although he was born in Texas.

e) All of the above.

Answer to Question 98

This is a trick question. All of the answers are wrong.

Answer a) is wrong because Johnson justified the war in Vietnam by a patently false claim about an incident that allegedly took place in the Gulf of Tonkin.

Answer b) is wrong because Bush pushed for Prescription Drug benefits (an expansion of Medicare) for the poor and middle class; also Bush, as President, cannot cut taxes (Congress does).

Answer c) is wrong because Johnson became President upon the assassination of John F. Kennedy in 1963; he retained his office by defeating Goldwater in 1964.

Answer d) is wrong because Bush was born in Connecticut and raised in Washington DC while his father was CIA Director and Senator; Johnson was born and raised in Texas.

As far as policy goes, there is no difference at all between L. B. Johnson and G. W. Bush. Both of them adopted the failed foreign policy of Woodrow Wilson (to try and solve every nation's problems) and the domestic policy of Franklin Roosevelt (minimize the liberties of the American people). It makes you wonder why the mainstream media loved one (Johnson) and hated the other (Bush). The answer should be obvious: Johnson was a Democrat.

We are seeing the same thing now in extended form with President Donald Trump. Some commentators have accused the mainstream media of having "Trump Derangement Syndrome" as the root cause of their hatred of Donald Trump. It is true that they hate Trump, but it's not personal. The mainstream media hates Trump because he is neither a fashionable card-carrying socialist nor a recognized member of the ruling elite.

-- § --

Question 99: Staff Work

Many members of Congress hire their spouses or other relatives to work on their permanent campaign staff or political action committees [1]. These people are paid by either the campaign funds or from contributions made to the political action committees. It is not necessary that the relatives, as employees, perform any particular task as part of their employment. It is legal for members of Congress to put relatives on their payroll for these jobs, but in what ways might it be considered unethical or immoral?
a) If it's legal, then it cannot be unethical or immoral, so this question is irrelevant.
b) It constitutes nepotism, in which family members get special treatment (good paying jobs) simply for being relatives.
c) It is possible that the relatives are no-shows, simply being paid as a means to enhance the family income without actual work being performed.
d) It is possible that the family member is less qualified than other people to perform these tasks, so the organization is not getting the best talent for the money.
e) Some combination of b), c), and d).

[1] Dick Morris and Eileen McGann, *Outrage*, New York: HarperCollins Publishers, 2007, pp. 111-115

Answer to Question 99

This is a trick question. The correct answer is "none of the above".

Answer a) is obviously wrong because there are many things that are not illegal (spending one's entire paycheck on gambling and not paying their other bills), but are certainly immoral.

Answers b), c), and d) are wrong because the relatives are being paid from contributions to the office-holder's campaign or contributors to the political action committee (PAC). In other words, the only people who are being ripped off are the ones dumb enough to contribute to a Congressman's campaign or PAC.

But what about the case where the campaign is funded is partly through the federal matching funds, which is taxpayer money? Isn't the taxpayer being ripped off? Of course, but that's why taxpayers exist (or so they believe in Congress). Besides, money spent on relative's salaries is that much less available for political ads, in which the Congressman lies to us about what a great job he's doing preserving our liberties as well as other assorted fables. We the taxpayers would be better off if all the campaign funds were simply diverted to the relatives, so long as we could be spared the political ads.

-- § --

Question 100: Multiple-Guess

Are multiple-choice questions the most accurate way to choose among possible alternatives?
a)   Yes
b)   No
c)   Maybe
d)   Sometimes
e)   Indeterminate, it depends on the subject of the question.

Answer to Question 100

This is not a trick question. As you no doubt have observed, all of the preceding questions on this test were trick questions. But in this case, there is no trick: the correct answer is b) No. Multiple choice questions, by their very nature, restrict the kind of answers that you can give.

Two-year-old children have a reputation for being very difficult. It is because they are first learning that such a thing as choice exists, and they want to exert some control by making choices. The best way to deal with children passing through this stage is to always give them a choice, so long as any of the choices are acceptable to you. Explain to them that they are big kids now, and so they should decide what to do (which plays into their impulses). For example, if you, the adult, has determined that it is their bedtime, give them a choice: a) eat a cookie, then take a bath, then brush their teeth, then go to bed; b) eat a cookie, then brush their teeth, then take a bath, then go to bed; c) take a bath, eat a cookie, then brush their teeth, then go to bed; or d) a spanking, and then go straight to bed without their teddy bear. As the adult, all the choices are acceptable to you, and it won't matter which one they pick. If they refuse to choose any of the options, choose either a), b), or c) for them. If they choose d), give them d); they will not choose it tomorrow. The main point is that you gave them limited choices which they desire (although they are not conscious of it), all of which reflected your desire to get them to go to sleep. So it is with multiple-choice questions. Each of the choices reflects the biases, preferences, and objectives of the person who made up the question. If the correct answer is not present in the list, it is because the person who made up the possible answers either: a) does not know the correct answer; b) does not want you to know or to give the correct answer; or c) does not want you to believe you are smart enough to think beyond the choices given.

Refer back to the introduction to the test. There it was stated "To make it more interesting, I have eliminated the essay format, and have instead adopted a multiple-choice question format." That statement is patently false. The multiple-choice question format does not "make it more interesting"; but it makes it easy for anyone who administers a test to maintain control over the acceptable answers.

-- § --

Question 101: Virtue of the Test

In your opinion, how useful was this test?
a) Completely useless
b) Mostly useless
c) So-so
d) Somewhat useful
e) Very useful

Answer to Question 101

This is another trick question. Note that the question explicitly asks for your opinion, not to determine a fact, a logical conclusion, or the best answer. Therefore, it does not have a correct answer, because an opinion is what it is. In the absence of underlying facts or relevant rules of logic, an opinion cannot be graded right or wrong.

3
Conclusion

I hope this little "test" was not as painful as your hardest class in school. As mentioned in the introduction, this "test" was organized entirely differently than the classes in school. First, you have seen firsthand that the questions covered a wide range of issues: economic, political, and social because all of these will come up in the course of your adult life.

Second, they were presented in random order, not neatly divided up by subject as is done in school. These issues throughout your life will also arrive in random order, usually at unexpected times.

Third, the questions required a variety of skills to analyze and solve; some are mathematical, some were logical, some are historical or political, and some rely on good old common sense. Some required a little research, and others rely on instinct. Common sense is not all that common. (Maybe it wasn't as common in the past either, as some would have you believe). I believe the influence of social and corporate media has contributed to a decline in the traditional habit of gathering facts, sorting them, and arriving at consistent conclusions. The media and the loud activist groups demand immediate reaction, hoping to bait you into a false conclusion.

These questions then were designed to check on how well your education prepared you for practical life, where you have to make your own decisions and live with the consequences. There won't be any cheerleaders other than your family, and no one will take responsibility in your place.

There are four reasons why I wrote this book. First, it was done to encourage you to think critically about everyday problems. I am confident that you are capable of critical thinking; I am not confident that our modern educational system has given you sufficient practice of it, or that you are confident of your abilities. Maybe this book will help change that.

Secondly, I left off all the correct answers to the first 99 questions to illustrate the point that real life consists mostly of trick questions. I am confident that most of you perceived that tactic early on; I encourage you to keep it in mind as you transition to the adult world. You probably have noticed that many of the answers are critical of socialism and "progressive" ideas. Those ideologies have never worked for regular people, and they never will work. Don't be afraid: when presented with a list of options that are consistent with some socialist notions, you can be sure that all those options are false and unworkable. In that respect, this little "test" was also a warning. The ruling elite are intent on turning America into a "progressive" socialist nation; if that happens, your freedom will be gone.

Third, I wanted to invoke a little humor in the course of analyzing these questions; hopefully some of you got a good laugh at the ridiculous suggested answers I provided. It is all harmless fun: I do not wish to embarrass anyone or make anyone feel like they are stupid. The main point is for you to be fooled once when it doesn't matter, so you won't be fooled in real life.

Fourth, and most importantly, I desired to help you recognize that you cannot believe much of what you see, read, and hear; everything needs to be examined closely, with supporting data. A great deal of what passes for "news" in these days of the internet and cable TV is mostly either propaganda or clever advertising. Some may perceive my answers as cynical; so be it. I am trying to show you the cold hard truth.